THE POLITICS OF ISLAM

To Feyza Gümüşlüoğlu

THE POLITICS OF ISLAM

The Muslim Brothers and the State in the Arab Gulf

Birol Başkan

EDINBURGH
University Press

Edinburgh University Press is one of the leading university presses in the UK. We publish academic books and journals in our selected subject areas across the humanities and social sciences, combining cutting-edge scholarship with high editorial and production values to produce academic works of lasting importance. For more information visit our website: edinburghuniversitypress.com

© Birol Başkan, 2021, 2023

Edinburgh University Press Ltd
The Tun – Holyrood Road
12 (2f) Jackson's Entry
Edinburgh EH8 8PJ

First published in hardback by Edinburgh University Press 2021

Typeset in 11/15 Adobe Garamond by
IDSUK (DataConnection) Ltd

A CIP record for this book is available from the British Library

ISBN 978 1 4744 9024 5 (hardback)
ISBN 978 1 4744 9025 2 (paperback)
ISBN 978 1 4744 9027 6 (webready PDF)
ISBN 978 1 4744 9026 9 (epub)

The right of Birol Başkan to be identified as author of this work has been asserted in accordance with the Copyright, Designs and Patents Act 1988 and the Copyright and Related Rights Regulations 2003 (SI No. 2498).

CONTENTS

Acknowledgements	vi
Introduction	1
1 Historical Background: Desert and its Legacies	18
2 Modern Sovereign State Building in the Gulf: From the 1950s to the 1970s	55
3 The Muslim Brotherhood in the Gulf	80
4 Modern Sovereign State Building in the Gulf: From the 1980s to the 2000s	111
5 Gulf States' Diverging Attitudes towards the Muslim Brotherhood	134
6 The Arab Spring	171
Conclusion	212
Bibliography	219
Index	242

ACKNOWLEDGEMENTS

This book is a product of my decade-long stay in Qatar. While writing it I have incurred enormous debt to so many people and institutions in and out of this country. I thank them all, especially my colleagues, friends and students, who have helped me better understand the region(s) of which Qatar is a part and microcosm. I also thank the editorial team of Edinburgh University Press and two anonymous reviewers. Finally, I thank her for being with me all along, from the very beginning to the end and afterwards. As my eternal gratitude I dedicate this book to her.

INTRODUCTION

In the summer of 2013 Egypt unleashed a massive crackdown on al-Ikhwan al-Muslimin, popularly known as the Muslim Brotherhood. The movement had previously endured similar repressions in its long history, most notably in its home country, Egypt, in the 1950s and 1960s. But the 2010s were different: in the 1950s and 1960s the Muslim Brotherhood found safe haven in all Gulf countries, but in the 2010s only in Qatar. Two of these countries, Saudi Arabia and the United Arab Emirates (the UAE), even designated the movement as terrorist in March 2014 and November 2014 respectively.[1] Neither designating the movement as terrorist, nor serving as safe havens for its members escaping repression in Egypt, Kuwait and Bahrain stood somewhere in-between these two extreme positions.

This book narrates this transformation,[2] accounting for why state–Muslim Brotherhood relations were cordial in all Gulf countries from the 1950s to the 1970s, but eventually deteriorated in Kuwait, the UAE and Saudi Arabia, but not in Qatar and Bahrain. The book argues that geopolitical developments, such as the rise and demise of pan-Arabism, the Iranian revolution, Iraq's invasion of Kuwait, the 9/11 attacks and finally the Arab Spring, as well as domestic

1. Hauslohner, 'Egypt's Muslim Brotherhood finds havens abroad'; Ajbaili, 'Saudi: Muslim Brotherhood a terrorist group'; 'UAE lists Muslim Brotherhood as terrorist group'.
2. The idea of writing this book was born out of my numerous conversations with Mazhar A. al-Zoby. I owe him a great intellectual debt.

circumstances dictated by necessities and challenges of (rentier) state building and regime formation, have shaped and reshaped the said transformation.

Yet, the book observes, there is a key difference between Saudi Arabia and the UAE on the one hand and Qatar on the other: the Muslim Brotherhood has become oppositional in the former, but not in the latter. The book also observes the same variation between Kuwait and Bahrain: the Brotherhood has become oppositional only in the former, not in the latter.

This variation across the five Gulf states is all the more interesting given the history of state–religion relations in the Gulf. As this book shows, Gulf rulers have never implemented any kind of forceful state secularisation reforms, the like of which has been observed elsewhere in the Middle East. As a consequence, all the Gulf states have been, and still are, quite religious states. And Saudi Arabia has been, and still is, more religious than the other Gulf states.[3] This difference in state religiosity between Saudi Arabia and the other Gulf states, this book claims, is due to the simple fact that among all Gulf countries only Saudi Arabia developed a native class of religious scholars, a class that nurtured a strong intra-group solidarity and played an active role in the foundation of the Kingdom.

Tracing the history of the five Gulf states' religious policies and their relations with the Muslim Brotherhood, this book arrives at a simple yet intriguing conclusion: *the level of state religiosity seems to have little impact on whether*

---

3. Gulf states' religiosity and Saudi Arabia's exceptionalism can also be seen in the Religious Support Index prepared by the Religion and State Project. This index combines a total of 52 variables and measures for every year from 1990 to 2014 on the 'different ways a government can support religion, including financial support, policies which enforce religious laws and other forms of entanglement between government and religion'. The Religious Support Index, if we take it as a measure of state religiosity, consistently ranks the five Gulf states among the top 20 most religious states in the world in the 1990–2014 period it covers. In fact, until 2001 the Index consistently ranks Saudi Arabia, Kuwait, Qatar and the UAE in the top ten, and Bahrain in the top 20. Still, Saudi Arabia stands out as exceptional, for it occupies the top spot in the Index, scoring 46 out of 52 every year from 1990 to 2014. For comparative purposes, consider Saudi Arabia's closest rivals; for example, in 2014, Malaysia scored 36, Brunei and Iran 35, Afghanistan and Indonesia 34. In the same year, Saudi Arabia's closest rival in the Gulf was Kuwait, which scored 30, while Qatar, the UAE and Bahrain scored 28, 27 and 24 respectively. The data is available at the project's website: the Religion and State Project, http://www.thearda.com/ras/.

Islamism generates opposition in a country or not. What to make of this conclusion? The forthcoming discussion elaborates and to this end revisits the literature on Islamism.

The Literature on Islamism[4]

There is now a well-established and still growing scholarly literature on Islamism.[5] This literature was once populated by a few highly specialised Middle East scholars, who penned what are now classics on the lives and ideas of such religious figures as Jamal al-Din Afghani, Muhammad Abduh and Rashid Rida, who are considered the intellectual founders of Islamism, especially in the Arab World.[6] The literature had paid much less attention to such twentieth-century Islamist figures as Hasan al-Banna, Abu'l Ula al-Mawdudi, Said Nursi and others, and the grassroots movements these figures initiated.[7]

After the 1979 Iranian revolution proved religion's vibrancy in the modern world, scholarly attention increasingly turned to religion, religious figures and movements; consequently, the literature on Islamism has grown exponentially.[8] In the post-1979 period the literature continued

---

4. I owe a great intellectual debt to Afyare Elmi for our numerous conversations on Islamism, Islam and politics over the course of many years.
5. Unless needed for the sake of discussion, I limit my examples from the literature to academic books written in or translated into English and on the Muslim Brotherhood or its branches. Needless to add that there are other Islamist movements both in the Arab world and elsewhere in the Muslim world and that the literature is rich in French and German as well as in regional languages such as Arabic, Persian and Turkish. But to have a sweeping review is beyond this author's capacity.
6. On the lives and ideas of these figures, see, for example, Adams, *Islam and Modernism in Egypt*; Gibb, *Modern Trends in Islam*; Hourani, *Arabic Thought in the Liberal Age*; Kerr, *Islamic Reform*; Kedourie, *Afghani and Abduh*; Keddie, *Sayyid Jamal ad-Din 'al-Afghani'*. For a broader geographical scope, see Rosenthal, *Islam in the Modern National State*.
7. Early exceptional studies on the Muslim Brotherhood movement are Worth-Dunne, *Religious and Political Trends in Modern Egypt*; Phelps-Harris, *Nationalism and Revolution in Egypt*; Mitchell, *The Society of the Muslim Brothers*.
8. A bibliography of books and articles written on Islamism testifies how the literature expanded so swiftly. See Haddad, Esposito and Voll (eds), *The Contemporary Islamic Revival*.

to revisit the ideas of the nineteenth-century intellectual forerunners of Islamism, but also devoted much closer attention to twentieth-century Islamist figures.[9] Beyond the lives and ideas of individual Islamist figures, the literature has also produced in-depth studies of grassroots Islamist movements, shedding light on their trials and tribulations under various secular-nationalist regimes, their resurgence in the 1970s and their political and social activism since then.[10]

Beyond mere description, the literature has also sought to address some thematic issues and theoretical questions. In the pre-1979 period the literature had been, for example, much more interested in tracing modern ideas and ideologies, such as secularism and nationalism, in the Middle East. In

---

9. There are two categories in this genre: the first category of studies takes a collection of Islamist figures and discusses their lives and ideas: see, for example, Enayat, *Modern Islamic Political Thought*; Esposito (ed.), *Voices of Resurgent Islam*; Rahnema (ed.), *Pioneers of Islamic Revival*; Abu-Rabi', *Intellectual Origins of Islamic Resurgence in the Modern Arab World*; Esposito and Voll, *Makers of Contemporary Islam*. The other category of studies focuses on the life and ideas of single Islamist figures. See, for example, Mousalli, *Radical Islamic Fundamentalism*; Euben, *Enemy in the Mirror*; Khatab, *The Political Thought of Sayyid Qutb*; Zollner, *The Muslim Brotherhood*; Calvert, *Sayyid Qutb and the Origins of Radical Islamism*; Krämer, *Hasan al-Banna*.

10. There are also two categories in this genre: the first category of studies discusses a number of Islamist movements in the same volume: see, for example, Kepel, *Muslim Extremism in Egypt*; Ayubi, *Political Islam*; Wiktorowicz, *The Management of Islamic Activism*; Rubin (ed.), *Revolutionaries and Reformers*; Kepel, *Jihad*; Burgat, *Face to Face with Political Islam*; Milton-Edwards, *Islamic Fundamentalism since 1945*; Ayoob, *The Many Faces of Political Islam*; Mandaville, *Global Political Islam*; Al-Mdaires, *Islamic Extremism in Kuwait*; Brown, *When Victory Is Not An Option*; Shehata (ed.), *Islamist Politics in the Middle East*; Osman, *Islamism*; Hamid and McCants, *Rethinking Political Islam*. The other category focuses singly on the Muslim Brotherhood: see, for example, Abd-Allah, *The Islamic Struggle in Syria*; Abu-Amr, *Islamic Fundamentalism in the West Bank and Gaza*; Brynjar, *The Society of the Muslim Brothers in Egypt*; Mishal and Sela, *The Palestinian Hamas*; Hroub, *Hamas*; Al-Awadi, *In Pursuit of Legitimacy*; Halverson, *Theology and Creed in Sunni Islam*; Pargeter, *The Muslim Brotherhood*; Rubin (ed.), *The Muslim Brotherhood*; Lacroix, *Awakening Islam*; Tadros, *The Muslim Brotherhood in Contemporary Egypt*; Lefevre, *Ashes of Hama*; Baron, *The Orphan Scandal*; Hamid, *Temptations of Powers*; Al-Anani, *Inside the Muslim Brotherhood*; Wolf, *Political Islam in Tunisia*; Freer, *Rentier Islamism*.

the post-1979 period the literature came to address more diverse issues and questions, such as the causes behind Islamism's resurgence after a period of decline under secular-nationalist regimes in the Middle East,[11] its modern or anti-modern features,[12] its conformity to or departure from traditional Islam,[13] its proclivity for violence,[14] its potential to lead democratisation in the Muslim world,[15] its ideological and behavioural transformation in or out of electoral systems,[16] and last, but not least, its impact on women's roles and identity.[17]

Despite its enormous size and wide scope, the literature has not specifically addressed the question of Islamism's oppositional character. Or, to put it differently, the literature has taken it for granted. Such a stance is understandable for the simple reason that Islamists had been marginalised under and even endured various hardships at the hands of the regimes that succeeded the Ottomans, the Qajars, the British or the French (the Kemalists in Turkey or the Pahlavis in Iran, the Nasserites in Egypt or the Baathists in Syria and Iraq or the Bourgubists in Tunisia).[18] Furthermore, these regimes continued in their predecessors' footsteps and pursued state secularising reforms, which

---

11. For the earliest attempts, see, for example, Dessouki (ed.), *Islamic Resurgence in the Arab World*; Voll, *Islam*; Esposito, *Islam and Politics*. There is also a broader literature addressing the global resurgence of religion, within which Islamic resurgence is also addressed: see, for example, Marty and Appleby (eds), *Accounting for Fundamentalisms* and their other volumes in the same series; Juergensmeyer, *The New Cold War?*; Kepel, *The Revenge of God*; Casanova, *Public Religions in the Modern World*; Tétreault and Denemark (eds), *Gods, Guns & Globalization*.
12. See, for example, Zubaida, *Islam, the People and the State*; Esposito, *The Islamic Threat*.
13. See, for example, Brown, *Religion and State*; Ayubi, *Political Islam*.
14. Lawrence, *Shattering the Myth*; Tibi, *Islamism and Islam*.
15. See, for example, Esposito and Voll, *Islam and Democracy*; Tibi, *The Challenge of Fundamentalism*; Tibi, *Islamism and Islam*; Baker, *Islam without Fear*; Bayat, *Making Islam Democratic*.
16. See, for example, Wickham, *Mobilizing Islam*; Ismail, *Rethinking Islamist Politics*; Schwedler, *Faith in Moderation*.
17. Mahmoud, *Politics of Piety*.
18. See, for example, Yavuz, *Islamic Political Identity in Turkey*; Arjomand, *The Shadow of God and the Hidden Imam*; Mitchell, *The Society of the Muslim Brothers*; Lefevre, *Ashes of Hama*; Wolfe, *Political Islam in Tunisia*.

curtailed the influence of religion in and over the state.[19] And these reforms stood in sharp contrast to what Islamism had been prescribing. Islamists appeared therefore as natural oppositional forces to these regimes.[20]

The Muslim Brotherhood operated in quite different circumstances in the Gulf. First, as Chapters 2 and 4 on modern state building in the Gulf show, the Gulf states have never undergone forceful state secularisation like Turkey, Iran, Egypt, Tunisia, Syria or Iraq did in the twentieth century.[21] In contrast, they have shown the utmost care in respecting the rules and norms of Islam and have remained among the world's most religious states. Furthermore, as Chapter 3 on state–Brotherhood relations from the 1950s to the 1980s shows, the Gulf states were quite friendly towards the Brotherhood, becoming safe havens for it and even offering jobs to Brotherhood figures who escaped repression in their own countries or sought better life conditions.[22] The five Gulf states, in short, have never been like Turkey, or Iran, or Egypt, or Tunisia, or Syria or Iraq in any period in their histories.

Despite this highly positive historical background though, as Chapter 5 on state–Muslim Brotherhood relations from the 1980s to the 2000s shows, the Brotherhood became oppositional in Kuwait and the UAE from the 1980s and in Saudi Arabia from the 1990s. Only in Bahrain and Qatar has the Brotherhood remained non-oppositional and even cooperative with the state.

---

19. For Turkey and Iran, see, for example, Berkes, *The Development of Secularism in Turkey*; Banani, *The Modernization of Iran, 1921–1941*. For the Arab world, see al-Azmeh, *Secularism in the Arab World*. Also see Anderson, 'Modern trends in Islam'; Crecelius, 'The course of secularization in modern Egypt'; Hinnebusch, *Syria*; Pierret, *Religion and State in Syria*; Micaud, Brown and Moore, *Tunisia*.
20. See Tamimi and Esposito (eds), *Islam and Secularism in the Middle East*; Ruedy, *Islamism and Secularism in North Africa*.
21. Yet we should not exaggerate the advent of secularism even in the non-Gulf Arab world. Mark Farha forcefully illustrates this through the case of Lebanon; see Farha, *Lebanon*. His book provides a treasure trove of valuable insights into the challenges of building and sustaining a secular state not only in Lebanon, but also in the whole Muslim world. Also see Farha, 'Arab secularism's assisted suicide'. I owe Mark a great intellectual debt for our extensive conversations on secularism and the politics of religion in Turkey and the Arab world.
22. Also see Lacroix, *Awakening Islam*; Freer, *Rentier Islamism*.

There are few studies that address the question of religious opposition inspired by the Muslim Brotherhood in Saudi Arabia.[23] These studies offer two sets of explanations: one set is economic and the other is ideological. The former relates the emergence of religious opposition in Saudi Arabia to the decline in oil prices in the 1980s and the consequent disillusionment especially among the religious youth, the latter to the essential ideological conflict between the Muslim Brotherhood and Wahhabism.

These studies shed critical light on the emergence of religious opposition in Saudi Arabia, but their conclusions have limited applicability to the other Gulf states.[24] First of all, like Saudi Arabia, the other Gulf states are also oil-rich and therefore suffered from the decline in oil prices in the 1980s. Yet the Brotherhood became oppositional in Kuwait and the UAE, but not in Bahrain and Qatar. Moreover, Wahhabism was not a factor in any other Gulf state, except Qatar, where the conflict between the Brotherhood ideology and Wahhabism has not generated a similar outcome.

This is not to claim that the two explanations do not have any relevance to the emergence of religious opposition in Saudi Arabia. But it is rather to claim that, metaphorically speaking, a relationship between the state or any group, religious or not, is like a marriage: not one single factor or incidence ruins it, but a number of them. Moreover, the specific combination of factors and incidences might change from one case to another. Or, as Leo Tolstoy has it: 'Happy families resemble one another; each unhappy family is unhappy in its own way.'[25] This is to suggest that for country-specific factors the Brotherhood became oppositional in Kuwait, the UAE and Saudi Arabia, but not in Bahrain and Qatar.

The variation among the Gulf states is still intriguing though. This is because, as the literature well documents, the states in the Middle East, even those avowedly secular-nationalist ones, have come to implement more

---

23. Teitelbaum, *Holier Than Thou*; Al-Rasheed, *Contesting the Saudi State*; Commins, *The Wahhabi Mission and Saudi Arabia*; Lacroix, *Awakening Islam*.
24. Freer, *Rentier Islamism*, is a valuable comparative study of the Muslim Brotherhood in Kuwait, Qatar and the UAE. But, unfortunately, Freer is theoretically interested in a different question: that is, the political influence of the Brotherhood, which according to the rentier state literature should not have existed in such super-rentier states.
25. Tolstoy, *Anna Karenina*, p. 3.

religious policies in the last four decades or so.[26] This so-called Islamisation of the state was, the literature suggests, by and large the outcome of otherwise secular regimes' concessions to Islamism.[27] Yet this book shows that the Gulf states had begun to implement religious policies in the 1950s, at a time when there was almost no pressure from Islamism. By the time the Muslim Brotherhood became oppositional in Kuwait, the UAE and Saudi Arabia, these Gulf states were already religious states. Saudi Arabia has in fact been and still is more religious than all others, but still the Brotherhood became oppositional in the Kingdom. Yet, even though Bahrain and Qatar have never been more noticeably religious (in terms of implementing more religious state policies) than others, the Brotherhood remained non-oppositional and even cooperative with the state in these two Gulf countries. Thus the paradoxical conclusion: *the level of state religiosity seems to have little impact on whether the Brotherhood becomes oppositional in a country.* The answer to this paradox must be sought within Islamism's ideological core.

Islamism as an Ideology[28]

Islamism is ultimately, if not exclusively, about the state, the modern state.[29] As far as the current discussion is concerned, the modern state's most defining characteristic is its ambitious drive to control or at the very least regulate all aspects of human life,[30] or to impose its so-called absolute sovereignty within a clearly demarcated territory.[31] Such a project of building and maintaining the modern state necessarily and inescapably concerns religion. This is, first

---

26. What legal scholars call the Islamisation of the law clearly illustrates states' turn to religion. This literature is in and of itself sizeable and requires an expertise of its own. See, as an example, Mayer, *Islam and Human Rights*; Peters, *Crime and Punishment in Islamic law*; Otto, *Sharia Incorporated*.
27. See Roy, *The Failure of Political Islam*, ch. 7; Kepel, *Jihad*; Esposito and Burgat (eds), *Modernizing Islam*. For an alternative perspective, see Nasr, *Islamic Leviathan*. Nasr claims that the Islamisation of the state served to strengthen the state.
28. For a powerful exposition, see Tibi, *Islamism and Islam*.
29. On the origin and development of the modern state, see Anderson, *Lineages of the Absolutist State*; Poggi, *The Development of the Modern State*; Tilly, *Coercion, Capital, and European States, AD 990–1992*.
30. See Pierson, *The Modern State*; Mann, 'The autonomous power of the state'.
31. See Grimm, *Sovereignty*, ch. 2.

and foremost, because even though absolute sovereignty is claimed over a limited territory, it is still a trait attributed solely to God especially in monotheistic religions.[32] Islam's Holy Book, the Qur'an, repeatedly describes God as such: verse 6 of the *al-An'am* chapter, for example, states, 'That is Allah, your Lord. There is no God, but Him, the creator of all things. So, worship Him. And He is overseer of all things.' Not surprisingly, Thomas Hobbes calls the modern state 'mortal God'.[33]

Such a monotheistic imagination of an absolutely sovereign God is intimately linked to another claim about God. That is, such a God intervenes in human affairs and even guides them through revelation to a few select individuals. Revelation then constitutes the holy sources of religions, which prescribe ultimate ideals for their adherents to pursue, and guidelines for them to regulate their religious and worldly affairs. God's prescriptions are not mere recommendations, but divine orders, and the choice of whether to follow some, if not all of them, is not left to human discretion.

It is not surprising, therefore, that as the modern state expands its jurisdiction and seeks to control or regulate more and more spheres of human life, one contentious political question that comes to the fore concerns the relevance of religion for state legislation and regulation. More broadly stated, the modern state defines what roles religion can play in politics, economics, society, culture, etc., and continuously upholds and makes changes, if necessary, in those defined roles. It is the modern state that continually defines and redefines 'the space that religion may properly occupy in society'.[34] And this process of defining and redefining religion's relevance for the modern state and modern life generates a political/ideological struggle.

---

32. As Carl Schmitt argued, theology and political theory of the modern state are closely linked, stating 'all significant concepts of the modern theory of the state are secularized theological concepts'. See Schmitt, *Political Theology*, p. 36. A classic on the topic is Kantorowicz, *The King's Two Bodies*. For a more recent treatment of the topic, see Elshtain, *Sovereignty*.
33. Hobbes, *Leviathan*, p. 227. As far as I know, religiously motivated individuals or groups in the Muslim world have not theologically questioned the modern state's claim to absolute sovereignty. A notable exception is, ironically, Hallaq, *The Impossible State*.
34. Asad, *Formations of the Secular*, p. 201.

In the Muslim world, Islamism emerged as one position among others in this still ongoing struggle. Islamism, simply stated, holds that the modern state must be subjected to Islam's rules and norms and at the very least must not act against them. This position rests upon a particular view of Islam. That is, this religion prescribes more than a set of beliefs and rituals for personal and communal piety. Islam is, in the words of one of Islamism's loudest and most influential voices, Hasan al-Banna, 'an all-embracing concept which regulates all aspects of life, providing for every one of its concerns and prescribing for it a fixed and detailed order'.[35]

Islamism holds, in other words, that Islam provides all the rules and norms that mankind might need any time in history and any place in the world, rules and norms that regulate and guide not only rituals, but also politics, economics, international relations, etc. The Islamic law is the obvious place to search for these rules and norms. This field of law contains rulings and norms that fall into four general topics: as named by jurists, these are 'rituals', 'sales', 'marriage' and 'injuries'. As its name suggests, 'rituals' covers such topics as preparations for prayers, such as praying, alms giving, fasting, undertaking pilgrimage and Muslim kosher requirements, and as such is generally outside the purview of the modern state and modern law. In addition, it should be noted that the bulk of the Islamic law concerns 'rituals'. However, the Islamic law also provides norms and rulings categorised under 'sales', 'marriage' and 'injuries' that concern both private and public laws. Yet, it has to be emphasised, the Islamic law does not provide detailed rulings and norms across all topics in these 'non-ritual' categories: it regulates personal status matters such as marriage, divorce, child custody and inheritance in more detail than other matters.[36]

Overall, the Islamic law provides detailed rulings for certain fields of the modern law and has some relevance to such diverse laws as contract law, commercial law, company law, property law, criminal law and tort law. In the regulations of these other matters, however, the Islamic law leaves rulers with

---

35. Cited in Krämer, *Hasan al-Banna*, pp. 146–7. For a detailed discussion of al-Banna's view of Islam, see ch. 4 of Krämer's book.
36. My discussion of the Islamic law depends on Hallaq, *An Introduction to Islamic Law*, pp. 28–30.

quite extensive judicial and executive discretion in, for example, regulating commerce and trade, protecting and securing public order, pursuing interstate diplomacy and international policy, and punishing individuals for their crimes against others.[37]

For Islamism, the question of whether the Islamic law in its most developed state can satisfactorily provide all laws and regulations that the modern state or modern life needs is misconceived. As a matter of fact, Islamism's intellectual founders reacted to and criticised the Islamic law's perceived insufficiency to provide all the necessary rules and norms modern life needed and called for a renewed reading and interpretation of Islam.[38]

Islamism, therefore, seeks to expand the scope of Islam beyond the specific areas explicitly covered by the Islamic law. Consequently it views the Islamic law as, at the very least, incomplete. For example, one might argue that both the Qur'an and the Prophetic Traditions (or Hadith) contain materials from which can be derived rules and norms that bind rulers in running internal and foreign affairs of state.[39] Yet, to repeat, the Islamic law is quite underdeveloped in deriving such policies and does not provide much guidance.

What Islamism sets forth as a task is that all rules and norms the modern state will ever need – currently or in the future – are to be derived from the sources of Islam: a task that is perpetually ongoing and ever-changing. As such, and perhaps more problematically, perhaps, that task is set to prove Sisyphean in nature.[40] It is not that Islamism is simply setting too high a level of religiosity as its standard for the modern state. It is more that that level is opaque and fluid, perpetually shifting and ever-changing. Or Islamism seeks to be in and at the same time above politics all the time and all the

---

37. Rohe, *Themes in Islamic Studies*, ch. 4.
38. See Enayat, *Modern Islamic Political Thought*.
39. See, for example, Hamidullah, *İslam'da Devlet İdaresi*. Some others might disagree with this claim, though. Nazih Ayubi, for example, claims that 'the original Islamic sources (the Quran and the Hadith) have very little to say on matters of government and the state'. See Ayubi, *Political Islam*, p. 1.
40. In Greek mythology, Sisyphus is eternally condemned by the gods to roll a rock to the top of a mountain and then to see it rolling back down to the bottom.

places.⁴¹ Therein lies Islamism's oppositional character. Even if the modern state aspires to, and to a certain extent implements, the existing Islamic law in its entirety, Islamism might still find it insufficiently religious, and therefore could still generate opposition on religious grounds.

The question is not really therefore what makes Islamism/Islamists, for example, the Brotherhood, oppositional? Islamism/Islamists, and hence the Brotherhood, can be oppositional for any reason. The question is what explains Islamism's/Islamists', or, the Brotherhood's, non-oppositionality? Based on the Brotherhood's acquiescence and cooperation with the Gulf states in the three decades prior to the 1980s and its continued acquiescence and cooperation in Bahrain and Qatar, one can argue that strategic/tactical reasons explain the non-oppositionality of the Brotherhood: in the three decades prior to the 1980s, most of the Brotherhood figures in the Gulf were foreigners, who escaped persecution in their home countries and fled to the Gulf, and therefore did not have the necessary social and cultural capital to be oppositional. Moreover, the Muslim Brotherhood figures were welcomed by almost all Gulf rulers and were to support them against their own arch-enemies, secular-nationalists, who were agitating for similar revolutionary steps in the Gulf. From the 1980s onwards, the Muslim Brotherhood figures remained non-oppositional in Bahrain and Qatar. Likewise, for strategic reasons in Bahrain, they were to support the ruling Sunni dynasty against the Shia majority; in Qatar, they continued to be weak in social, political and economic capital in order to generate any opposition to the ruling dynasty and hence chose instead to be acquiescent and cooperative.

It is critical to add that Islamism as an ideology can condone such strategic/tactical considerations. In other words, Islamism can also be quite acquiescent with the modern state that implements no Islamic law or does it at a very basic level. This is because Islamism does not take the implementation of the Islamic law as its sole yardstick to judge political legitimacy and instead looks for or often prioritises features beyond the implementation of the Islamic law. Hence, supporting a friendly regime against hostile forces or not fighting a

41. With all due respect, the task Islamism sets forth might even be absurd: or, what Islamism wants to see in Islam might not actually exist in Islam. Recognition of this absurdity, in the way Albert Camus recommends, is obviously not a solution for Islamism, for it is Islamism's own suicide. Hence, Islamism's leap of faith in Islam. See Camus, *The Myth of Sisyphus*.

losing battle for the sake of survival can trump other considerations. In short, *the level of state religiosity might not have any real impact on the emergence of an Islamist opposition.*

Comparative Logic behind the Cases

The cases studied in this book are very similar in many different ways.[42] First, all five Gulf states are wealthy and can afford higher standards of living for their citizens, reflected in the fact that they all sit in the United Nations' category of 'very high' Human Development.[43] Second, modern state building in the Gulf is oil-financed. There is a sizeable literature on rentier states[44] and this literature suggests that opposition hardly forms against rentier states.[45] Even though this suggestion applies to Bahrain and Qatar in the case of the Muslim Brotherhood, it does not to Kuwait, Saudi Arabia and the UAE.

There are other factors that might be proposed to account for the observed variation among the Gulf states. Religion or sect cannot be such a factor because all the Gulf states accept Islam as their religion, and all of their ruling elites belong specifically to the Sunni branch of Islam. Another factor to consider might be the colonial past. A number of studies find that colonialism has long-term negative consequences for colonies, regarding their prospects for issues such as democratisation, economic development and ethnic harmony.[46]

---

42. Oman is kept out of this study because even though the Muslim Brotherhood also expanded to this country, the movement did not take deep root in the society and disappeared by the late 1970s. The fact that the ruling family of Oman and the majority of its population are not Sunni, but Ibadi, must have seriously limited the Brotherhood's spread.
43. The UN 2016 Human Development Report ranks Qatar 33rd, Saudi Arabia 38th, the UAE 42nd, Bahrain 47th and Kuwait 51st. See United Nations, *Human Development Report 2016*, p. 198.
44. Courtney Freer's aforementioned study challenges the rentier state literature. This literature suggests that civil society remains weak in rentier states and therefore the Muslim Brotherhood shouldn't have any political influence. But Freer's study shows to the contrary that the Brotherhood indeed has political influence. See Freer, *Rentier Islamism*.
45. Ross, 'Does oil hinder democracy?'.
46. This literature is sizeable and likely to grow in the future. For some exemplary studies, see Huntington, 'Will more countries become democratic?'; Young, 'The African colonial state in comparative perspective'; Acemoğlu, Johnson and Robinson, 'The colonial origins of comparative development'; Lange, 'British colonial legacies and political development'.

Saudi Arabia has no colonial past, while Kuwait until 1961, and Bahrain, Qatar and the UAE until 1971 were protected states of Britain.[47] Therefore, the colonial past does not explain why the Brotherhood became oppositional in Kuwait and the UAE, but not in Bahrain and Qatar.[48]

It must also be added that all five Gulf states are Arab states, geographically close to one another (and therefore have historically faced the same natural constraints) and 'dynastic monarchies'.[49] Finally, when they set out to become modern, all five Gulf states lacked the necessary human capital and therefore relied heavily on expatriate populations.

According to most similar systems design, 'systems as similar as possible with respect to as many features as possible constitute the optimal samples for comparative inquiry'.[50] Having so many similarities, the five Gulf states are therefore perfect cases for a comparative historical analysis.

Sources and Transliteration

The broader topic of state–religion relations in Saudi Arabia has attracted considerable scholarly attention. Therefore, a number of detailed analyses are available in English. For the most part I benefited from these secondary sources in my account.[51] In addition to them, I also relied on the available biographies of religious scholars and figures, especially those in a major biographical source, Abdullah Abd al-Rahman al-Bassam's six-volume *'Ulama'*

---

47. See Onley, 'Britain and the Gulf shaikhdoms, 1820–1971'.
48. Britain was usually less interventionist than other colonial powers in the domestic politics of its colonies. In the Gulf, Britain was even less interventionist than elsewhere. After the discovery of oil, Britain became more interventionist in the Gulf, but by then was not the global superpower it had once been. Nathan Brown persuasively illustrates how Britain failed in steering the development of the legal system in the Gulf, despite its best efforts to do so. See Brown, *Rule of Law in the Arab World*.
49. See Herb, *All in the Family*.
50. See Przeworski and Teune, *The Logic of Comparative Social Inquiry*, p. 32.
51. I would like to cite especially al-Rasheed, *Contesting the Saudi State*; Commins, *The Wahhabi Mission and Saudi Arabia*; Hegghammer, *Jihad in Saudi Arabia*; Lacroix, *Awakening Islam*; Mouline, *The Clerics of Islam*. There are also many articles and book chapters that can be added to this list: I would like to mention in particular Steinberg, 'The Wahhabi ulama and the Saudi state'. Steinberg, *Religion und Staat in Saudi-Arabien – Die Wahhabitischen Gelehrten 1902–1953* is unfortunately in German.

Najd Khilal Thamaniya Qurun [Ulama of Najd During Eight Centuries], or simply *Ulama Najd*.⁵²

Unfortunately the topic of state–religion relations in other Gulf states has not attracted the same level of attention. There are some notable exceptions and I benefited from them.⁵³ The prime archival source of the history of the Gulf states, the reports and letters of British officials stationed in the Gulf, contains few pieces of information regarding religion and religious figures.⁵⁴ The Turkish/Ottoman sources that I could consult do not contain much useful information either: for example, Sadık Albayrak's five-volume *Son Devir Osmanlı Uleması* [The Ottoman Ulama of the Last Period] contains no single entry of a religious scholar from Kuwait, Qatar or the eastern Arabian peninsula. Fortunately, other sources exist. Adnan Salim al-Rumi's *'Ulama' al-Kuwait wa A'lamuha Khilal Thalatha Qurun* [Kuwait's Ulama and Leading Personalities During Three Centuries], or simply *Ulama al-Kuwait*, provides many biographies of religious scholars from Kuwait.⁵⁵ For other Gulf states, to my knowledge, there is unfortunately no compilation of biographies of religious figures. Therefore I relied on biographies available on websites such as IkhwanWiki.com, al-qaradawi.net,⁵⁶ numerous tribal/family websites or those provided by relatives. Finally, in analysing how some prominent Brotherhood figures and organisations from the Gulf viewed the Arab Spring, I relied heavily on their Twitter posts.⁵⁷

Finally, I should add that the field of Gulf Studies is flourishing and producing high-quality academic treatments of the domestic and international politics of the modern Gulf. For the most part I relied on these in my

---

52. Al-Bassam, *'Ulama' Najd Khilal Thamaniyat Qurun [Ulama Najd]*. I thank Nadeen El-Ashmawy and Aya al-Makki for their research assistantship on this multi-volume book. Al-Rumi, *'Ulama' al-Kuwait wa A'lamuha [Ulama al-Kuwait]*.
53. Some notable exceptions are Freer, *Rentier Islamism*; Al-Mdaires, *Islamic Extremism in Kuwait*; Awadh, *Islamic Political Groups in Kuwait*; Al-Zumai, *The Intellectual and Historical Development of the Islamic Movement in Kuwait*; Hamed, *Islamic Religion in Qatar during the Twentieth Century*.
54. Many of the archival materials are available at Qatar Digital Library: https://qdl.qa/en.
55. Al-Rumi, *Ulama al-Kuwait*.
56. I thank Intidhar Amri for her research assistantship on these and similar sources.
57. I thank Nourhan Elsayed for her research assistantship on Twitter posts.

historical narrative and account of modern state building in the Gulf. In order to complement these secondary sources, I consulted two other sources: the laws promulgated by the Gulf states,[58] and the annual reports submitted by the Gulf states to the United Nations Educational, Scientific and Cultural Organization (UNESCO).[59]

As for transliteration, I adopted a simplified version of Encyclopedia of Islam's method. However, I further simplified this method. First, in transliterating person, family or tribal names into English I put no diacritical mark for the Arabic letters ayn and hamza and made no distinction between long and short vowels. I also used the same Latin letters for those Arabic letters that sound similar for many non-Arabs: I transliterated both the third and sixteenth letters as T, the sixth and twenty-sixth as H, the eighth and fifteenth as D, the eleventh and seventeenth as Z, and the twelfth and fourteenth as S.[60] If an Arabic word or a person name or place name is commonly used in English, I use its common form. Hence it is written as ulama, not 'ulama, or shariah, not shari'ah, or Abu Dhabi, not Abu Zabi. I also dropped the Arabic prefix al- from the names of places. Hence, it is Hasa, not al-Hasa, or Bahrain, not al-Bahrain. Finally, I transliterated Arabic person or place names as locally pronounced. Hence, it is Jassim, not Qassim, or Sharjah, not Sharqah.

Outline

The task at hand is to trace two historical processes: the development of the Gulf states' religious policies and of their relations with an Islamist movement, the Muslim Brotherhood. The book thus aims to show that even though the Gulf states have always been religious states, with Saudi Arabia

---

58. Some of these laws are available online. For Saudi Arabia's laws, visit the website of the Bureau of Experts at the Council of Ministers at https://www.boe.gov.sa; for Bahrain's laws, visit the website of the Bahrain Government at https://www.bahrain.bh; for Kuwait's laws, visit the website of the Kuwait Government at https://www.e.gov.kw/sites/kgoenglish/Pages/HomePage.aspx; for Qatar's laws, visit the website of the Qatar Legal Portal at http://www.legal.gov.qa/Default.aspx?language=en; for the UAE's laws, visit the website of the Ministry of Justice at http://www.elaws.gov.ae/EnLegislations.aspx.
59. These reports are accessible at the website of UNESCO's International Bureau of Education at http://www.ibe.unesco.org/en/ibedocs/national-reports.
60. I apologise in advance for this simplification, which might seem outrageous to speakers and experts of this beautiful language.

being even more religious than the others, the Muslim Brotherhood became oppositional irrespective of this fact.

The argument is laid out in the following six chapters. Chapter 1 provides the crucial historical background for the subsequent discussion. It describes the natural conditions in the Arabian peninsula, provides a political history of the region, and more critically discusses the emergence of a native class of religious scholars in Saudi Arabia with an intra-group solidarity, but not in other Gulf states. The chapter also introduces Islamism and the Gulf's early exposure to it.

Chapter 2 discusses the first stage of modern state building in the Gulf, a period lasting from the early 1950s to the late 1970s. Focusing on Gulf rulers' efforts in two fields historically occupied by religious scholars – justice and education – this chapter shows that all the Gulf states have never undergone strict state secularisation and explores how Saudi Arabia soon distinguished itself from the other Gulf states in its efforts to incorporate religious scholars.

Chapter 3 describes the geopolitical context the Gulf states faced in the 1950s and 1960s, and argues that this context and its domestic repercussions led the Gulf states to welcome the Muslim Brotherhood. The chapter then details how the Brotherhood expanded to the Gulf.

Chapter 4 investigates the second stage of modern state building in the Gulf, from the early 1980s until the late 2000s, and discusses Gulf rulers' continuing efforts in justice and education. The chapter illustrates that Gulf rulers have not changed their religious policies in any radical ways, but rather have continued along the same paths they set out in the 1950s. Any change introduced by the Gulf states in this period was not really substantive, but more rhetorical and symbolic, as they began to emphasise their religious credentials more strongly than before.

Chapter 5 describes the changing geopolitical context in which the Gulf states found themselves starting in the 1980s and explores the domestic repercussions of this context, more specifically, illustrating how state–Muslim Brotherhood relations deteriorated in Kuwait, Saudi Arabia and the UAE, but not in Bahrain and Qatar.

Chapter 6 focuses on the Arab Spring. It claims that the Arab Spring paved the way for the rise of the Muslim Brotherhood to political prominence across the region and as such was particularly troubling for Saudi Arabia, the UAE and Kuwait, where the Brotherhood had an oppositional history. The final chapter, Conclusion, briefly summarises the book and raises some theoretical points.

1

HISTORICAL BACKGROUND: DESERT AND ITS LEGACIES

The Desert

The basic fact about the Gulf is that it is a desert. Without modern technology it is an extremely harsh habitat for humans. Covered by sand and a variety of rock formations, this land mass receives little annual rain[1] and has no river of any size. As a result, it has scarce arable land, where agricultural activity has been historically restricted to date palm cultivation and a few other products, and can support only sparse vegetation. The Arabian peninsula has overall an extremely limited natural capacity for agriculture and husbandry.[2]

---

1. In 2012 Bahrain had 83 mm of precipitation, Kuwait 121 mm, Qatar 74 mm, Saudi Arabia 59 mm and the UAE 78 mm. For comparative purposes, the driest countries that year were Egypt with 51 mm of precipitation and Libya and Liechtenstein with 56 mm each. Four Gulf Arab states followed: Saudi Arabia, Qatar, the UAE and Bahrain. Kuwait was the twelfth-driest country, coming after Algeria, Mauritania and Jordan. Source: The World Bank, *World Development Indicators*.
2. Only modern technology has helped to improve this capacity over the last half a century. The table below illustrates the improvement from 1961 to 2012. The table also shows that the Arab Gulf states were well below the world average in both years.

   Arable Land (% of land)

	1961	2012
Bahrain	1.44	2.10
Saudi Arabia	0.53	1.46
Qatar	0.08	1.11
Kuwait	0.05	0.56
The UAE	0.05	0.56
World	9.55	10.75

   Source: The World Bank, *World Development Indicators*.

Due to this limited capacity in husbandry and agriculture, the peninsula has historically been extremely poor in both economic and human resources. Severe droughts, famine and various epidemics further crippled the peninsula's potential to nurture human life. Furthermore, the available economic and human resources were scattered across a huge land mass, concentrated in oases, where natural reservoirs of underground water came out of or were closer to the surface.

The distribution of oases is not uniform across the peninsula. Certain regions have more oases than others. The interior region, or Najd, for example, has numerous oases, scattered across a sizeable arc-shaped area extending for about 800 miles from the Great Nafud Desert in the north-west to Rubʻ al-Khali (the Empty Quarter) Desert in the south-east. The eastern part of the peninsula includes Hasa and Qatif in what is today Saudi Arabia, Liwa and Ain in what is today the UAE, and Bahrain.

The isolation of these oases is also partly responsible for why this part of the peninsula became a safe haven for those, especially religious minorities, who rebelled against and escaped from central authorities based in Iraq or Syria. Not surprisingly, the peninsula became early on in Islamic history a hotbed for the rebellious Kharijite and Shia movements that had been regularly oppressed by the ruling dynasties.[3] The Shias eventually came to dominate the oasis towns of Hasa and Qatif and the island of Bahrain in terms of population.[4]

In all these regions, oases spread over a territory much smaller in size than that of Najd. The island of Bahrain, for example, is about 300 square miles, but the oases are concentrated on the northern edge of the island only, constituting less than 2 per cent of the total territory. Hasa consists of oases spreading over an L-shaped area of around 120 square miles and Liwa spreads over an arc-shaped area around 80 miles from one end to the other.

The rest of the Arabian peninsula is even more difficult to inhabit: in the past, only the roaming Bedouin Arabs, with their precise knowledge of water wells and impeccable sense of direction, could survive in this

---

3. The mountainous regions of what are today Oman and Yemen were also safe havens for rebellious religious minorities. A Shia sect, Zaidism, flourished in Yemen and a Kharijite sect, Ibadism, in Oman. On the origins of Ibadism, see Wilkinson, *Ibadism*.
4. Cole, 'Rival empires of trade and Imami Shi'ism in eastern Arabia, 1300–1800'.

harsh environment with the meagre resources they had through animal husbandry and barter trade with the settled populations.[5]

The parts of the coast where Kuwait, Qatar and the UAE are located today are not naturally endowed with reservoirs of drinkable water in great quantities. They could not therefore support sizeable human settlements other than some fishing villages. The capitals of these countries, Kuwait City, Doha and Abu Dhabi, were founded in the eighteenth century and grew in size throughout the nineteenth century as the global demand for pearls increased.[6] Yet, even by the beginning of the twentieth century, they still had quite modest populations: Kuwait had a population of 37,000, Qatar, consisting of several towns, 27,000 and Abu Dhabi 11,000, with Dubai having a population of 10,000 and Sharjah 18,750. On the other hand, Bahrain, with its better resources, had a considerably higher population of 100,000.[7]

The Arabian peninsula, in short, had been able to support a weak economic base and feed a sparse population for a long period of time. This fact had at least two long-lasting legacies. First, the desert made political centralisation across the peninsula extremely difficult, if not impossible. Second, the desert delayed, if not prevented, the formation of a professional class of religious scholars.[8] The forthcoming discussion elaborates.

---

5. On the living conditions of the Bedouin Arabs of the Arabian peninsula, see Cole, *Nomads of the Nomads*.
6. On the growth of the pearling industry in the eighteenth century, see Yapp, 'The nineteenth and twentieth centuries'; Carter, 'The history and prehistory of pearling in the Persian Gulf'.
7. See Carter, 'The history and prehistory of pearling in the Persian Gulf', p. 199.
8. I must emphasise that the desert, or broadly speaking geography, climate or topography, does not abrogate human will. Rather, as I see it, it shapes and reshapes the material context within which humans make their choices. This applies not just to the peoples of the Arabian peninsula but to all peoples. Karl Marx spoke of traditions when he said, 'Men make their own history, but they do not make it as they please; they do not make it under self-selected circumstances, but under circumstances existing already, given and transmitted from the past.' But this statement equally applies to geography, climate or topography.

Late Political Centralisation: The Formation of the Modern State System in the Gulf

Because it was a harsh habitat for humans, the Gulf had historically been an unfavourable environment for any sort of political centralisation. Centrifugal forces such as the physical distance between oases, difficulty of transportation and the existence of Bedouin Arabs had been too strong to overcome and little, if no, centripetal force had been in place. A merchant class developed in the region, but it was situated in just a few major oasis towns. Given the weak economic and population base of the region, these merchants were unlikely to be in a position to support financially any unifying force.[9] Therefore, they either relied on private protection or directly bribed the nomads in order to continue their businesses, which in turn added to political decentralisation.

Well into the eighteenth century, the Najd region remained unaffected by any initiative towards political centralisation; political authority remained extremely localised and fragmented.[10] In the eastern region, where Hasa and Qatif are situated, some larger political units formed, which came to control sizeable territories. But these units were themselves highly unstable as they were merely tribal confederations, not bureaucratic empires or states, the likes of which had risen and fallen in the neighbouring, more fertile regions, such as Iran, Iraq, Anatolia, Syria and Egypt.[11]

This pattern ended in the eighteenth century with the rise of an ambitious political unification campaign led by Al Saud family in Najd. At the beginning of that century, a Sunni tribal confederation, Bani Khalid, controlled much of the eastern part of the peninsula from Kuwait to Qatar. Bahrain was under the control of the Iran-based Safavid Empire. The south shore of the Gulf, known as the coast of Oman, was under the suzerainty of the Yariba Imamate based in the interior of Oman. No single tribe or tribal confederation dominated the interior region, known as Najd. Almost every oasis town in Najd had its own ruling family, each vying and fighting with the others for supremacy.

---

9. For a detailed account of such an oasis town, see Altorki and Cole, *Arabian Oasis City*; Al-Rasheed, *Politics in an Arabian Oasis*.
10. Retz, *The Birth of the Islamic Reform Movement in Saudi Arabia*.
11. Cole, 'Rival empires of trade and Imami Shi'ism in eastern Arabia, 1300–1800'.

By the mid-eighteenth century, this scene had changed.[12] Bani Khalid was suffering from internal dissent, loosening its control over Kuwait. Benefiting from this, Al Sabah emerged as the ruling family of Kuwait and turned it into a trading town. Both the Safavids in Iran and the Yariba Imamate in Oman had already collapsed. After changing hands several times, Bahrain eventually fell under the rule of an Arab tribe, Al Madhkur, based in Bushire in southern Iran. Three decades later, Al Madhkur would lose the island to a new family, Al Khalifa. Originally from Najd, Al Khalifa was Sunni and has since then ruled over the predominantly Shia inhabitants on the island.

A new dynasty, Al Busaidi, rose to power in Oman, yet was not able to extend its rule over the coast of Oman. There, two competing powers vied for supremacy: Al Qawasim, a naval power based in Ras al-Khaimah in the north, and Bani Yas, a land power based at the Liwa Oasis in the south. The latter moved to the coast in the last quarter of the eighteenth century and settled in Abu Dhabi under the leadership of Al Nahyan family.

In this fluid regional political landscape, Al Saud, the ruling family of a small oasis town in Najd, began to rise in the mid-century. Al Saud's rise was at first slow: it took twenty-eight years to subdue the closest town, Riyadh, and more than forty years to control the whole Najd region. Yet, after subduing Najd, the rest succumbed to Al Saud much more swiftly. In the late eighteenth century, Al Saud defeated the by then already weakened Bani Khalid and added Hasa and Qatar to its possessions. By the early nineteenth century, the family extended its rule over the coast of Oman and over Hijaz in the western Arabian peninsula.

With the latter move, however, Al Saud became a force to be reckoned with for the regional and global powers, the Ottoman and British empires, which had otherwise shown no interest in this historically resource-poor region. By extending its control over Hijaz, Al Saud seriously harmed the Ottoman Empire's prestige in the Islamic world, a prestige coming from its suzerainty over the Holy Cities of Mecca and Medina.[13] By extending its

12. The following is a general account: see Commins, *The Gulf States*; Vassiliev, *The History of Saudi Arabia*; Zahlan, *The Making of the Modern Gulf States*; Rahman, *The Emergence of Qatar*; Abu Hakima, *History of Eastern Arabia*; Heard-Bey, *From Trucial States to United Arab Emirates*.
13. On Ottoman–Saud relations, see Kurşun, *Necid ve Ahsa'da Osmanlı Hakimiyeti*.

control over the coast of Oman, Al Saud challenged the British, who had been the dominant naval power in the Indian Ocean and were concerned with the safe passage of ships through the Gulf. Al Saud began to pose a threat to the British as it formed an alliance with Al Qawasim, a naval power in the Gulf.

After embarking on several, but limited, campaigns in the early 1800s, the British finally launched a major and decisive operation in 1819 and decimated the naval power of Al Qawasim. Almost simultaneously, the Ottomans took steps to confront Al Saud starting in the early 1800s, asking their powerful governor in Egypt, Muhammad Ali, to deal with the challenge. The Egyptian army, commanded by Muhammad Ali's son, first ousted Al Saud from Hijaz and then totally destroyed its power base in Najd by 1818.

The destruction of Al Saud and the decimation of Al Qawasim left the region in a political vacuum as neither the Ottomans/Egyptians nor the British had any interest in extending any sort of political authority. Having eschewed direct Al Saud rule, Al Sabah in Kuwait and Al Khalifa in Bahrain were relieved and continued to rule their small chiefdoms. Meanwhile, on the coast of Oman, the Bani Yas Federation, having resisted Al Saud, revived its fortunes, but failed to prevent the emergence of Dubai as an independent chiefdom under the rule of Al Maktoum family. Having lost its powerful ally, Al Saud, and being decimated by the British, Al Qawasim went into a period of decline and lost control of towns including Umm al-Quwain and Ajman, followed by Fujairah later in the century. Al Mualla, Al Nuaimi and Al Sharqi families came to rule these towns respectively. In the second half of the nineteenth century, Al Qawasim also suffered internal fragmentation and as a result Sharjah and Ras al-Khaimah became two separate chiefdoms under the rule of different branches.

Interested only in the security of the Indian Ocean and of the Gulf connected to it, the British imposed a treaty on Al Qawasim and forbade plunder and piracy on the sea.[14] The British imposed the same treaty on the ruling families of other towns on the coast of Oman. As the treaty was viciously enforced by the British, these towns increasingly turned to pearling as a

---

14. On British hegemony in the Gulf, see Onley, 'Britain and the Gulf Shaikhdoms, 1820–1971'. See also J. E. Peterson, 'Britain and the Gulf'.

source of income. By the mid-1830s, pearling had become such a critical source of income that the rulers of the coastal towns agreed to a truce to cease maritime warfare during the six-month pearling season.

The truce was renewed every year and became a ten-year truce in 1843. In 1853 the truce became perpetual. The British were the enforcer, protector and mediator in what had come to be called the Trucial System. The signatories of the truce became the Trucial States and the coast of Oman the Trucial Coast.

Eight years later, in 1861 Bahrain became part of the Trucial System. The British further increased their influence over Bahrain and the Trucial States in the last quarter of the nineteenth century as the latter agreed to Exclusive Agreements, according to which the rulers of Bahrain and the Trucial States agreed not to cede, sell or lease any territory to any other country except Britain and left the management of all of their external relations in the hands of the British.

Meanwhile, in Najd the political vacuum took longer to fill, as Egyptian forces did not remain in the region. The Egyptian army withdrew from Najd soon after it destroyed Al Saud and left the region in turmoil. In the ensuing vacuum, Al Saud family recovered and founded in the mid-1820s its second state, now based in Riyadh. Yet this state failed to recover the former's glory and could not extend its power beyond Najd. Primarily due to internal dissent, the family gradually lost ground to a newly rising family, Al Rashid, based in another Najd town, Hail. After Al Saud lost a decisive battle in 1891, the last ruler, Abd al-Rahman, left Najd and settled in Kuwait.

During the same period, Al Thani family had been on the rise in Qatar. Yet, having helped Al Khalifa capture Bahrain, it was still subordinate to Al Khalifa, except for a brief period during the Saudi period. The conflict between Al Khalifa and Al Thani eventually led to hostilities at sea, which Britain sought to halt. In 1868 the British imposed an agreement on Qatar and obliged it to keep the maritime peace in the Gulf and refer any trouble back to Britain. Even though the agreement was imposed on Qatar, Britain clearly recognised Al Thani as the ruling family. Bahrain's claim over Qatar continued, however, and troubled Al Thani for decades.

Al Thani's rise to power and the concomitant emergence of Qatar as an independent chiefdom were confirmed in the 1870s. By then the governor of the Baghdad province in the Ottoman Empire was Mithat Pasha, who was seeking to expand Ottoman control over the central and eastern Arabian peninsula. To this end, he utilised the internal dissent raging within Al Saud and in a swift military operation imposed Ottoman rule over the region in 1871. Kuwait, Najd, Hasa and Qatar were defined as separate administrative units and placed under the newly formed province of Basra.[15]

Ottoman rule confirmed Qatar's independence from Bahrain and consolidated Al Thani's position, as the Ottomans acknowledged it as the ruling family of Qatar. Qatar remained under Ottoman rule until 1913, the year the Ottoman Empire signed a treaty with Britain and left Qatar. It withdrew from the region two years later, during the First World War. In 1916 the new ruler of Qatar, Abdullah bin Jassim, signed the Exclusive Agreement with Britain and entered the Trucial System, delegating all external affairs to the British.

During their brief stay in the Gulf, the Ottomans stationed a small military force in the region and delegated much of the administration to the existing ruling families. Hence, they did not pay full attention to regional developments. They did not even notice that the ruler of Kuwait, formally an Ottoman territory, had secretly signed the Exclusive Agreement with Britain in 1899 and entered the Trucial System. The Ottomans also did not take any action when the son of the last Al Saud ruler, Abd al-Aziz bin Abd al-Rahman Al Saud, popularly known as Ibn Saud, captured Riyadh in 1903 and founded the third Saudi state.

This third Saudi state soon recovered its strength under the energetic, ambitious and shrewd leadership of Ibn Saud. The Ottomans withdrew from Hasa in 1913. Benefiting from the vacuum, Ibn Saud immediately moved in and added Hasa to his domain. During the next twelve years, Ibn Saud first defeated al-Rashid based in Hail and then the Sharif of Mecca. In January 1926 he proclaimed himself King of Hijaz and Sultan of Najd. Further expanding his domain, he annexed the Asir region in the south of Hijaz in 1930. Two years later, he unified all of his domains into one kingdom, which he called the Kingdom of Saudi Arabia.

15. Kurşun, *Basra Körfezi'nde Osmanlı-İngiliz Çekişmesi*. See also Anscombe, 'The Ottoman role in the Gulf'.

Ibn Saud was unwilling to provoke the British. Therefore he did not attack the smaller chiefdoms on the shore of the Gulf, even though the British provided maritime defence only and not land defence. However, the British soon began to show signs of changing this policy. At the beginning of the First World War, for example, they began to provide land defence to Kuwait against a possible Ottoman attack.

The discovery of oil in the region in the 1930s changed the British attitude. After losing concessions to an American oil company in Bahrain and Saudi Arabia in 1932 and 1933 respectively, the British began to offer full maritime, land and air defence to entice the other Gulf rulers to grant concessions to a British company. Qatar was the first chiefdom to grant an oil concession to a British oil company and in return began to receive full British protection. The British extended the same protection to the Trucial States in return for oil concessions in 1951.

By the mid-twentieth century, British protection over the Gulf was fully in place. However, after the Second World War, Britain was no longer the world superpower and began to relinquish control over its colonies. In the Gulf, Kuwait was the first, becoming a fully independent state in 1961. But the ruling family, Al Sabah, paid an unforeseeable price for this move. The neighbouring and much stronger Iraq renewed its territorial claim over Kuwait. To ward off Iraq's challenge, the ruling family agreed to a constitution that envisaged a parliament with legislative powers. Even though the parliament was often dissolved and faced closure for years, it has survived to this day and has become a unique feature of Kuwait's political system in the Gulf.[16]

In 1968 the British declared they would withdraw from the Gulf by 1971. Before completing the withdrawal, however, they worked to unite the remaining states, with partial success. Bahrain and Qatar decided not to join and became independent states in their own right in 1971. In the same year, six other Trucial States, Abu Dhabi, Dubai, Sharjah, Ajman, Umm al-Quwain and Fujairah, formed the UAE and became an independent state. A few months later, in 1972, Ras al-Khaimah joined the UAE. As the largest and wealthiest chiefdom, Abu Dhabi became the capital of this new state and its ruler the president.

---

16. See Herb, *The Wages of Oil*.

Late Formation of Religious Scholarship in the Gulf[17]

The desert also delayed the formation of an indigenous class of religious scholars in the Arabian Gulf region. This was to change in the Najd region, where a native class of religious scholars began to develop in the sixteenth century. The region had an even sparser population before the twelfth century, for the Najd tribes participated in the swift conquests of Egypt, Mesopotamia and Iran made by the early Muslim Arabs. The region's population began to increase again in the twelfth century, and by the sixteenth century had a considerable sedentary population in its oases.[18]

As the oasis towns became more populous, their own ruling families emerged which oversaw and undertook certain public functions such as protecting the settlement, adjudicating disputes and dispensing justice. The rulers usually resorted to tribal law in undertaking the last two of these, which must have been sufficient to solve problems in the usually small settlements. However, as the settlements grew in size, religious law came to supplement tribal law. We do not precisely know when this happened, but eventually there was a demand for religious scholars and other religious functionaries.

Al-Bassam's *Ulama Najd* mentions twenty-eight names of religious scholars from the sixteenth century,[19] providing separate entries for seventeen of them. The other names are mentioned in the biographies as either students or teachers. Based on the available biographies, it is possible to argue that there were a few pioneers who travelled to Damascus and Cairo to pursue a religious education and then returned to Najd to serve as a fountain of religious knowledge.[20] The most productive of them, in terms of the number of religious students he trained, appears to be Ahmad bin Yahya bin Atwah, who

---

17. For a broader look at the ulama class, see Zaman, *The Ulama in Contemporary Islam*.
18. Al-Juhany, *Najd Before the Salafi Reform Movement*.
19. Those religious figures who died during the sixteenth century are counted as being from that century.
20. Among the seventeen religious figures, five of them are reported to have travelled to Damascus and Cairo: Ahmad bin Yahya bin Atwah (v.1), Hasan bin Ali bin Abdullah (v.2), Zamil bin Mousa bin Jadwah (v.2), Ahmad bin Muhammad bin Musharraf (v.1), Muhammad bin Ibrahim Abi Humaidan (v.5). See al-Bassam, *Ulama Najd*: respective volumes stated in parentheses.

directly and indirectly taught at least half of the twenty-eight names reported to have lived in the sixteenth century.[21]

This shows that prior to the sixteenth century the region must have had almost no tradition of religious education. By the mid-eighteenth century, however, the Najd region had developed its own small centres of religious education in some of the major oasis towns such as Ushaiqir, Unaizah and Diriyah.[22] Ushaiqir was one of the earliest. Eleven of the seventeen religious scholars about whom al-Bassam provides separate biographical entries were from this town: some of them settled there and trained new students while serving as religious judges.

As time passed, the Najd region produced even larger numbers of religious scholars. Al-Bassam provides thirty-three biographical entries for religious scholars from the seventeenth century and ninety-one from the eighteenth century. While Ushaiqir continued to produce the highest number, some other towns also began to produce religious scholars. While twenty of the thirty-three religious figures about whom al-Bassam provides biographical entries were born in Ushaiqir in the seventeenth century, nine of them were born in another Najd town, Uyainah. In the eighteenth century, two other towns joined Ushaiqir and Uyainah: Unaizah and Mujammah, both of which surpassed Uyainah in terms of number of religious scholars. Out of ninety-one religious figures, more than half came from these three towns: eighteen from Ushaiqir, fourteen from Unaizah, nine from Mujammah and six from Uyainah.

Several features of this education must be noted. First, religious education took shape around certain individuals. Religious education was, in other words, restricted to what these individuals could offer. Second, from the very beginning, religious education was not the primary occupation of these religious scholars; rather, they were first and foremost religious judges in their towns. They also led prayers and delivered Friday sermons in the town's main mosque. If any time was left, they could use it to educate religious students. Hence, an elaborate religious specialisation, which could be observed elsewhere in the Islamic world, had not developed in Najd by the sixteenth

21. Ahmad bin Yahya directly taught nine of them. Five of them were students of his students. See al-Bassam, *Ulama Najd*, v.1, pp. 544–52.
22. Note that Diriyah acquired this status only after Muhammad ibn Abd al-Wahhab settled there in 1744. Al-Uthaymin, *Muhammad ibn Abd al-Wahhab*.

century. Not surprisingly, therefore, aspiring religious students continued to travel to Iraq, Syria and Egypt to pursue higher degrees in religious sciences, even late in the nineteenth century. Specialisation among religious scholars in Najd remained absent even as late as the mid-twentieth century.[23]

In tandem with this increasing diversification of geographical background, religious scholars also came from diverse tribal stock. Of seventeen religious figures from the sixteenth century, for example, twelve were from the al-Wahib clan of Bani Tamim, two from other clans of Bani Tamim and one from Bani Hanifa. The al-Wahib clan of Bani Tamim continued to produce the highest number of religious scholars: 15 of 33 religious scholars from the seventeenth century and 34 of 91 from the eighteenth century were from this clan. Bani Tamim's other clans produced another six religious scholars in the seventeenth century and sixteen in the eighteenth century. Even though Bani Tamim dominated religious scholarship, other major tribes also made their presence felt, such as Bani Khalid, Bani Zaab, Bani Qahtan and others. For example, Bani Khalid produced two religious scholars in the seventeenth century and four in the eighteenth century; Bani Zaab three and three; Bani Qahtan three and four; Bani Anaza six in the eighteenth century; Shammar two in the eighteenth century; and Bani Zaid, Bani Utaibah, Bani Hamdan, Bani Hajir, Al-Sabae and Al-Ibrahim each one religious scholar in the eighteenth century.[24]

In addition to tribal ties, religious scholars were joined through familial and master–student relationships. Yet it is still difficult to assess whether they had become a distinct class in Najd by the eighteenth century. They were too few in number, lived in different oasis towns and were extremely dependent on the whims of the rulers of those towns in which they lived.[25]

It was the major achievement of Wahhabism to create such a distinct class of religious scholars. It was also the Wahhabi movement that gave a decisive advantage to Al Saud family, otherwise an insignificant ruling family based in

23. Commins, *The Wahhabi Mission and Saudi Arabia*.
24. I was unable to map two figures from the seventeenth century and eleven from the eighteenth century in the tribal network based on the available information in al-Bassam.
25. The life of Muhammad ibn Abd al-Wahhab is a striking case in point. See Retz, *The Birth of the Islamic Reform Movement in Saudi Arabia*; DeLong-Bas, *Wahhabi Islam*; Commins, *The Wahhabi Mission and Saudi Arabia*.

the small oasis town of Diriyah in Najd, over its much stronger rivals. Wahhabism's founder was a religious scholar by the name of Muhammad bin Abd al-Wahhab who was born in the early eighteenth century in the oasis town of Uyainah in Najd. Belonging to the al-Wahib clan of Bani Tamim, ibn Abd al-Wahhab was raised in a scholarly family: both his father, Abd al-Wahhab bin Sulaiman, and his grandfather, Sulaiman bin Ali, had served as religious judges. Ibn Abd al-Wahhab first studied under his father and then travelled to Mecca, Medina and Basra to pursue higher education in religious studies.

It was during this period that ibn Abd al-Wahhab developed his puritanical views. To him the central tenet of Islam was the belief that 'there is no god, but God'. For ibn Abd al-Wahhab, this statement entailed more than acknowledging that there was no god, but God. It also entailed denying to any other being other than God any God-like feature. For ibn Abd al-Wahhab, it was critical that Muslims held this belief in the way ibn Abd al-Wahhab understood it, and behaved accordingly. A person holding a belief or undertaking a behaviour that contradicted this central tenet of Islam as understood by ibn Abd al-Wahhab was not committing a simple sin. He was committing the gravest of all sins, that is, associationism with God, and was therefore an apostate, for whom the punishment was capital.

For ibn Abd al-Wahhab pretty much all Muslims of his period, the Shias and the Sunnis alike, practised associationism. Ibn Abd al-Wahhab believed that he was living in an age described by a famous Prophetic Tradition, which stated, 'Islam began as something strange and will revert to being strange as it began.'[26] His mission was to call the Muslims to the truest and purest Islam, which could be found only in the original sources of Islam and the practices of the early Muslims, known as Salaf al-Salihin.

From Basra, ibn Abd al-Wahhab returned to Najd in 1738 and and settled in Huraimilah, where his father was serving as a religious judge. Ibn Abd al-Wahhab did not initially publicise his reformist views. Only on his father's death in 1740 did he become more vocal in preaching his puritanical understanding of Islam. His criticisms of the prevailing religious practices in Najd drew a strong reaction and as a result he was forced to leave the town, fearing that his life was in danger. From Huraimilah, ibn Abd al-Wahhab moved to

---

26. Commins, *The Wahhabi Mission and Saudi Arabia*, p. 16.

Uyainah in 1742. The town's ruler, Uthman bin Muammer, initially welcomed him, even marrying his sister to him and allowing him to preach and eradicate practices ibn Abd al-Wahhab deemed un-Islamic. But, unable to ward off increasing pressure from Sulaiman bin Muhammad, the ruler of Hasa, ibn Muammer asked ibn Abd al-Wahhab to leave.

Ibn Abd al-Wahhab settled in Diriyah in 1744, where he found a loyal disciple and ally in Muhammad bin Saud, the ruler of the town. Declaring the populations of the Arabian Desert as polytheists, the two Muhammads embarked on a religious mission to re-Islamise the Arabian peninsula. Such a mission brought a fundamental change in the politics of the Arabian Desert. Ibn Abd al-Wahhab's message worked as a subversive force, gaining the first Wahhabi–Saudi state fifth columns all across Najd. Yet, even though Ibn Abd al-Wahhab's message was powerful, it was also disturbing, gaining not only friends but also enemies. Furthermore, even though his ally was loyal, he was not the most powerful chief in the Desert. The movement's development therefore was not smooth. As mentioned previously, it took twenty-eight years to subdue the closest town, Riyadh, and more than forty years to take the whole Najd region. However, sixty-five years after the original pact between ibn Abd al-Wahhab and ibn Saud, the Wahhabi state was ruling over much of the Arabian peninsula.

Al Saud's success at political unification across the peninsula was remarkable. Nevertheless, it had obvious limitations. The first Wahhabi–Saudi state never aspired to establish a centralised bureaucratic state over the scattered populations of the Arabian Desert. It was more like a confederacy of oasis towns. It sufficed for the rulers for the settled and nomadic populations to declare their adherence to Wahhabism to be considered within the fold. In return, business went on more or less as usual. Furthermore, the state depended less on the regular extraction of resources from the population than on the unreliable and irregular booty acquired through constant military expansion. Hence, territorial expansion did not go hand in hand with institution building. Once the state reached the natural limits of its expansion, not surprisingly, it collapsed rather easily in the face of a determined and more superior enemy.

The only unifying element in this state was Wahhabism. When a town declared adherence to Wahhabism, Al Saud appointed to that town a religious judge, hand-picked from religious scholars who were trained in or embraced

Wahhabism. Those who refused to embrace Wahhabism were forced to leave Al Saud's domains.

The collapse of the first Wahhabi–Saudi state dealt a major blow to Wahhabi religious scholars in Najd: some of them were killed in battle, some of them, especially the immediate family of Muhammad bin Abd al-Wahhab, were forcibly deported to Egypt. Fortunately for the movement, some religious scholars survived. Soon after the Egyptian army withdrew from Najd, a member of Al Saud family revived the second Saudi state in the mid-1820s, but it never attained the power and geographical extent of the first. Moreover, it frequently suffered from political instability and eventually collapsed in the early 1890s. But with the critical support it provided in the meantime, the surviving Wahhabi religious scholars were able to thoroughly Wahhabise the Najd region and successfully thwart all attempts by non-Wahhabi scholars and Sufis to penetrate it.[27]

More critically, perhaps, this ordeal hardened Wahhabi religious scholars and transformed them into a distinct class, strongly and self-consciously committed to the teachings of Muhammad bin Abd al-Wahhab. This class, unlike their colleagues elsewhere, was neither deeply entrenched in an institutionalised state structure nor in control of wealthy economic resources like their Ottoman, Egyptian or Iranian colleagues. But they still constituted a group, united through informal ties including class identity, marriage and education, and organised under an informal hierarchy of the leadership of the descendants of Muhammad bin Abd al-Wahhab, known as Al al-Sheikh.[28]

Al al-Sheikh, literally meaning the family of the Sheikh, descended from the al-Wahib clan of Bani Tamim. This branch continued to dominate religious scholarship in the nineteenth century. Of 158 religious figures about whom al-Bassam provides biographical information,[29] forty-seven came from the al-Wahib clan. Other branches of Bani Tamim also continued to produce religious scholars, twenty-seven in total in the nineteenth century. But religious scholars came from even more diverse tribal backgrounds, including such major tribes

27. Commins, *The Wahhabi Mission and Saudi Arabia*; Commins, 'Traditional anti-Wahhabi Hanbalism in nineteenth-century Arabia'.
28. Ibid.; also see Mouline, *The Clerics of Islam*.
29. This number does not include sixteen names from Zubair, Iraq and twenty-seven names I was unable to map in the tribal network.

as Dawasir, Bani Anaizah, Bani Hanifah, Bani Ajman, Bani Khalid, Bani Zaid, Shammar, Bani Lam and Bani Khazraj, each producing between three and nine religious functionaries in the nineteenth century.

By the twentieth century, the teachings of ibn Abd al-Wahhab were firmly established among the populations of the Najd region. More importantly, his disciples, looking like a tribal confederacy but still united under an informal hierarchy, constituted the only organised group in the Arabian peninsula with an identity transcending all localising tribal identities. They served as religious judges, prayer leaders and teachers – the same person generally occupying all these roles at the same time – and as such were the only group who had easy and regular access to scattered populations.

Having no military power of their own, Wahhabi religious scholars could not bring political unity back to the region. But they could provide critical help to a potential candidate in unifying and consolidating a realm. This was their contribution to the unification campaign launched by the future King of Saudi Arabia, Abd al-Aziz Al Saud, in 1902. His first act after capturing Riyadh sent a powerful message to Wahhabi religious scholars across Najd: he married Tarfa bint Abdullah al-Sheikh, the daughter of the religious judge of Riyadh, Abdullah bin Abd al-Latif al-Sheikh, a descendant of Muhammad ibn Abd al-Wahhab and by then the leader of the Wahhabi religious scholars.[30] Longing for a powerful and ambitious ruler, Wahhabi religious scholars flocked to Abd al-Aziz's cause.

The strong religious legitimacy the Wahhabi religious scholars accorded to Abd al-Aziz Al Saud saved him precious time in strengthening his family's legitimacy to rule and greatly reduced the role of brute force in unifying Najd. The Wahhabi religious scholars waged intense religious propaganda for Abd al-Aziz, portraying him, for example, as the defender of true Islam.[31]

In addition to waging religious propaganda, the Wahhabi religious scholars also provided a critical service to Abd al-Aziz in the creation of a fearsome

---

30. For an alternative interpretation of Abd al-Aziz al Saud's marriages, see al-Rasheed, *A History of Saudi Arabia*.
31. Abdullah al-Anqari, a prominent Wahhabi religious scholar, wrote: 'God granted Muslims a religious government, represented by the imam Abd al-Aziz ibn Abd al-Rahman ibn Faysal [al Saud], God grant him victory and give him the strength to enforce the Law and destroy blameworthy innovations.' Cited in Mouline, *The Clerics of Islam*, p. 95.

military force from the nomadic populations of Najd, or the Bedouins. The Bedouins were encouraged to settle permanently in certain oases under Abd al-Aziz's control. Wahhabi religious scholars were then sent to these settlements to indoctrinate the now settled Bedouins in Wahhabism. Embracing Wahhabism rather fanatically and driven by a zeal to spread it, this military force, known as the Ikhwan (Brothers), greatly contributed to Abd al-Aziz's military campaigns.[32]

Finally, the Wahhabi religious scholars compensated for one critical disadvantage Al Saud family faced against their rivals: the Rashidis came from a major nomadic family from Najd, Shammar, and the Hashimis enjoyed religious charisma as they descended from the family of the Prophet of Islam through his grandson, Hasan. As emphasised previously, the Wahhabi religious scholars also came from the major tribes of Najd, thus providing Al Saud family with what Madawi al-Rasheed calls 'tribal depth'.[33]

The new Wahhabi–Saudi state was no different from the previous ones in terms of its administrative capacity. It was a tribal state par excellence with no bureaucracy and no standing army. The state lived off booty and, with the incorporation of Mecca and Medina, pilgrimage revenues. However, neither source of revenue was regular. Once the state reached its natural limits of expansion, booty was no longer an option. In fact, when Abd al-Aziz strategically stopped further expansion so as not to confront Britain, his own forces, the Ikhwan, turned against him. Abd al-Aziz was only able to eradicate the Ikhwan threat through a bloody confrontation during which leading Wahhabi religious scholars stood by Al Saud and thus legitimated his action. The Great Depression and the Second World War further reduced pilgrimage revenues.

In such dire financial circumstances, the Saudi state didn't have the necessary resources to expand its services beyond public order and justice: along with provincial governor-princes and their strong men, Wahhabi religious scholars provided justice in their courts, which were usually in a mosque or sometimes even a house. Religious scholars also continued to provide religious education in the time-honoured master–disciple tradition. During the formation of the kingdom in the first quarter of the century, religious scholars also took on responsibility for the regulation of public morality and

---

32. See Habib, *Ibn Sa'ud's Warriors of Islam*; Mouline, *The Clerics of Islam*, pp. 97–107.
33. Al-Rasheed, *A History of Saudi Arabia*, p. 25.

founded the nucleus of what would become Hay'at al-'amr bi'l ma'ruf wa'l nahyi 'an'il munkar (Committee for the Promotion of Virtue and the Prevention of Vice), or the religious police.

By the time oil began to transform Saudi Arabia in the 1950s, the Wahhabi religious scholars already had a firm control over justice, education and public morality. They were also the native literate class, having excellent relations with the ruling family.

Religious Scholarship in Other Gulf States

The tribes of eastern Arabia also participated in the conquests of early Muslim Arabs, which led to a considerable decline in the population in this region. However, Hasa and Bahrain, in particular, with their better economic opportunities, soon began to attract populations as they turned into safe havens for those persecuted by successive Muslim dynasties. Eventually a Shia sect, Ismailism, came to dominate in Bahrain and Hasa.[34]

From time to time, Sunni tribal federations dominated Bahrain and Hasa, but the majority of the populations in these two places have remained Shia, not as Ismaili though, but as Twelver, another sect of Shiism, which was adopted and spread into the region by the Safavid Empire.[35] Hence, with the relatively better economic conditions, Hasa and Bahrain developed their own native class of Shia religious scholars. They also continued to import Shia religious scholars from or send religious students to Iraq and Iran.[36] Even though the populations in Hasa and Bahrain were and still are predominantly Shia, Hasa nevertheless became a centre of Sunni religious education in the Arabian peninsula around the same time that Najd did. The region not only attracted religious students from but also exported religious scholars to the other Gulf states, in particular Kuwait, Bahrain and Abu Dhabi.[37] Still, Hasa could not be compared to the Holy Cities of Mecca and Medina and other

---

34. See Cole, 'Rival empires of trade and Imami Shi'ism in eastern Arabia, 1300–1800'.
35. See ibid.
36. See Louër, *Transnational Shia Politics*.
37. From Qatar too, students went to Hasa to pursue religious education. Abdullah al-Ansari, for example, studied in Hasa. Abdullah's father was a religious judge in Khor, a town north of Doha, who migrated to Qatar from the Persian side of the Gulf. On his return to Qatar, Abdullah al-Ansari served in the Ministry of Education, responsible for rural affairs. See Mukhtar, *'Allamah Qatar al-Sheikh 'Abdullah Bin Ibrahim al-Ansari*.

Arab countries such as Egypt, Iraq and Syria, or even to Najd, in terms of prestige and size as a centre of Sunni religious education. Only a few families dominated religious scholarship in Hasa, one of the most prominent being the al-Mubarak family, which originated in Najd. As the available biographies illustrate, members of this family often travelled outside Hasa to pursue higher religious education. Mubarak bin Ali, the person after whom the family was named, for example, was in Baghdad when he died.[38] Hasa became part of Saudi Arabia in 1913.

Bahrain,[39] on the other hand, did not become a centre of Sunni religious education. Throughout the nineteenth century and the first half of the twentieth, two families dominated the religious judiciary in Bahrain: the al-Jame family in the first half of the century and al-Mahza family afterwards. The first member of the al-Jame family in Bahrain was Uthman bin Jame, who was born and studied in Najd and then migrated to Bahrain.[40] Uthman's son, Ahmad, took over the judiciary and left it in the hands of his own son, Muhammad, when he himself settled in Zubair, Iraq.[41] Muhammad also left Bahrain and settled in Zubair to take over the judiciary after his father died.[42] The al-Mahza family moved to Bahrain from the other coast of the Gulf in the mid-nineteenth century. In terms of religious education, Qasim bin Mahza and his nephew, Abd al-Rahman bin Mahza, studied in Hasa and Ahmad bin Mahza, Qasim's brother, in al-Azhar in Egypt. Bahrain also imported religious scholars from Hasa, several members of the al-Mubarak family serving as religious judges, prayer leaders and preachers on the island.[43]

Kuwait had also not become a centre of Sunni religious education, even though it was closer to Iraq's major urban centres such as Basra and Baghdad

38. There is information on al-Mubarak family on the family website: www.almubarak.org.
39. For a history of Bahrain, see Joyce, *Bahrain from the Twentieth Century to the Arab Spring*.
40. Al-Bassam, *Ulama Najd*, v.5, pp. 109–12.
41. Al-Bassam, *Ulama Najd*, v.1, pp. 492–3.
42. Al-Bassam, *Ulama Najd*, v.5, pp. 496–7.
43. See Salih bin Muhammad al-Mubarak, al-Bassam, *Ulama Najd*, v.2, p. 539; Abdullah bin Abd al-Rahman al-Mubarak, al-Bassam, *Ulama Najd*, v.4, p. 210; Abdullah bin Abd al-Aziz al-Mubarak, al-Bassam, *Ulama Najd*, v.4, p. 262; Hamad bin Abd al-Latif bin Mubarak, Muhammad bin Abd al-Latif bin Mubarak and Yusuf bin Rashid al-Mubarak, Nasab Mubarak at www.almubarak.org.

and to the Najd and Hasa. Religious scholars from the Najd and Hasa often settled in Kuwait and served as religious judges and prayer leaders. It is claimed that the first religious judge of Kuwait, Muhammed bin Abd al-Wahhab bin Fairuz, was from Ushaiqir in the Najd region.[44]

At the beginning of the twentieth century Kuwait was less populous than Bahrain, but more so than Qatar and the individual Trucial towns. With a population concentrated in a smaller territorial space and enjoying close geographical proximity to major Iraqi towns, Kuwait was more attractive as a destination and not surprisingly developed a much stronger merchant class than Qatar and the UAE: in Qatar the merchants were small in number and in the UAE the Indian merchants dominated trade under British protection.[45]

Among those who found Kuwait more attractive were a number of religious scholars/figures who also often engaged in commerce. Descendants and students of these early figures[46] became interested in pursuing higher levels of religious knowledge and to this end travelled to other places such as Zubair, Basra, Hasa, Mecca, Medina, Cairo and Damascus. The fact that Kuwait had become a state of merchant families whose networks spanned all these regions must have helped seekers of religious knowledge there.

By the end of the nineteenth century Kuwait had its own native religious scholars who served as prayer leaders and preachers in various mosques and also ran their private religious schools, known as *Kuttab*, teaching basic religious topics and arithmetic.[47] More significantly, Kuwait did not have to import religious judges from elsewhere, as Qatar and the Trucial States did:

---

44. See al-Bassam, *Ulama Najd*, v.6, pp. 267–9.
45. See Crystal, *Oil and Politics in the Gulf*; Davidson, *Dubai*; Davidson, *Abu Dhabi*; Al-Fahim, *From Rags to Riches*.
46. Such as Abd al-Jalil al-Tabatabai, Muhammad al-Adsani, Muhammad bin Faris, Khalaf al-Dahyan, Muhammad al-Farsi and Ahmad al-Badah. For biographical information on these names, see al-Rumi, *Ulama al-Kuwait*.
47. Among them are Sulaiman Ali al-Rifai, Hamad bin Abd al-Rahman al-Bawwadi, Ahmad bin Muhammad al-Qattan, Muhammad bin Ibrahim al-Tabatabai, Muhammad bin Junaidal, Abd al-Wahhab bin Yusuf al-Haniyan, Abdullah al-Khalaf al-Dahyan, Ahmad bin Muhammad al-Farsi and Ali Ibrahim al-Ibrahim. For biographical information on these names, see al-Rumi, *Ulama al-Kuwait*.

in the late nineteenth and early twentieth centuries several al-Adsani family members served as religious judges in Kuwait.[48] There were also other Kuwaitis who served as religious judges.[49] There was only one foreigner, Abd al-Muhsin Aba Batain, who served as a religious judge in Kuwait in the 1930s. He remained in Kuwait very briefly and was replaced by Abd al-Aziz bin Qasim bin Hammadah.[50]

Yet religious scholars in Kuwait never played the role religious scholars in Saudi Arabia played: the ruling Al Sabah family did not rely on them in consolidating its power or legitimising its authority. Religious scholars in Kuwait developed familial links with the growing merchant class: for example, al-Adsani family came to be known as a merchant family.[51] Furthermore, while religious scholars in Saudi Arabia were deeply local, all Najdi, and attached to one school of jurisprudence, Hanbalism, religious scholars in Kuwait came from different regions, such as Najd, Hasa, Basra or even Iran, and therefore followed different schools of jurisprudence. Last, but not least, even though they developed a master–disciple relationship among each other, they still did not develop an aristocratic scholarly family, like al-Sheikh family in Saudi Arabia, who could have served as their leader and representative.

Among all the coastal states, Qatar had possibly the weakest population and agricultural base[52] and emerged as an independent political entity much later than the others. If any properly trained religious scholar existed in Qatar in the late nineteenth century, it is likely he was a religious judge appointed by the Ottomans. Al-Bassam records Jassim bin Muhammad, the merchant-ruler, as a Wahhabi religious scholar of the Najd.[53] However, his recognition must be due not to the fact that Jassim was truly a religious scholar but rather to his being the first Al Thani ruler who embraced Wahhabism. The Ottomans appointed a certain es-Seyyid Abd al-Latif as a religious judge under

---

48. See the biographical information on Abdullah al-Adsani in al-Rumi, *Ulama al-Kuwait*.
49. Such as Yusuf bin Isa al-Qinai, Ahmad Atiyya al-Athari and Abd al-Aziz bin Qasim bin Hammadah. See biographical information on these names in al-Rumi, *Ulama al-Kuwait*.
50. See biographical information on Abd al-Aziz bin Hammadah in al-Rumi, *Ulama al-Kuwait*.
51. See Assiri and al-Monoufi, 'Kuwait's political elite'.
52. On the poor agricultural base of Qatar, see statements from Ottoman officials in Kurşun, *Basra Körfezi'nde Osmanlı-İngiliz Çekişmesi*, pp. 3–6.
53. Al-Bassam, *Ulama Najd*, v.5, pp. 405–10.

Muhammad bin Thani. Except in certain years, the Ottomans continued to appoint a religious judge to Qatar until their departure in 1913.[54] Biographical information is available for only four Ottoman-appointed religious judges who served in Qatar:[55] they were all Iraqi, which shows again that Qatar did not have native religious scholars.

According to the Qatari narrative, which is different to the Ottoman narrative, a certain Muhammad ibn Hamdan served as a religious judge from 1862 to 1887. After bin Hamdan's departure, Abdullah al-Dirham became the religious judge in 1893 and remained in post until 1914.[56] I could find no biographical information on Muhammad bin Hamdan. Al-Dirham's ancestors were originally from Najd, but he was born in Qatar; however, he received his religious education in Najd.[57] Al-Dirham was succeeded as religious judge by Muhammad bin Abd al-Aziz al-Mana. Al-Mana was originally from the Najd region, but studied in Iraq and Egypt. During his stay in Qatar until 1939, al-Mana also gave religious lessons to students not only from Qatar, but also from the region.[58] However, religious education at the school revolved around the personality of al-Mana, who could not devote all of his time to teaching. Not surprisingly, when he left Qatar in 1939, the school could not continue to function and was closed down.

Like other coastal states that had developed in response to the boom in pearling, Qatar suffered severely from the collapse of the industry in the 1930s. Some religious figures left in search of better opportunities: for example, Muhammad bin Abd al-Aziz al-Mana left Qatar for Saudi Arabia. Qatar's next religious judge, Abdullah bin Zaid al-Mahmoud, was also a foreigner, born in Hawtah in the Najd region and brought to Qatar from Mecca by Abdullah bin Jassim Al Thani, the ruler of Qatar. Al-Mahmoud served first as the religious judge and then as the president of religious courts in Qatar until the mid-1990s.[59]

54. See the names of religious judges and their terms in Qatar in Kurşun, *Basra Körfezi'nde Osmanlı-İngiliz Çekişmesi*, Appendix.
55. See Albayrak, *Son Devir Osmanlı Uleması*.
56. See Hamed, *Islamic Religion in Qatar During the Twentieth Century*, p. 220.
57. I thank Aisha al-Dirham, a descendant of Abdullah al-Dirham, for this biographical information. The text containing this information is available from the author.
58. See al-Bassam, *Ulama Najd*, v.6, pp. 726–8.
59. See al-Bassam, *Ulama Najd*, v.4, pp. 120–33.

Like Qatar and Kuwait, those coastal towns that make up the UAE today emerged in response to the growth of pearling. They gained their first religious judges in the early twentieth century. Lacking a native class of religious scholars, Dubai and Abu Dhabi brought their religious judges from Morocco and Tunisia, while Sharjah and Ras al-Khaimah brought them from the Najd region.[60] In later decades, these states continued to import religious judges: for example, Muhammad bin Ahmad al-Shanqiti, who served as the chief judge in Dubai, was a graduate of al-Azhar and possibly, as his family name suggests, from Mauritania. Ahmad bin Abd al-Aziz al-Mubarak, who was appointed in 1969 as the head of the Shariah division in Abu Dhabi's judiciary and served as an advisor to the ruler, was also not a native but from Hasa.[61] Only later did local inhabitants become religious judges in these states. However, they still had to travel abroad for their religious studies. For example, Mubarak bin Ghobash, who served as Ras al-Khaimah's religious judge, and Abdullah al-Shaibah, Ajman's native religious judge, studied in Qatar under Muhammad al-Mana.[62]

Unlike Saudi Arabia, in short, the other Gulf states did not develop a native class of religious scholars. Those in Kuwait were natives, but had not developed group solidarity. Religious scholars in Bahrain, Qatar and the UAE were few in number and mostly foreigners. Moreover, neither in Kuwait nor in Bahrain, Qatar or the UAE had they played any meaningful political roles in the rise of the ruling families and their consolidation of power. However,

---

60. According to Heard-Bey, *From Trucial States to United Arab Emirates*, pp. 452–3, the first judge of Dubai was Muhammad bin Abd al-Salam al-Maghrebi from Morocco, who died in Dubai in the 1940s. Abd al-Rahman bin Hafiz, an Arab from Lingah, and Mubarak bin Ali bin Bashit, a Dubai citizen, succeeded him. In Abu Dhabi, first Muhammad Ali Buzainah from Tunisia and then Badr bin Yusuf from Bahrain served as the religious judges. The religious judges of Ras al-Khaimah and Sharjah were Ahmad bin Humaid al-Raghbani and Abd al-Rahman bin Abdullah bin Faris, both from Najd. There is an alternative claim as to the first judges of Dubai, however. A native of Dubai, a certain Khamis, is claimed to be the first religious judge of Dubai, who went to Hasa to study religion and came back to serve as a religious judge. This alternative claim cites Muhammad bin Abd al-Salam as the third religious judge, not the first. See Dubai Courts, 'Nabdhat Tarikhiyya'.
61. Available at www.almubarak.org.
62. See Abd Allah, *The United Arab Emirates*.

some, if not all, of them were instrumental in bringing Islamism to the Gulf. The next section introduces Islamism and discusses its penetration in the Gulf.

Islamism and the Muslim Brotherhood

Islamism originated as a set of ideas, rather than a social movement, in the nineteenth century.[63] It was in this century that some Muslim intellectuals realised the stark and growing disparity in power between the West and Muslim countries. Until the late eighteenth century, this disparity had been ignored because it did not yet create a hostile international environment for the Muslim states. However, the European powers, especially Britain, France and Russia, became increasingly aggressive in the nineteenth century and began to colonise the Islamic world.

Various rulers across the Muslim world took steps to thwart this process and implemented reforms to remodel their state institutions using European examples. Even so, the Mughals could not escape direct British colonisation in the mid-nineteenth century. Likewise, the Qajars could not prevent Russian and British advances and the eventual division of Iran into two spheres of influence in the early twentieth century. In North Africa, two semi-autonomous provinces of the Ottoman Empire, Egypt and Tunisia, undertook possibly the most successful state reforms in the Muslim world, but still could not escape British and French colonisation respectively in the late nineteenth century.

The Ottomans also initiated and pursued extensive and ambitious reform of the army, bureaucracy, education and the legal system. Still, the Empire could not prevent territorial losses in the Balkans, Caucasus and North Africa. Not only the superpowers of the period, Britain, France, Russia and Austria-Hungary, but also Ottoman minorities such as the Greeks, Bulgarians and Serbians, cut their own territorial pieces out of the Empire. By the end of the nineteenth century, other remaining religious and ethnic groups, such as Albanians, Armenians, Arabs and Kurds, also began to long for their own states and imagined a total break from the Empire.

---

63. Islamism originated in the nineteenth century as an idea, but developed as a grassroots social movement in the twentieth century. For a more detailed discussion, see Lapidus, *A History of Islamic Societies*, Part III; Hefner, *The New Cambridge History of Islam*.

The nineteenth century also witnessed European ideas and ideologies such as materialism, positivism and rationalism penetrating the Muslim world and gaining adherents. This wholesale ideational invasion came with a parallel development, a serious questioning of Islam as a religion. Various European thinkers had spoken negatively about Islam prior to the nineteenth century. Now they did it from a position of superior power.

In a lecture delivered at Paris' Sorbonne University in 1883, Ernest Renan, for example, held Islam responsible for the backwardness of the Muslims:

> Anyone with even the slightest education in matters of our time sees clearly the current inferiority of Muslim countries, the decadence of states governed by Islam, the intellectual sterility of races that derive their culture and education from that religion alone. All who have been to the Orient or to Africa are struck by what is the inevitably narrow-mindedness of a true believer, of that kind of iron ring around his head, making it absolutely closed to science, incapable of learning anything or of opening itself up to any new idea.

For Renan, 'Islam' was 'an indistinguishable union of spiritual and temporal', 'the reign of dogma' and 'the heaviest chain that humankind has ever borne'.[64] And as such it was the prime reason for the backwardness of the Muslims.

Islamism was born in this milieu as an intellectual effort to defend Muslims and their religion, Islam, against what seemed to be an unjustified and total European assault. From Egypt to Iran, from Tunisia to Syria and Iraq, from Ottoman Turkey to India, many contributed to the development of Islamism. For sure, these figures differed from each other across several dimensions: literalism versus rationalism, scripturalism versus Sufism. But nevertheless, Islamism had a core set of claims about Islam to which a large majority of its adherents subscribed. These included a reform of Islam, even though what kind, for what purpose and to what extent could be disputed.

Islam, as Jamal al-Din Afghani, the undisputed luminary of Islamism in the nineteenth century, would argue with Renan, could indeed be an obstacle to science. But this was not because of Islam itself; it was because of how Islam was understood and practised by ordinary Muslims. As Christians

---

64. Renan, *Islam and Science*, p. 3.

threw off the yoke of their religion and advanced 'rapidly on the road of progress and science', Muslims could do the same, 'breaking [Islam's] bonds and marching resolutely in the path of civilisation someday after the manner of Western society'.[65] But Islam needed a reformation for Muslims to do this, as had happened in Christianity.

If appropriately reformed, Islam could therefore be made compatible with science. Islamism eventually came to claim more than this, however. Islam could be reformed so as to become a great source not only for generating progress and development, but also for solidifying relations among Muslims at all levels, individual, communal, national and international.

The problem was that the Muslims of the period were not tapping the great potential in Islam and for that very reason were weak politically, economically and culturally, dominated by the West. The Muslims once untapped Islam's potential and created a great civilisation in the seventh to the sixteenth centuries. They did so because they subscribed to and lived up to the true Islam, the Islam represented by the Prophet and those who succeeded him, the Salaf. As time passed, however, Islamism claims, Muslims had strayed from that Islam and as a result were weakened, becoming both internally divided and externally powerless.

To recover it, Muslims needed to understand and live by the true Islam, which could only be found in Islam's primary sources, the Qur'an and the Prophetic Traditions. By doing so, Islam could be remade relevant to Muslims' lives. Islam, conceived as such, was more than a religion. It was not just for regulating the relations between God and God's servants. It also regulated all of human life. Islamism started as an elite project. Its early proponents sought initially to influence the rulers. But it also envisioned a social transformation: Muslims had to be retaught as Islam was reformed. As such, Islamism found its loudest voice in Hasan al-Banna.

Hasan al-Banna: The Founder of the Muslim Brotherhood

Al-Banna was born in 1906 in Mahmoudiyah, Egypt. His father, Ahmad, was a local cleric and a watch repairer. Widely read in different religious fields, Ahmad had even written a commentary on a famous collection of

---

65. Cited in Keddie, *An Islamic Response to Imperialism*, p. 183.

Prophetic Traditions, the Musnad of Ahmad bin Hanbal. Hasan received his early education in a school attached to a mosque in Mahmoudiyah. In 1919 he enrolled in an elementary-level teachers' college in Damanhur and then moved to Dar al-'Ulum (House of the Sciences) College in Cairo, completing his education in 1927.

During his Cairo years, Hasan al-Banna was exposed to the Islamist literature that had been developing since the late nineteenth century in the writings of such figures as Jamal al-Din Afghani, Muhammad Abduh and Rashid Rida. When al-Banna was in Cairo, Rida was alive and still publishing his famous journal, *al-Manar*. Al-Banna not only attended Rida's meetings and became an avid reader of *al-Manar*, but also befriended Muhib al-din al-Khatib, a Syrian journalist who settled in Cairo in the 1920s and founded a publishing house and a bookshop, from where he propagated Salafism, which called for a return to unadulterated Islam.

Hasan al-Banna viewed Islam as 'a perfect system of social organization which encompasses all the affairs of life'.[66] Islam was a comprehensive religion (al-din al-shamil). Comprehensiveness meant that Islam concerned not only the afterlife, but also everything in this life. Islam set forth the fundamentals of belief and prescribed in detail the duties of humans to their creator and sustainer, Allah. However, Islam was, in al-Banna's view, beyond this. It also set forth guidelines for Muslims to follow while regulating all other social, economic, political and even international affairs.

Hasan al-Banna stated his view of Islam repeatedly. While addressing a group of students, he said, for example:

> Tell me, Brothers: if Islam is something other than politics, society, economy and culture, what is it then? Is it only prostrations devoid of a pulsating heart? . . . Did the Qur'an reveal a perfect, fixed and detailed system just for that? . . . It is precisely to such a weak and narrow understanding of Islam that the enemies of Islam try to confine the Muslims so that they can mock them and say to them, 'We left you your freedom of religion.'[67]

---

66. Al-Banna, *Five Tracts of Hasan Al-Banna (1906–1949)*, p. 30.
67. Cited in Krämer, *Hasan al-Banna*, p. 51.

In another piece, titled *To What Do We Summon Mankind?*, al-Banna said:

> The Noble Qur'an is an all-inclusive book in which God has gathered together the fundamentals of religious doctrine and the basis of social welfare, as well as the broad generalities of secular legislation, containing both commands and prohibitions.[68]

Al-Banna believed that, if properly used, Islam could be an awesome source of progress and welfare, not only spiritually, but also materially by providing solutions to all the problems Muslims and non-Muslims alike face. In *To What Do We Summon Mankind?*, al-Banna said:

> God ... incorporated within this true religion [Islam] all the fundamentals necessary for the life of nations, their advancement and their prosperity ... If you examine the teachings of Islam, you will find that it promulgates the soundest principles, the most suitable regulations and the most precise laws for the life of the individual, man or woman, for the life of the family both during its formation and its dissolution, and for the life of nations during their growth, their strength, and their weakness, and sanctions ideas before which even reformers and leaders of nations have stood hesitant.[69]

What distinguished Hasan al-Banna from other Islamist reformists and intellectuals before him was that he initiated a mass movement to undertake that re-education. Al-Banna was not only a man of intellect, but also a man of action. In fact, he was more the latter than the former. He was also a skilled leader and an excellent organiser. In Ismailiyya, where he was appointed as a schoolteacher after he finished his education at Dar al-'Ulum, al-Banna started a mass movement in 1928 and called it the Muslim Brotherhood. With his superb organisational skills, seemingly endless energy, deep belief in his own righteousness, strong commitment and simplicity in his message, the Brotherhood rapidly expanded. By the time al-Banna was assassinated in 1949, the Brotherhood had an elaborate organisation with offices and a membership base spanning the whole of Egypt.

68. Al-Banna, *Five Tracts of Hasan Al-Banna (1906–1949)*, pp. 69–70.
69. Al-Banna, *Five Tracts of Hasan Al-Banna (1906–1949)*, p. 87.

The Brotherhood, as imagined by al-Banna, was definitely a religious movement, which undertook missionary activities to re-educate the masses in Islam and improve their morals. In fact, al-Banna's first Islamist activisms were of this kind. During his school years in Mahmoudiyah, he joined an association called Jam'iyyat al-Akhlaq al-Adabiyya (the Society of Literary Virtues). The members of this association engaged in practical activities of moral improvement such as praying together and imposing fines on all kinds of misdemeanours. In Cairo, too, al-Banna engaged in similar activity, joining, in 1924, at age of eighteen, Jam'iyyat Makarim al-Akhlaq al-Islamiyya (the Society of the Noble Islamic Virtues).[70]

The Muslim Brotherhood, as imagined by Hasan al-Banna, was not only a religious movement, but also a liberation movement. The Brotherhood's fundamental objective was the liberation of 'the Islamic fatherland from all foreign domination' and the establishment of a free state in that fatherland, a state 'acting according to the precepts of Islam, applying its social regulations, proclaiming its sound principles, and broadcasting its sage mission to all mankind'.[71]

The Islamic fatherland al-Banna spoke of was not just Egypt. It also included 'the Arab domain' and 'every land which God has made fortunate through the Islamic creed: a religion, a nationality, and a creed uniting all Muslims'.[72] The society under that state, the Islamic nation or the ummah, must also be exemplary so that society would deserve to 'be associated with the Islamic Sacred Law'. To this end, the Muslim Brotherhood was meant therefore to wage total jihad against all social and economic problems such as 'poverty, ignorance, disease and crime'.[73]

Islamism originated as an intellectual defence of Islam and remained so until it inspired the grassroots religious movement, the Muslim Brotherhood. It held that Islam was not responsible for the political, economic, cultural and military weakness of Muslims with respect to Europeans. It was the opposite. Muslims were in a state of total weakness because they were not true Muslims. This simple message also reached the Arab Gulf.

70. See the discussion in Krämer, *Hasan al-Banna*, pp. 1–24.
71. Al-Banna, *Five Tracts of Hasan Al-Banna (1906–1949)*, pp. 31–2.
72. Al-Banna, *Five Tracts of Hasan Al-Banna (1906–1949)*, p. 32.
73. Al-Banna, *Five Tracts of Hasan Al-Banna (1906–1949)*, p. 32.

The Arab Gulf Region's Exposure to Islamism

The Arab Gulf region did not produce any Islamists who made a contribution to the development of Islamism. Nevertheless, the region was not out of touch with this ideological current. In particular, two groups served as carriers of Islamist literature to the Gulf: merchants and religious scholars.

The development of religious scholarship in the region has already been discussed. As for the development of merchants, the region had suffered serious limitations. It was too poor in economic and human resources. Naturally, the region had limited trade potential. Yet other factors alleviated the problem. An ancient pilgrimage route from Iraq to the Hijaz, where the two Holy Cities of Mecca and Medina were located, passed through Najd. The nomadic and sedentary populations produced complementary goods and had therefore been in a symbiotic relationship. Moreover, they produced valuable export items such as camels, horses and dates. In certain oasis towns in Najd, such as Buraidah, Unaizah, Hail and Riyadh, merchant families emerged who engaged in regional trade, thus connecting Najd to Egypt, Syria, Iraq and India.

The Gulf coast was better situated than Najd in terms of potential trade for the Arabian Gulf was suitably located in the middle of international trade routes connecting China and India on the one hand and Mesopotamia, Egypt and Europe on the other. However, three factors greatly limited the coast's potential. First, only a few places had enough water sources to support even a small population. Second, trade via the Red Sea had always been an option, making trade via the Arabian Gulf extremely reliant on political stability in Iran and Mesopotamia. More critically, perhaps, the other side of the Gulf had a better hinterland, Iran. All in all, therefore, except for Bahrain, much of the shore of the Arabian peninsula on the Gulf was not suitable for trading towns supporting merchant families.

This changed, however, starting in the eighteenth century, as coastal communities began to engage more heavily in pearling and attract populations from the interior. As mentioned previously, today's major towns in Kuwait, Qatar and the Trucial States (later the UAE) began to develop at this time. Furthermore, Britain had turned the Gulf into a safe zone for pearling and trading, which created a perfect environment for the emergence of merchants in the mushrooming coastal towns. By the late nineteenth century,

Kuwait, Qatar and the Trucial States already had burgeoning merchant families. However, in terms of the composition of the merchants, they differed: Kuwait had more numerous and wealthier native merchants than Qatar and the UAE.[74] This was in large part because Kuwait had a better port and a more central location on regional and international trade routes than Qatar. There was an added problem in the Trucial States: because they had been under British hegemony longer than the others, Indian merchants, rather than the local population, came to dominate the pearling trade, as they were under British protection.

As discussed previously, Islamism originated in the nineteenth century and developed in major cities such as Cairo, Damascus, Baghdad, Basra and Bombay, where Islamist revival literature was available and some prominent figures of the Islamist movement resided, such as Muhammad Abduh, Rashid Rida, Abd al-Qadir al-Jazairi, Jamal al-Din al-Qasimi, Khair al-Din al-Alusi, Mahmud Shukri al-Alusi and Sayyid Ahmad Khan.

In the same period, Najd, Hasa, Kuwait, Bahrain, Qatar and the Trucial States already had religious scholars and native merchants, some, if not all, of whom had been connected through multiple channels to the traditional centres of religious scholarship and trade in Egypt, Syria and Iraq, and India. These merchants and religious scholars from or working in the Arab Gulf had been exposed to Islamist literature and served as conduits through which Islamism found adherents in the Gulf. Additionally, certain aspects of Islamism, especially its radical critique of the religious beliefs and practices of ordinary Muslims and call for a return to the essentials of Islam, resonated among the Wahhabi religious scholars, for Muhammad bin Abd al-Wahhab had made a similar call in Najd more than a century before.

The early exposure of some merchants and religious scholars from or working in the Arab Gulf to Islamist revival literature eventually created a receptive audience in the Gulf for the Muslim Brotherhood. Particularly, schools founded by these merchants and religious scholars played critical roles. In Bahrain, the first such school, named al-Hidayah, was founded in 1919 by a member of the ruling Al Khalifa family, Abdullah bin Isa, who collected

---

74. Crystal, *Oil and Politics in the Gulf*.

donations from the ruling family and wealthy Sunni merchants to finance it.[75] This school's first director was Hafiz Wahba, who had great sympathy for Muhammad ibn Abd al-Wahhab and Muhammad Abduh.[76] He was also a friend of two prominent Islamists of the period, Rashid Rida and Muhib al-Din al-Khatib. Hafiz Wahba didn't live in Bahrain for long as he was adamantly anti-British. Not surprisingly, he was deported a year later and settled in Saudi Arabia, serving the kingdom for many years in different posts.[77]

The ideological orientation of the school's directors and teachers during and after Hafiz Wahba can only be speculated on. They were for sure either Syrians or Egyptians. After Wahba, for example, a Syrian, Uthman al-Hourani, became the school's director. If this was the same Uthman al-Hourani who was a cousin of the prominent Syrian politician and pan-Arabist Akram al-Hourani, then he was not an Islamist but rather a pan-Arab socialist.

Yet it must be taken into consideration that Islamism and Arab nationalism by then had not evolved into two distinct, hostile and opposing ideologies. Muhib al-Din al-Khatib, for example, started his political career as an Arab nationalist.[78] As Ira Lapidus noted:

> Arab nationalist thinkers of the 1920s and 1930s stressed the close identification of Arabism and Islam. The vocabulary of Arab nationalism was infused with words such as ummah (community of Muslims) and millah (religious community), which have strong religious overtones but were used to express national solidarity. Even Christian writers considered Arabism and Islam to be two expressions of the same ideal.[79]

More importantly, in the context of the 1920s and the 1930s, both Islamism and pan-Arabism were strongly anti-imperialist as the Arab countries had been under direct European domination.

---

75. This was a school for Sunnis only. Prior to this school, Bahrain had schools that provided a modern education. One was founded and run by the American Mission and the other by the Persian community in Bahrain. See Rumaihi, *Bahrain*.
76. Wahba, 'Wahhabism in Arabia'.
77. Rumaihi, *Bahrain*, p. 194.
78. Rizvi, *Muhibb ad-Din Al Khatib*.
79. Lapidus, *A History of Islamic Societies*, p. 623.

Bahrain's first modern school, al-Hidayah, must have therefore produced a student body that would become receptive to all ideological currents, including the Muslim Brotherhood version of Islamism. One of these graduates was Abd al-Rahman bin Ali al-Jawdar from a leading Sunni merchant family in Bahrain. Born in the 1920s, Abd al-Rahman al-Jawdar studied at al-Hidayah and was among the founders of the Nadi al-Talabah (the Student Club) in 1941. In the mid-1940s, he went to Egypt to pursue higher education. During his stay in Cairo he met Hasan al-Banna and witnessed firsthand the Brotherhood's organisation and activities in Egypt. This meeting was most likely arranged by Brotherhood-affiliated teachers in Bahrain in the early 1940s. Meanwhile, the Student Club changed its name to Nadi al-Islah (al-Islah Club) in 1948 and to al-Islah Society in 1980, which has since 1948 served as the Brotherhood's branch in Bahrain. Abd al-Rahman al-Jawdar served as deputy chair of al-Islah Club/Society for many years.

Like Bahrain, Kuwait had also faced direct British domination since the early twentieth century and had witnessed missionary activities.[80] A member of a leading Sunni tribe in Kuwait and a son of a pearl merchant, Yusuf bin Isa al-Qinai played a critical role in the spread of Islamist ideas in Kuwait.[81] Al-Qinai was born in Kuwait in 1876 and began his education under local religious figures. He then went to Hasa, Basra and Mecca to pursue more advanced education in religion. During this period he must have encountered the newly developing Islamist literature and sympathised with Jamal al-Din Afghani and Muhammad Abduh. He also became a friend of Rashid Rida, exchanging letters with him. Al-Qinai was also among the founders of a literary club in Kuwait, which circulated Rashid Rida's *al-Manar* journal, thus helping to spread Islamist ideas. Al-Qinai also founded Kuwait's first modern schools, al-Mubarakiyyah in 1911 and al-Ahmadiyyah in 1921.

Like al-Qinai, Abd al-Aziz al-Rashid also contributed to the spread of Islamist ideas. He was born in Kuwait in 1887. He began his education in Kuwait and then studied in Zubair and Baghdad. In the latter he met and studied under Mahmoud Shukri al-Alusi, a prominent Islamist of the late

---

80. Also see Freer, *Rentier Islamism*, ch. 4.
81. For a biography of Yusuf al-Qinai, see al-Jaser, *Al-Sheikh Yusuf bin 'Isa al-Qina'i*.

nineteenth and early twentieth centuries. When he returned to Kuwait, al-Rashid taught in al-Mubarakiyyah and later in al-Ahmadiyyah.[82]

Abdullah bin Ali al-Mutawa, who became a leading figure in the Brotherhood in Kuwait, graduated from al-Ahmadiyyah. Abdullah's elder brother, Abd al-Aziz, was probably the first Kuwaiti to meet Hasan al-Banna in Egypt and became the Brotherhood's general guide in Kuwait. In 1952 Abd al-Aziz founded the movement's first organisation in Kuwait, Jam'iyyat al-Irshad al-Islami (the Islamic Guidance Society) or al-Irshad Society. It is interesting to note that while Abd al-Aziz became the general secretary of al-Irshad Society, Yusuf bin Isa al-Qinai became its chair.[83] Al-Qinai and the Mutawa brothers had familial relations: al-Qinai and al-Mutawa families descended from the same tribe, al-Salih, and intermarried intensively. Abd al-Aziz al-Mutawa, for example, married Yusuf al-Qinai's niece.[84]

Unlike Bahrain and Kuwait, Qatar had a much weaker merchant class and therefore did not have a modern school until the state founded one in the early 1950s.[85] Yet Qatar had already been exposed to the Islamist literature of the late nineteenth and early twentieth centuries. A religious scholar played a critical role in this exposure: Muhammad bin Abd al-Aziz al-Mane.[86] Al-Mane was born in Unaizah in Najd into a family of merchants and religious scholars. His father was a religious scholar, serving as a judge in Unaizah. Al-Mane also pursued his father's career and took his early lessons in religion in Najd. After the age of eighteen he travelled to study under prominent religious figures in Basra, Baghdad, Damascus and Cairo. During his travels he met Muhammad Abduh, Jamal al-Din al-Qassimi and Mahmoud Shukri al-Alusi. After years of studying, al-Mane finally settled in Bahrain at the invitation of a merchant from Najd. After four years he moved to Qatar in 1913 at the invitation of Qatar's ruler, Abdullah bin Jassim. Over the next twenty-five years, al-Mane stayed in Qatar and served as a religious judge. In addition to his judgeship, he gave religious lessons to prominent figures from Qatar.

---

82. Al-Mdaires, *Islamic Extremism in Kuwait*. For a detailed discussion, see al-Rashoud, *Modern Education and Arab Nationalism in Kuwait, 1911–1961*, ch. 1.
83. Mousa and Desouki, 'Tarikh al-Ikhwan al-Muslimun fi'l Kuwait'.
84. I thank Ali al-Kandari for this information. I also thank Talal al-Rashoud.
85. Also see Freer, *Rentier Islamism*, ch. 4.
86. For more on his life, see al-Bassam, *Ulama Najd*, v.6, pp. 100–13.

Several students of Muhammad al-Mane were to play critical roles in the future. His student from Najd, Abdullah bin Zaid al-Mahmoud, for example, became a religious judge in Qatar after al-Mane left the country and later served as the president of religious courts. Another student of al-Mane, Abdullah al-Ansari, served as the Director of Religious and Rural Affairs in the Ministry of Education, responsible for the spread of modern education to rural areas in Qatar.[87] Two other students of al-Mane, Qasim Darwish and Abdullah bin Turki al-Subae, both of whom were wealthy merchants, served on the Educational Committee formed by Qatar's emir, Ali bin Abdullah, which designed the state educational system.

These individuals were not themselves Islamist, but at the very least were familiar with and sympathetic to Islamist ideology. Not in vain, when Qasim Darwish went to Egypt to hire a Director of Education for Qatar did he consult Muhib al-din al-Khatib, himself a prominent Islamist and a friend of Hasan al-Banna. On the recommendation of al-Khatib, a member of the Muslim Brotherhood, Abd al-Badi al-Saqr, was appointed Director of Education in Qatar, who would be instrumental in bringing teachers affiliated with the movement to Qatar.[88]

In the Trucial States, a wealthy merchant, Ali al-Mahmoud, played a critical role in the spread of Islamist ideas. In 1911 he founded a school in his native town, Sharjah, and put it under the administration of two brothers, Abd al-Wahhab and Abd al-Samad al-Wuhaibi, who were originally from Najd but had pursued their religious education in Egypt. While in Egypt, the brothers studied at al-Azhar and frequented the circle of the prominent Islamist, Rashid Rida. Al-Mahmoud also sent a number of students to Qatar to study under Muhammad bin Abd al-Aziz al-Mane. One of these students was Muhammad bin Said bin Ghobash, who also pursued higher religious education at al-Azhar, again financed by Ali al-Mahmoud. After al-Azhar, Muhammad bin Ghobash returned to his native town, Ras al-Khaimah, and became its religious judge.[89]

87. For more on Abdullah al-Ansari, see Mukhtar, '*Allamah Qatar*.
88. Kobaisi, *The Development of Education in Qatar, 1950–1977*.
89. Abd Allah, *The United Arab Emirates*, pp. 107–9. Ali al-Mahmoud was not the only merchant who founded schools in the Trucial States. Among them, however, he seemed the most sympathetic to the newly developing Salafi-Islamist current of the period.

Yet to what extent this early exposure prepared a receptive audience in the Trucial States to the Muslim Brotherhood is difficult to assess. This is because the wealth of the merchants in the Trucial States depended almost exclusively on pearling. Starting in the 1910s, Japanese cultured pearls began to invade the international market and drove prices down. The global economic depression in 1929 dealt the final blow to the already weakening pearling industry in the Gulf. Kuwait and Bahrain were fortunate that oil was discovered there soon after the pearling market crashed. But the Trucial States had to wait another three decades, during the course of which many left for better opportunities elsewhere. For example, the merchant Ali al-Mahmoud left for Saudi Arabia and Muhammad bin Ghobash for Qatar. Still, as will be discussed later in this book, the Brotherhood found an opportunity to expand to the Trucial States.

Saudi Arabia had also been exposed to the Islamist ideas of the late nineteenth and early twentieth centuries, as some religious scholars made trips to Cairo, Damascus, Baghdad, Basra and Bombay (Mumbai) to pursue a more advanced education in religious sciences. Because these were also centres where Islamist literature was developing, Wahhabi religious scholars became familiar with that literature.

Wahhabism, Saudi Arabia's official religious understanding, shared striking similarities with Islamist ideas. Both viewed their Muslim contemporaries as seriously deviating from the true Islam, an Islam that could only be founded in the original sources of Islam and the practices of the Prophet and his immediate successors, or Salaf al-Salihin. Both were Salafi, therefore, and preached a return to Islam's original sources and the practices of the early Muslims.

Furthermore, Saudi Arabia's founding king, Abd al-Aziz, surrounded himself with Islamists from other Arab countries as advisors, such as Hafiz Wahba, who also helped Abd al-Aziz Al Saud polish his image in both the Muslim and non-Muslim worlds. The Kingdom's first Director of Education was in fact Hafiz Wahba, who laid the foundations for the development of a state educational system in the mid-1920s. One of the figures Hafiz Wahba sought to hire was none other than Hasan al-Banna, who was introduced to him by Wahba's friend, Muhib al-Din al-Khatib.

In 1925 Saudi Arabia annexed Islam's two Holy Cities, Mecca and Medina, which had been frequently visited by prominent Islamist figures.

Hasan al-Banna visited almost annually to perform pilgrimage, making his first visit in 1936. During these visits he not only undertook pilgrimages, but also propagated his own understanding of Islam and sought to recruit individuals for his movement. During one of these visits, he even met Abd al-Aziz Al Saud, the King of Saudi Arabia; a photograph taken at this meeting shows al-Banna kissing Abd al-Aziz's hand. It is claimed that al-Banna asked Abd al-Aziz to establish a branch of the movement in the Kingdom, but he was gently refused. Despite this refusal, the Muslim Brotherhood would later find an opportunity to enter Saudi Arabia and gain adherents.

2

MODERN SOVEREIGN STATE BUILDING IN THE GULF: FROM THE 1950S TO THE 1970S

This chapter discusses the first phase of modern state building in the Gulf, which lasted from the 1950s to the 1970s. Because modern state building is a comprehensive task, which involves building and maintaining a number of institutions such as standing armed forces, internal security forces, courts, schools, hospitals, etc., the following looks at only two fields, education and justice, that are most concerned with religion, religious institutions and religious figures. This chapter aims to show that the Gulf states did not undergo any forceful state secularisation: on the contrary, they relied as much as possible on religion and religious figures in building their educational and judicial systems. The chapter also shows that Saudi Arabia implemented more religious policies than others in pursuing the same aim.

Pre-oil Period: Limited Efforts to Build Modern States

To start with Saudi Arabia. When the kingdom annexed the Hijaz region in 1925, it inherited some modern state institutions from the Hashimites and the Ottomans. Over the next three decades Hijaz became a testing ground for Saudi Arabia's future state-building efforts.[1] Rather than totally dismantling the court system it found in Hijaz, for example, Saudi Arabia worked to

---

1. For a more detailed discussion, see Vassiliev, *The History of Saudi Arabia*, ch. 13; Al-Rasheed, *A History of Saudi Arabia*, ch. 3.

improve it: however, unlike the Ottoman Empire, which expanded its new courts, called the *Nizamiye*, at the expense of the Shariah courts throughout the nineteenth century,[2] Saudi Arabia modernised the Shariah courts. To this end, for example, in 1927 the kingdom issued a regulation that created a three-tier Shariah court system in Hijaz: Summary Shariah Courts, Great Shariah Courts and the Judicial Supervisory Board. In an attempt to introduce some measure of uniformity, Shariah courts were ordered to follow the Hanbali School of Jurisprudence and base their decisions on certain specifically designated Hanbali treaties.[3]

Saudi Arabia also kept the Ottoman/Hashimite-period schools and opened new ones in Riyadh and in other large towns. The kingdom also founded a religious school, called al-Ma'had al-Islami (the Islamic Institute), in 1926 under the administration of a Syrian religious scholar. However, the school soon failed. Two decades later, Saudi Arabia founded another one, named Dar al-Tawhid (House of Unitarian Theology), in the city of Taif in the Hijaz region under the administration of the same Syrian religious scholar. This school survived, but has not grown much or expanded to other regions. More significantly, Saudi Arabia founded a College of Shariah in Mecca in 1949.[4]

With the limited resources at its disposal, Saudi Arabia could not build an extensive state apparatus. The relatively modern court system had remained exclusive to Hijaz: elsewhere in the Kingdom, the old dual system had survived, the governors and religious judges delivering justice in their respective jurisdictions with no written record or codified laws.[5] In expanding the modern school system, Saudi Arabia made limited progress: in 1952 there were only 142 primary schools and five secondary schools throughout the Kingdom.[6]

2. For Ottoman modernisation, see Berkes, *The Development of Secularism in Turkey*.
3. For a detailed discussion, see Yargı, *Suudi Arabistan'ın Yargı Sistemi*, ch. 4; Vogel, *Islamic Law and Legal System*, ch. 3.
4. Mouline, *Clerics of Islam*, p. 111.
5. The Islamic Law is the collection of all legal opinions derived from the sources of Islam on diverse topics ranging from rituals to commerce. Because these legal opinions have not been issued by a central agency, but by individuals, they often contain different rulings on the same issue. As such, the Islamic Law has to be codified to serve the modern state's need for homogenous laws.
6. UNESCO, *International Yearbook of Education*, v.19, p. 336.

During this period certain actions of King Abd al-Aziz proved to be the early signs of future state–religion relations in Saudi Arabia. For example, the Fundamental Provisions of the Kingdom of Hijaz he issued in 1926 stated that the Kingdom of Hijaz was an Islamic state and that its government 'shall be bound by the provisions of the glorious Shariah'.[7] Abd al-Aziz collected *Zakat*, (a mandatory payment Islam imposes on Muslims) and *Jizya* (a mandatory payment Islam imposes on non-Muslims), distributed gifts and subsidies to religious scholars, asked their religious opinions, fatwa, on major issues and, as mentioned previously, delegated religious education and religious justice to them. Even the secular educational institutions he founded were not free from religion: for example, in 1950 religious classes made up close to 80 per cent of the teaching time in primary schools and 25 per cent in secondary schools.[8] Last, but not least, he founded in 1926 what later became the notorious religious police to enforce collective prayers and public morality, and, more significantly, put it under the administration of religious scholars.

Due to their smaller populations and geographical areas, other Gulf countries had – institutionally – even simpler states than Saudi Arabia. All educational initiatives were, for example, private initiatives in the pre-oil period.[9] In the provision of justice, the rulers acted as judges or appointed their own relatives as judges. On commercial issues they relied on commercial courts formed by merchants who knew the market and the prevailing commercial customs. The rulers also employed religious judges and submitted to them matters that fell under the Islamic Shariah. In interpreting the Shariah, religious judges were totally autonomous, being given no clear guidelines or codes by the rulers.[10]

The rulers of other Gulf states also had opportunities to observe the organisation and practices of the modern state, as they had been either part of the Ottoman Empire or under the protection of Britain. Yet the Ottoman Empire had no incentive to invest in these states and help their rulers develop their state capacities.[11] Britain pursued primarily a strategic objective in the

---

7. Vassiliev, *The History of Saudi Arabia*, p. 601.
8. Vassiliev, *The History of Saudi Arabia*, p. 634.
9. Al-Misnad, *The Development of Modern Education in Bahrain, Kuwait and Qatar*.
10. Brown, *The Rule of Law in the Arab World*.
11. See Kurşun, *Basra Körfezi'nde Osmanlı – İngiliz Çekişmesi*.

Gulf and never aimed to intervene in the states' internal affairs or improve their administrative capacities, but still made some limited contributions especially to the development of a more modern legal system: for example, Britain issued a series of Orders in Council for Bahrain in 1913, Kuwait in 1925, Qatar in 1935 and the Trucial States in 1945, and secured from the rulers extraterritorial jurisdiction over its subjects and other foreigners.[12] In its fully developed form, Britain founded a three-tiered court system for the Gulf: the chief court, headed by the political resident based in Bushire, Iran, and the country courts, headed by the political agents based in each country. These courts would apply the British colonial codes. The Orders in Council also prescribed the establishment of joint courts, which were to be headed by both British and local judges and try cases involving foreigners and locals.

Yet Britain's efforts in the Gulf states were half-hearted: only in Bahrain did Britain fully establish a court system, the Bahrain Order in Council. In addition to the British courts, Bahrain had a joint court, a customary court that tried cases concerning the pearl industry, and religious courts, which had branches for Sunnis and Shias. However, within the new system religious courts' autonomy was curtailed and their jurisdiction restricted: in penal cases, for example, a representative of the British political agent had to be present at the trial and the court's decision could be appealed to the political agent.[13] Still, though, religious courts continued to operate without any codified laws and hence kept some autonomy in the interpretation of the Islamic Shariah.

In other Gulf countries the implementation of the Orders in Council was limited. Kuwait did not accept a joint court. A joint court in Qatar, even though it was accepted by the ruler, was not established. Until 1949 Qatar did not have a resident political agent; prior to this, cases involving foreigners were referred to the political agent in Bahrain. The Trucial States also agreed to a joint court, but did not have any until the 1960s, even

12. The composition of who 'other foreigners' were changed from country to country: it was widest in the UAE and narrowest in Kuwait. See Liebesny, 'Administration and legal development in Arabia', p. 36.
13. Radhi, *Judiciary and Arbitration in Bahrain*, p. 33.

though there was a British political agent based in Sharjah. In all these cases, the rulers continued to deliver justice in collaboration with merchant courts and religious courts.

Only in Bahrain and Kuwait were efforts made to improve the legal system. In Bahrain, the ruler's courts developed into a two-tiered structure of Courts of First Instance and Courts of Appeal, with other customary courts marginalised: Shariah courts' jurisdiction became restricted to personal matters in the early 1950s. On the other hand, members of the ruling family continued to staff the rulers' courts.[14] In Kuwait, an important step was taken in 1939: the Ottoman civil code, the *Majalla*, based on the Hanafi School of Jurisprudence, became the law of the land: yet this code did not cover all civil matters, especially leaving out personal matters, matters that are detailed in the Islamic Shariah. Commercial customs and conventions were also codified,[15] and a two-tier court system was put in place with lower and upper courts.[16]

In the pre-oil period, there were also efforts to improve the educational system: in Bahrain, for example, the state expanded its role into education. There were already a few modern schools in Bahrain in the 1920s. These schools were financed by private funds and administered by committees of private individuals.[17] The state in Bahrain provided financial aid to these schools initially, but fully took them over in 1930. The state also founded new schools in the 1930s. By 1941 there were twelve schools in Bahrain, eight for boys and four for girls.[18] Kuwait also expanded its role into education: in 1936 the state took over the existing private schools and introduced a new curriculum adapted from other Arab countries. In the succeeding years, Kuwait also opened new schools, raising the number to fifteen in 1944/45.[19]

---

14. See Brown, *The Rule of Law in the Arab World*, ch. 5.
15. Liebesny, 'Administration and legal development in Arabia', p. 39.
16. Brown, *The Rule of Law in the Arab World*, ch. 5.
17. One of these individuals was a member of the ruling family, Sheikh Abdullah bin Isa.
18. Al-Misnad, *The Development of Modern Education in Bahrain, Kuwait and Qatar*, p. 57.
19. Al-Misnad, *The Development of Modern Education in Bahrain, Kuwait and Qatar*, p. 69.

Oil-financed Modern State Building in the Gulf

Oil was first discovered in Bahrain in 1932, in Saudi Arabia and Kuwait in 1938, in Qatar in 1939 and in the Trucial States in 1958. But it was only after the Second World War, which delayed the development of the oil industry in the region, that unprecedented wealth was brought to this once poverty-stricken region, helping Gulf rulers overcome many nature-imposed restrictions and build their modern state institutions. As they built their modern state institutions, Gulf rulers also invested in their educational and justice systems.

Education

Funded by oil revenues, Gulf rulers expanded, or created almost ex nihilo, public education systems in their countries. The table below shows the expansion of public education systems in Saudi Arabia, Bahrain, Kuwait and Qatar.

Expansion of Saudi Arabia's Public Education System

	Number of Students		Number of Teachers	
	1952	1965	1952	1965
Primary*	73,600	254,779	2,250	11,517
Secondary**	2,218	24,429	248	1,323

Expansion of Bahrain's Public Education System

	Number of Students		Number of Teachers	
	1954	1965	1954	1965
Primary	5,395	31,579	248	1,215
Secondary**	327	5,994	29	479

Expansion of Kuwait's Public Education System

	Number of Students		Number of Teachers	
	1954	1965	1954	1965
Primary	13,354	49,562	793	2,316
Secondary**	679	29,494	79	1,783

Expansion of Qatar's Public Education System

	Number of Students		Number of Teachers	
	1954	1965	1954	1965
Primary	560	26	248	1,215
Secondary**	NA***	1,236	NA***	109

Notes:
* Data for 1954.
** Secondary stage includes secondary and tertiary levels of education.
*** Secondary education was not available in Qatar in 1954.

Sources: UNESCO, *International Yearbook of Education*, vol. 19; UNESCO, *International Yearbook of Education*, vol. 29.

Oil was discovered in the Trucial States, the future UAE, almost two decades after the other Gulf states. Kuwait and Qatar financially and logistically helped some of the Trucial States open modern schools in the 1950s and 1960s. Bahrain and Egypt also helped these states by providing teachers. After Sheikh Zayed bin Sultan Al Nahyan became its ruler in 1966, the oil-rich emirate of Abu Dhabi took the lead in expanding public education in the Trucial States. As the table below illustrates, within a short time the UAE's public education system dramatically expanded.

Expansion of the UAE's Public Education System

	Number of Students		Number of Teachers	
	1968	1974	1968	1974
Primary	12,373	41,529	513	1,540
Intermediate	1,659	18,178	208	863
Secondary	485	586	41	110

Source: UAE Ministry of Education, *Education in UAE*.

The Gulf states also invested in higher education. Saudi Arabia was the front-runner. As previously mentioned, Saudi Arabia founded in 1949 the College of Shariah in Mecca to train theology teachers and religious judges. Up to the end of the 1970s Saudi Arabia founded a number of higher education institutions such as the College of Shariah and College of Arabic in 1953 in Riyadh, King Saud University in Riyadh in 1957, the College of Petroleum and Minerals in Dhahran in 1964, King Abd al-Aziz University in Jiddah in 1967 and King Faisal University in Hofuf in 1975.

Other Gulf states also founded higher education institutions, but later than Saudi Arabia: Kuwait University was founded in 1966, Bahrain's Gulf Polytechnic in 1969 and the University College of Arts, Sciences and Education in 1979 (the two merged to become the University of Bahrain in 1986), Qatar's College of Education in 1973 (Qatar University from 1977) and the University of the United Arab Emirates in 1976.

Within their public education systems, the Gulf states also opened religious schools, known as Ma'had al-'Ilmi (the Religious Scientific Institute) in Saudi Arabia and Ma'had al-Dini (the Religious Institute) elsewhere. These schools differed from ordinary schools in that they devoted more time to religious classes. Saudi Arabia was again the first, opening a school of this type in 1926, which failed, but was later reincarnated in 1945 as Dar al-Tawhid in the city of Taif. More significantly, Saudi Arabia founded a Ma'had al-'Ilmi in 1950, first in Riyadh and then in other Saudi towns. Over the next two decades Saudi Arabia opened more religious schools: by 1974 there were thirty-six.

At the higher-education level, Saudi Arabia had already founded two colleges of Shariah, in Mecca and Riyadh. To these were added another College of Shariah and two other higher institutions of religious education: the Islamic University of Medina founded in 1961 and al-Ma'had al-'Ali Li'l Qada' (the Higher Institute for Jurisprudence), founded in 1965 in Riyadh. In 1974 the College of Shariah, College of Arabic and the Higher Institute of Jurisprudence, all in Riyadh, merged to become the Islamic University of Imam Muhammad bin Saud.[20] Two years later, all religious schools across the kingdom were attached to and have since then been part of the university.

Other Gulf states also opened religious schools, known as Ma'had al-Dini: Bahrain opened a religious school in 1943, Kuwait in 1947 and Qatar in 1960. In the Trucial States, Saudi Arabia opened a religious school in Ras al-Khaimah in the late 1960s. But religious schools did not expand much in these states. In the 1966–7 school year, for example, religious schools had just

---

20. For an extensive discussion, see Mouline, *Clerics of Islam*.

146 students in Bahrain, 309 students in Kuwait and 92 students in Qatar. By comparison, in the same school year, secondary schools had 4,646 students in Bahrain, 23,829 students in Kuwait and 1,236 students in Qatar.[21]

Bahrain, Kuwait, Qatar and the UAE did not institute a separate higher institution for religious education, but instead attached it to their national universities: the College of Law and Shariah was established at Kuwait University in 1967, the College of Shariah, Law and Islamic Studies at Qatar University in 1977 and the College of Law and Shariah at the United Arab Emirates University in 1978: the University College of Arts, Sciences and Education in Bahrain established the Department of Arabic and Islamic Studies in 1978.

The Gulf states have always included religious classes in their curriculums. In 1947 the primary school programme in Saudi Arabia, for example, had several religious courses such as the Qur'an, Recitation of the Qur'an, Unitarian Theology, Religious Law and the Prophetic Traditions: these classes took 71 per cent of weekly class time in the first grade, 55 per cent in the second and third grades, 44 per cent in the fourth, 35 per cent in the fifth and 32 per cent in the sixth.[22] Around the same time, the primary school programme for boys in both Bahrain and Kuwait had only one religious course, titled Qur'an: in Bahrain this course took around 13 per cent of weekly class time in the first, second and third grades, around 11 per cent in the fourth grade, and around 6 per cent in the fifth, sixth and seventh grades. In Kuwait the course took around 12 per cent in the first, second and third grades and 9 per cent in the fourth, fifth, sixth and seventh grades.[23]

As they expanded their public education systems, the Gulf states also adjusted their curriculums. As of the late 1970s, however, they retained religious courses. Saudi Arabia, for example, taught Qur'an, Islamic Theology and Islamic Traditions at all grades in its primary schools, adding Qur'an

---

21. For secondary school figures, see UNESCO, *International Yearbook of Education*, v.28; for religious school figures, see al-Misnad, *The Development of Modern Education in Bahrain, Kuwait and Qatar*, p. 228.
22. Trial and Winder, 'Modern education in Saudi Arabia', p. 129.
23. The primary school programme for girls in Bahrain and Kuwait also had a course titled Qur'an and took up fewer weekly class hours both in Bahrain and Kuwait. See al-Misnad, *The Development of Modern Education in Bahrain, Kuwait and Qatar*, pp. 111–12.

Exegesis at Grades 4–5 and Islamic Jurisprudence at Grades 5–6. In its intermediate schools, it taught all five of them. In its secondary schools, it taught Recitation of the Holy Qur'an, Islamic Tradition and Culture and Islamic Theology at all grades and sections, adding Islamic Jurisprudence at Grades 1–2 at all sections.[24]

In the late 1970s, other Gulf states, on the other hand, taught only one religious course: Bahrain taught a religious course titled Religious Education in its primary schools, Islamic Studies in its intermediate schools and Islamic Education in its secondary schools. Kuwait taught a religious course titled Islamic Religion in its primary schools and Islamic Education in its intermediate and secondary schools. Qatar taught a religious course titled Qur'an and Islamic Religion in its primary schools, Islamic Education in its intermediate schools and Qur'an and Islamic religion in its secondary schools.[25]

To add further detail, Saudi Arabia devoted more class hours to religious classes than others. For example, it devoted a total of nine class hours across all grades of primary school to religious classes, which made up 30–32 per cent of the total weekly class hours; eight class hours across all grades of intermediate schools, which made up around 22 per cent of total weekly class hours; and four class hours across Grades 1–2 and three hours at Grade 3 of secondary schools, which made up 8–14 per cent of total weekly class hours.[26] In the late 1970s Saudi Arabia's closest rival was Qatar, which devoted a total of six class hours across all grades of primary school to religious classes, which made up 20 per cent of the total weekly class hours; five class hours across all grades of intermediate schools, which made up around 14 per cent of total weekly class hours; and five class hours at Grade 1, four class hours at Grade 2 and three class hours at Grade 3, which made up 8–14 per cent of total weekly class hours.[27]

24. Saudi Arabia Ministry of Education, *The Bi-Annual Report of the Ministry of Education 1976 and 1977*.
25. Al-Misnad, *The Development of Modern Education in Bahrain, Kuwait and Qatar*, pp. 115–17, 147–56.
26. Saudi Arabia Ministry of Education, *The Bi-Annual Report of the Ministry of Education 1976 and 1977*.
27. Al-Misnad, *The Development of Modern Education in Bahrain, Kuwait and Qatar*, pp. 115–17, 147–56.

Justice

In addition to expanding their public education systems, the Gulf states also reformed and modernised their legal systems. Saudi Arabia had already been developing a modern Shariah court system in the Hijaz region and began to extend it across the whole country in 1957, unifying all Shariah courts under the Presidency of the Judiciary in Riyadh in 1960. Two years later, Saudi Arabia established Hay'at al-Tamyiz (the Board of Review), to serve as the Court of Appeal for the Shariah courts.[28]

In another major reorganisation, Saudi Arabia began to disestablish the Presidency of the Judiciary in 1970, distributing its functions to newly created agencies such as the Ministry of Justice and Majlis al-Qada' al-A'la (the Supreme Judicial Council). While the former assumed the administration of Shariah courts, the latter came to serve as the highest judicial authority in the Kingdom, standing above the newly reorganised Courts of Appeal and First Instance Courts.[29]

Following another track of legal modernisation, Saudi Arabia had in 1955 instituted the Board of Grievances (Diwan al-Mazalim). The Board's duty was to investigate all complaints it received, report its findings to the appropriate authorities, and suggest actions to be taken. In the early 1960s the Board was given authority to look into criminal cases, such as bribery and commercial fraud. The Board's jurisdiction further extended to cases of unethical or corrupt conduct of state employees in the early 1970s. In the late 1970s the Board further expanded its role to look into contractual disputes involving the government.[30]

Unlike Saudi Arabia, other Gulf states took steps that eventually marginalised Shariah courts in the expanding court system.[31] As mentioned previously, Bahrain had already expanded the jurisdiction of the ruler's court and restricted that of Shariah courts in the early 1950s. In the wake of independence in 1971, it reorganised its court system, dividing the courts into

---

28. Yargı, *Suudi Arabistan'ın Yargı Sistemi*; Vogel, *Islamic Law and Legal System*, ch. 3.
29. For a description, see al-Ghadyan, 'The judiciary in Saudi Arabia'.
30. See Long, 'The Board of Grievances in Saudi Arabia'; Sfeir, 'An Islamic Conseil d'Etat'.
31. Unless otherwise stated, the following discussion owes to Brown, *The Rule of Law in the Arab World*, ch. 5.

two main categories: civil courts and Shariah courts with Sunni and Shia branches. While the former had general jurisdiction, the latter had jurisdiction over personal-status matters only.[32]

Having made some progress in legal reform, Kuwait hired professional judges to serve in its courts but restricted their cases to personal-status matters. Like Bahrain, Kuwait's ruling family members continued to look into other cases. In a significant step, Kuwait introduced a major reorganisation of its court system in 1959, completely unifying Kuwait's legal system and establishing an appeal court and a judicial council, which was to make appointments and promotions in the court system.

Unlike Bahrain and Kuwait, Qatar had not made much progress in the pre-oil period and, more critically, its ruling family members had not developed the same level of interest in establishing and maintaining their monopoly over the courts. This might have been for a number of reasons: first, Al Thani family came to power in Qatar much later than Al Sabah family in Kuwait and Al Khalifa family in Bahrain. It was a much larger family and therefore didn't have the same level of intra-family cohesion. Furthermore, the population of Qatar was more mobile than those of Kuwait and Bahrain, and therefore could rely on more traditional agents of justice, especially tribal leaders.

In any case, in 1950 Qatar established a new court and appointed two members of the ruling family as judges. In 1957 it also moved to reorganise its Shariah court and to this end established the Presidency of Shariah Courts: as part of this reorganisation, Shariah courts were reorganised in a two-tiered structure: the Supreme Shariah Court, headed by the president of the Shariah courts, and the Shariah Court. In the early 1960s, Qatar established a labour court with a jurisdiction over cases regulated by labour law. Qatar then took a major step in 1971 and established 'Adliyya (Justice) Courts: the court system included at the bottom tier a two-tiered criminal court, a civil court and a labour court. Above these courts was the Court of Appeal, its chief judge also serving as the president of all 'Adliyya Courts.[33] In the next decade and a half Qatar issued a number of laws and granted their jurisdictions to the 'Adliyya Courts, thus expanding their jurisdictions. Yet the Shariah courts continued

---

32. Radhi, *Judiciary and Arbitration in Bahrain*, ch. 2.
33. Law No. 13 of 1971 on the System of the Courts of Justice.

to look at civil and criminal cases until the late 1980s, especially those cases involving Muslims.

The Trucial States did not make any progress in their legal systems until the late 1960s: Abu Dhabi, the emirate where oil was discovered, led the reform in 1968 by establishing civil courts in addition to the existing Shariah courts. Abu Dhabi also established an appeal court above civil and Shariah courts. Two years later, Dubai introduced a similar reform, establishing civil courts in addition to Shariah courts. Yet, unlike Abu Dhabi, Dubai did not establish any appeal court for Shariah courts, while it organised civil courts as the First Instance Courts and the Court of Appeal. When Abu Dhabi and Dubai joined other Trucial States and formed the United Arab Emirates in 1971, the Federal Constitution envisioned a unified judiciary and established the Federal Supreme Court. In 1978 the UAE established the Federal Courts of Appeal and the Federal Courts of First Instance, to which four emirates, Abu Dhabi, Sharjah, Ajman and Fujairah, transferred the jurisdictions of their corresponding courts. The law, it is important to add, left their Shariah courts outside the federal court system. As of the late 1970s, the UAE still had to make considerable progress to realise the vision set out in the constitution.[34]

Legislation

Historically, Gulf rulers had ruled their subjects by uncodified customs, conventions and the Islamic Shariah. The necessities of modern sovereign state building and modern economic life posed two fundamental challenges for the Islamic Shariah. First, new matters had arisen for which Shariah had no specific rulings. Second, originally Shariah was uncodified and therefore could have multiple rulings on the same matter: codification was inescapably going to be selective.

While building their modern state institutions, Gulf rulers had to address these two challenges. In Saudi Arabia, Shariah courts became the backbone of the whole court system and eventually came to claim general jurisdiction theoretically over all matters. Yet when the Islamic Shariah did not cover a matter, Saudi Arabia promulgated a new law, calling it *Nizam* (regulation) or

---

34. Al-Muhairi, 'The development of the UAE legal system and unification with the judicial system'.

Marsum (decree), to regulate that matter. Saudi Arabia issued tens of regulations and decrees up to the late 1970s, such as the 1931 Commercial Law, 1946 Labour Law, 1959 Penal Law of Money Counterfeit, 1962 Law of Commercial Agencies and 1963 Law of Commercial Papers.[35] But religious scholars refused to judge according to these man-made laws. In fact, they made it clear to the founding king of Saudi Arabia as early as 1925 that only the Islamic Shariah had to be applied in Hijaz and all laws inherited from the Ottoman period had to be cancelled. Religious scholars' intransigence to judge according to newly issued regulations and decrees led Saudi Arabia to establish new bodies that would judge according to them: for example, to apply the 1931 Commercial Law, Saudi Arabia established a Commercial Court. This court operated until its dissolution in 1954. Ten years later, the Commercial Dispute Committees were established by the Ministry of Commerce to serve the same function. The jurisdiction of these committees later expanded so that they also began to apply the Patent Law, Commercial Papers Law, Commercial Corporate Law and some others. In a similar vein, Saudi Arabia established the Tariff Committees for the implementation of the Customs Law and the Labour Dispute Committee in 1969 for the Labour Law. The Board of Grievances also assumed jurisdiction over such newly issued ordinances and decrees as the 1962 Forgery law and the 1962 Bribery Law.[36]

Other Gulf states had also promulgated laws and regulations, especially gaining momentum in their legislative activities in the years leading up to or immediately after their independence. In the two years before its independence in 1961, Kuwait, for example, passed the Law of Real Estate Registration, Law of Commercial Registration, Law of Commercial Companies, Penal Law, Civil Procedure Law and Criminal Procedure Law. In the independence year, Kuwait passed two critical laws: the Commercial Law and Tort Law. In the 1960s and 1970s, Qatar also passed a number of significant laws, such as the Law of Commercial Registration System and Labour Law in 1962, Law of Real Estate Registration in 1964 and Law of Civil and Commercial Articles and Criminal Procedure Law in 1971. The UAE did not pass any significant legislation until the 1980s: the only significant exceptions

---

35. These laws and many others are available at http://www.boe.gov.sa.
36. Al-Jarbou, 'The role of traditionalists and modernists on the development of the Saudi legal system'.

were that Abu Dhabi passed the Criminal Procedure Law and Penal Law in 1970, Dubai passed the Penal Law in 1970 and the UAE passed the Law of Commercial Registration in 1978.

Earlier than other Gulf states, Bahrain adopted a Penal Law in 1955, but this law was British-made and prepared for application in British courts in the Gulf. Bahrain repealed this law and adopted a new Penal Law in 1976, which included articles punishing offences against religion. In addition, Bahrain passed a number of laws, such as the Law of Commercial Registration in 1961, Ordinance of Civil Wrongs in 1970, the Civil and Commercial Procedures Act in 1970 (amended in 1971), Commercial Companies Law in 1975, Labour Law in 1976 and Land Registration Law in 1979.

Unlike Saudi Arabia, however, other Gulf States did not institute specialised tribunals to apply these laws, but rather authorised their non-Shariah courts. As also happened elsewhere in the Middle East, these courts began to expand at the expense of Shariah courts as more and more laws were issued, and eventually dominated them. Like Saudi Arabia, other Gulf states had been reluctant to codify the Islamic Shariah. Among them only Kuwait adopted the Ottoman Civil Code, the *Majalla*. The *Majalla* was superseded by Kuwait's Commercial Law of 1961 in certain matters, but remained the civil law of Kuwait until the late 1970s. However, the *Majalla* did not cover all matters, and therefore, especially those concerning personal status, family and inheritance remained uncodified until the late 1980s.

Finally, unlike Saudi Arabia, the other Gulf states issued their constitutions immediately after they became independent states: Kuwait issued its constitution in 1962, the UAE in 1971, Qatar in 1972[37] and Bahrain in 1973. These constitutions all declared Islam as their state religion and the Islamic Shariah as either a or the chief source of legislation.[38]

In short, all the Gulf states issued man-made laws to regulate increasingly complex modern life. This does not suggest, however, that they intentionally pursued state secularisation. It rather suggests that the Islamic law is insufficiently developed to regulate all, new or old, fields of human life and in

---

37. Qatar's constitution is called provisional, not permanent.
38. Only Qatar declared Islamic Law as the source of law. For a comparative analysis, see Ballantyne, 'The Constitutions of the Gulf states: a comparative study'. Also see Lombardi, 'Constitutional provisions making Sharia "A" or "The" chief source of legislation'.

fact grants to rulers extensive discretion to regulate a range of them. The fact that Saudi Arabia, which kept the Shariah courts as its general courts, issued as many man-made laws as the others is telling in this regard. Saudi Arabia, however, had been more religious than the others. This was because only Saudi Arabia had developed a native class of religious scholars and this class retained its influence in and over the modern state of Saudi Arabia.

Religious Scholars and the Modern State

As discussed in Chapter 1, religious scholars played critical roles in the unification of Saudi Arabia and the consolidation of Al Saud's authority. As the only literate class in Saudi Arabia, religious scholars also took part in modern sovereign state building in the Kingdom. First and foremost as mentioned before, Saudi Arabia established a religious police, later to be called the Committee for the Promotion of Virtue and the Prevention of Vice, to perform a Qur'an-sanctioned religious duty called *Hisbah*.[39] Whatever the exact origin of the religious police in Saudi Arabia,[40] it was well in place by the late 1930s, organised under two major presidencies: one for the western regions of Hijaz, Asir and Jazan and the other for the central and eastern regions of Najd and Hasa.

Through the religious police, the Saudi state took over a religious duty, which if left in private hands might result in a disruption of public order, especially outside of Najd where populations were not then thoroughly Wahhabised. In fact, the establishment of the religious police was a measure to counter the Ikhwan, Al Saud's puritanical Bedouin forces, who repeatedly took into their hands the supervision and enforcement of public morality in the new regions annexed to the Kingdom. Several religious scholars issued religious opinions that sanctioned the state's exclusion of all others from undertaking this religious duty.

More significantly, religious scholars took administrative roles in the religious police and served at the highest levels: Umar bin Hasan al-Sheikh was head of the religious police in the central region of Najd from the 1920s to the mid-1970s and Abdullah bin Hasan al-Sheikh and Abd al-Aziz bin

---

39. For a detailed historical account of the evolution of the term, see Cook, *Commanding Right and Forbidding Wrong in Islamic Thought*.
40. See Cook, *Commanding Right and Forbidding Wrong in Islamic Thought*, ch. 8; Al-Hedaithy, *Modernization and Islam in Saudi Arabia*.

Abdullah al-Sheikh were the heads of the religious police in the western regions of Hijaz, Asir and Jazan from the late 1930s to 1952 and from 1952 to 1976 respectively. In 1976 the religious police were unified under the administration of another religious scholar, Abd al-Aziz bin Abdullah al-Sheikh, the son of the former head of the religious police in the western regions. Other religious scholars also worked in the religious police, as indicated in the table below.

In addition to serving as religious judges elsewhere in the Kingdom, religious scholars from Najd worked in the reorganised judiciary of the Hijaz region in such cities as Mecca, Medina, Taif and Jiddah, as shown in the table below. More critically, a religious scholar from Najd, Abdullah bin Hasan al-Sheikh, became head of the judiciary of the whole Hijaz region: it was he, as mentioned before, who was also the head of the religious police of the Hijaz region. When the organisation of the judiciary in Hijaz was extended to the whole country in the late 1950s, therefore, the religious scholars of Najd were not introduced to something with which they were totally unfamiliar.

When the judiciary was totally unified in 1960, it was put under the leading Wahhabi religious scholar from Najd, Muhammad bin Ibrahim al-Sheikh. Only after the demise of Muhammad bin Ibrahim in 1969 did Saudi Arabia put the judiciary under the Ministry of Justice in 1970. However, another religious scholar, Muhammad al-Harakan, then the chief religious judge of Jeddah, became the first Minister of Justice of Saudi Arabia and served until 1975.[41] In that year, Ibrahim bin Muhammad al-Sheikh, the son of Muhammad bin Ibrahim, became the Minister of Justice, thus taking the post his father once filled.

Religious scholars also worked in Diwan al-Mazalim (the Board of Grievances). When the Board was formed in 1955, its president was a member of the royal family: Musaid bin Abd al-Rahman Al Saud, a brother of the king. However, a religious scholar, Abdullah bin Sulaiman al-Masari, became his deputy. Six years later, al-Masari became the president of the Board and

41. Muhammad bin Ali was born in Medina but his family was originally from Najd: his father was a merchant who had traded between Unaizah, a major town in Najd, and Medina and eventually settled in Medina. Muhammad bin Ali al-Harakan also studied under Unaizah religious scholars and therefore must have had the necessary Wahhabi credentials. Al-Bassam, *Ulama Najd*, v.6, pp. 317–20.

served until 1975.[42] Other religious scholars also served on the Board, as shown in the table below.

Many religious scholars also worked in religious schools and even in ordinary state schools, which heavily taught religion at all levels, as administrators and teachers, as shown in the table below. More significantly, a prominent religious scholar, Hasan bin Abdullah al-Sheikh,[43] became Minister of Education in 1962 and oversaw the expansion of the public education system. Needless to say, religious schools, all Religious Scientific Institutes, Colleges of Shariah, the Higher Institute of Jurisprudence and the Islamic University of Medina were put under the presidency of the leading Wahhabi religious scholar, Muhammad bin Ibrahim.[44]

In the 1970s, especially after the demise of Muhammad bin Ibrahim in 1969, Saudi Arabia dismantled the office of the grand mufti and distributed the authority associated with it to other newly founded ministries and committees. As part of this reorganisation, Shariah courts, for example, were put under the Ministry of Justice. Saudi Arabia also established Hay'at Kibar al-'Ulama (the Committee of Senior Religious Scholars) to assume the prime function of the one-man office of the grand mufti, issuing religious opinions, fatwa.[45]

In a similar vein, Saudi Arabia established the Ministry of Higher Education and put all universities, including the Islamic University of Medina and Imam Muhammad bin Saud University, under its administration. But religious scholars continued to play a critical role after this reorganisation. A prominent religious scholar, Abd al-Aziz bin Abdullah bin Baz, became the president of the Islamic University of Medina: since its foundation, he had already served as deputy president. When bin Baz left the the presidency of the university in 1975, the presidency went to his student, Abd al-Muhsin bin Hamad al-Abbad, a graduate of the Religious Scientific Institute and College of Shariah in Riyadh where Abd al-Aziz bin Baz had taught. Likewise, the president of Imam Muhammad bin Saud University, founded in Riyadh 1974 and subsequently annexing the Colleges of Shariah in Riyadh, was also a religious scholar, Abd al-Aziz bin Muhammad bin Ibrahim

---

42. 'Al-'Alim al-Jalil'.
43. Al-Bassam, *Ulama Najd*, v.2, pp. 40–5.
44. Mouline, *Clerics of Islam*, p. 138.
45. For a more detailed discussion, see Mouline, *Clerics of Islam*.

al-Sheikh, another son of the former grand mufti, who previously presided over the Colleges of Shariah. More critically, a religious scholar, Hasan bin Abdullah bin Hasan al-Sheikh, who had served since 1962 as Minister of Education, became the Minister of Higher Education.

Religious Scholars who Worked in Different State Institutions in Saudi Arabia

The Religious Police

Name	Volume, pages
Ibrahim bin Muhammad al-Jardan	v.1, pp. 394–5
Salih bin Abdullah al-Jarid	v.2, pp. 497–8
Sulaiman bin Abd al-Rahman al-Sane	v.2, pp. 301–7
Abd al-Rahman bin Abd al-Aziz al-Hassain	v.3, pp. 72–5
Abdullah bin Mutlaq bin Fuhaid	v.4, pp. 509–15
Ali bin Abd al-Aziz al-Ajaji	v.5, pp. 219–20
Muhammad bin Ibrahim al-Abd al-Latif	v.5, pp. 460–1
Faisal bin Muhammad al-Mubarak	v.6, pp. 303–4

The Reorganised Judiciary (Mecca, Medina, Taif, Jiddah)

Name	Volume, pages
Sulaiman bin Abd al-Rahman al-Umari	v.2 pp. 308–19
Sulaiman bin Abd al-Rahman bin Hamdan	v.2, pp. 295–300
Abdullah bin Sulaiman al-Bulaihid	v.4, pp. 138–50
Abdullah bin Salih al-Khalifi	v.4, pp. 176–81
Mubarak bin Abd al-Muhsin bin Baz	v.5, pp. 325–6
Muhammad bin Ali al-Turki	v.6, pp. 333–9
Muhammad bin Abd al-Muhsin al-Khayal	v.6, pp. 258–65
Muhammad bin Uthman al-Shawi	v.6, pp. 275–86
Muhammad bin Ali al-Biz	v.6, pp. 326–30

The Board of Grievances

Name	Volume, pages
Abd al-Rahman bin Hamad al-Fouzan	v.3, pp. 43–4
Naser bin Muhammad al-Wuhaibi	v.6, pp. 486–90
Muhammad bin Abd al-Aziz bin Halil	v.6, pp. 84–8

Religious Schools

Name	Volume, pages
Abd al-Aziz bin Abdullah bin Baz[46]	
Sulaiman bin Ibrahim al-Bassam	v.2, pp. 265–8
Abd al-Aziz bin Ibrahim al-Abd al-Latif	v.3, pp. 289–90
Abd al-Latif bin Ibrahim al-Sheikh	v.3, pp. 550–2
Abd al-Rahman bin Abdullah al-Bulaihid[47]	v.3, pp. 96–7
Abdullah bin Matlaq bin Fuhaid	v.4, pp. 510–16
Abdullah bin Salih al-Khuleifi[48]	v.4, pp. 176–81
Abdullah bin Abd al-Aziz al-Khudeiri	v.4, pp. 283–7
Abdullah bin Muhammad al-Awhali	v.4, pp. 503–5
Abd al-Muti bin Muhammad al-Khuwaitir	v.5, pp. 36–7
Uthman bin Ibrahim al-Haqil	v.5, pp. 66–9
Falih bin Mahdi al-Mahdi	v.5, pp. 370–2
Muhammad bin Abd al-Rahman bin Abbad	v.6, pp. 50–1
Muhammad bin Ali bin Turki	v.6, pp. 333–9
Muhammad bin Fayyiz al-Habti	v.6, pp. 352–4
Yusuf bin Abd al-Aziz al-Kharab	v.6, pp. 503–6

Ordinary State Schools

Name	Volume, pages
Ibrahim bin Abdullah al-Huwaish	v.1, pp. 358–71
Ahmad bin Abd al-Muhsin al-Aba Hussein	v.1, pp. 488–9
Salih bin Hamad al-Zugheibi	v.2, pp. 447–8
Sulaiman bin Uthman bin Ahmad	v.2, pp. 362–3
Sulaiman bin Muhammad al-Shebl	v.2, pp. 394–7
Abd al-Aziz bin Sulaiman al-Farih	v.3, pp. 366–9
Abdullah bin Jarallah al-Jarallah	v.4, pp. 55–60
Abdullah bin Muhammad al-Khalifi	v.4, pp. 472–9
Uthman bin Abd al-Rahman al-Aba Hussein	v.5, pp. 83–6
Abdullah bin Mutlaq bin Fuhaid	v.4, pp. 510–16
Muhammad bin Khalaf al-Rashid	v.5, pp. 528–9
Ali Bin Abdullah al-Hassain	v.5, pp. 221–2
Mansur bin Salih al-Dhalan	v.6, pp. 438–41

Source: Al-Bassam, *Ulama Najd*.

---

46. 'Liqa' Hawl Sirat al-Sheikh wa Masiratahu'.
47. Al-Bulaihid taught at Dar al-Tawhid in Taef.
48. Al-Khuleifi taught at Dar al-Tawhid in Taef.

As shown, religious scholars continued to play their historical roles in Saudi Arabia, but now within the expanding modern state institutions. Nowhere else in the Gulf did religious scholars achieve a similar level of influence in the modern state even though Shariah courts survived and modern religious schools, known as Ma'had al-Dini, and Colleges of Shariah became part of the public education system.

Four other Gulf states – Bahrain, Kuwait, Qatar and the Trucial States (the future UAE) – employed individuals trained in religion in their Shariah courts and religious schools. As I will discuss later, they had to import professionals from other Arab countries to run them. The question of what happened to those already in the country, who had been serving as religious judges and religious teachers, needs further empirical evidence to be addressed. But there is no reason to argue that given the rentier nature of the modern state they were expelled from the country. Most likely they continued their services in the newly reorganised Shariah courts and religious schools. For example, Qatar's religious judge, Abdullah bin Zaid, continued to serve as the president of Shariah courts until his death in 1993. Better biographical evidence comes from the case of Kuwait. Those religious figures who had been giving private religious class in their homes or running primitive religious schools were employed in state schools as teachers of the Qur'an, Arabic and religion.[49]

Yet it is critical to note that even in Kuwait, which had a number of native religious scholars, no one scholar seems to have played a critical role in shaping the justice and education systems. Nor did Shariah courts or religious schools become the backbone of the systems that eventually took shape.

Religious scholars' weakness in Bahrain, Qatar and the UAE stemmed from the fact that they were few in number and also foreigners. Kuwait did

---

49. For example, Abd al-Badah al-Mutairi, Maruf al-Sarhan, Saoud al-Saqr, Uthman al-Uthman, Sayer al-Atiqi, Abd al-Aziz al-Atiqi, Muhammad al-Ibrahim and Abd al-Qader al-Sarhan taught at new state schools; Muhammad bin Abd al-Rahman al-Faris, Abdullah Nuri, Abd al-Badah al-Mutairi, Abd al-Aziz Hammadah and Ali Hammadah taught in the state-run religious school, Ma'had al-Dini; Idris al-Idris worked in the Directorate of Customs and Ports; Mizal al-Salal worked in the judiciary and municipality; Abd al-Rahman al-Tirkit worked in the Directorate of General Security as a religious judge; Ahmad al-Khamis al-Jabran was a religious judge and advisor in the Court of Cassation (Mahkamat al-Tamyiz); Maruf al-Sarhan and Ahmad al-Mutawa were religious judges and teachers. For the biographical information, see the relevant titles in al-Rumi, *Ulama Al Kuwait*.

have a number of native religious scholars by the time it initiated its modern sovereign state building. But they had not become a class unified by and zealously pursuing a religious mission. Their grandfathers, fathers or even they themselves came from different parts of the Muslim world, had pursued higher religious education in different places, such as Hasa, Iran, India, Egypt or Iraq, and trained in different schools of jurisprudence: Maliki, Shafi, Hanbali. Furthermore, they often came from families with different class backgrounds: Kuwait was a commercial city-state, whose economy heavily relied on the extremely exploitative pearling industry. Some prominent religious scholars were members of merchant families; others were not. Moreover, religious scholars had not played any significant political role in the founding of Kuwait and the consolidation of the ruling Al Sabah family. Last, but not least, religious scholars in Kuwait could not produce a single leader due to the lack of an aristocratic scholarly family to produce such religious-scholar leaders.[50]

Religious scholars in Saudi Arabia did not suffer from these weaknesses. As suggested in the previous chapter, religious scholars in Saudi Arabia were more homogenous in several ways. For sure they let in some foreigners, who even rose to the top of the religious establishment in Saudi Arabia. A case in point is Abd al-Razzaq al-Afifi, who was born in Egypt in the early twentieth century. He graduated from the prestigious al-Azhar with a doctorate in Jurisprudence. In the late 1940s he moved to Saudi Arabia and taught at Dar al-Tawhid in Taif. In the following decades he rose up and eventually became a member of the Kingdom's highest religious council, the Committee of Senior Religious Scholars.[51] But, as Nabil Mouline illustrates, religious scholars who were members of this Committee between 1971 and 2010 came predominantly from

---

50. Donald E. Smith mentions this as a generic feature of Islam, an observation that must be qualified. Twelver Shia Islam has produced a semi-hierarchical ulama body. See, for example, Said Amir Arjomand, *The Shadow of God and the Hidden Imam* (Chicago: University of Chicago Press, 1984). The Ottoman Empire also organised its Sunni ulama in a hierarchical way. However, this did not occur endogenously, but rather was state-imposed. Still, though, Smith's observation is valid. See Donald E. Smith, *Religion and Political Development* (Boston: Little, Brown Company, 1970).
51. This biographical information is available at Alifta.Gov.Sa, the portal of the General Presidency of Scholarly Research and Ifta' as 'His Eminence Shaykh Abd al-Razzaq ibn Afify ibn Atiyyah'.

the major tribes of Saudi Arabia and from the Najd region: in the said period, 79 per cent of members of the Committee had family background in major sedentarised tribes and 73 per cent of the members originally came from the Najd region.[52]

As discussed in the previous chapter, Najd was the region where Wahhabism was born and came to be the dominant theology to the exclusion of all other alternatives by the late nineteenth century. The agents who made this possible were religious scholars who zealously embraced Wahhabism as the original version of Islam and rejected all other understandings as corrupt versions. As David Commins perceptively notes, they truly perceived themselves as the last stronghold of Islam and justified this perception with a prophetic tradition: 'Bada' al-Islam ghariban wa saya'udu ghariban kama bada'.' Or, 'Islam began as a stranger and it will return as it began (stranger).' Muhammad ibn Abd al-Wahhab believed that 'he lived at a time in history when Islam had become a stranger'. He and his followers were those strangers of his time, the Prophet blessed at that end of the same reported prophetic statement or Hadith: 'tuba li'l ghuraba.'[53] Or, 'heaven is for the strangers.'

This element of serving a zealous mission of purifying Islam was clearly missing among religious scholars in Kuwait. Yet in Saudi Arabia that mission had driven religious scholars. The idea of serving that mission also pushed them into the arms of Al Saud family. As the discussion in the previous chapter illustrated, religious scholars supported Al Saud family in every way they could in all three Al Saud attempts to found and then refound the Saudi state.

As a puritanical religious movement, Wahhabism owed its birth to one man, Muhammad bin Abd al-Wahhab. He left behind several sons, some of whom had studied under their father and become religious scholars, such as Ali, Hussein, Ibrahim and Abdullah.[54] His descendants have since produced many religious scholars and become an aristocratic scholarly family, to whom other religious scholars turned and under whom students of religion studied. It is illustrative that Ibn Abd al-Wahhab's descendants adopted the family name, Aal al-Sheikh, literally meaning the family of the sheikh, the word

---

52. See Mouline, *Clerics of Islam*, ch. 7.
53. Commins, *The Wahhabi Mission and Saudi Arabia*, p. 16.
54. Al-Bassam, *Ulama Najd*, v.1, p. 167.

sheikh being the honorific title adopted by prince-rulers and religious scholars. Muhammad bin Abd al-Wahhab also trained others as religious scholars, who along with his descendants transmitted Wahhabism down the generations. By the early twentieth century, three major Najdi towns – Riyadh, Buraidah and Unaizah – were the centres of religious education in the peninsula. Tens of biographies of religious scholars who lived to see the foundation of the Kingdom of Saudi Arabia in 1932 and witnessed the state-building efforts of successive Saudi kings visited these towns and studied under prominent religious scholars settled there.[55]

It is also noteworthy no single teacher could teach all religious sciences. Therefore students of religion took classes from several of them, often traveling from town to town to expand and deepen their knowledge. We do not know how students of religion financed their studies before the state began to run religious schools out of its own budget. Some students came from merchant families and presumably could finance their own studies; some were sons and relatives who often started their religious education with their fathers and uncles; others still must have relied on their teachers' own financial resources. Whatever the case, religious education relied on personal relations.

In all likelihood, religious scholars formed densely interwoven networks of personal relations. This was especially true for prominent religious scholars. For illustrative purposes, we can look at Muhammad bin Abdullah bin Salim, one of the most productive religious teachers based in Buraidah. Muhammad bin Abdullah was born in Buraidah in 1824 and studied under several prominent

---

55. In Riyadh were, for example, Ishaq bin Abd al-Rahman al-Sheikh, Ibrahim bin Abd al-Latif al-Sheikh, Muhammad bin Ibrahim bin Mahmoud, Hasan bin Hussein al-Sheikh, Abdullah bin Abd al-Latif al-Sheikh, Hamad bin Faris, Sulaiman bin Muslih bin Sahman, Saad bin Hamad bin Atiq, Muhammad bin Abd al-Latif al-Sheikh and Muhammad bin Ibrahim al-Sheikh; in Buraidah, for example, were Muhammad bin Abdullah bin Salim, Abdullah bin Muhammad bin Salim, Abd al-Aziz bin Ibrahim al-Abadi, Umar bin Muhammad bin Salim and Muhammad bin Umar Bin Salim; in Unaizah, for example, were Ibrahim bin Hamad al-Jassir, Salih bin Uthman al-Qadi, Abdullah bin Muhammad bin Mane, Sulaiman bin Abd al-Rahman al-Amri and Abd al-Rahman bin Nasser al-Sadi. In addition, there also appear repeatedly as religious scholars, Abdullah bin Sulaiman bin Bulaihid, Abdullah bin Abd al-Aziz al-Anqari and Muhammad bin Abd al-Aziz al-Mane.

religious scholars.[56] Two other prominent religious figures from Buraidah, Abdullah bin Muhammad and Umar bin Muhammad, were his sons,[57] and another, Abd al-Aziz al-Abadi, was his son-law.[58] Muhammad bin Abdullah studied under Abd al-Rahman bin Hasan, who was the father of Ishaq bin Abd al-Rahman al-Sheikh from Riyadh, and Abd al-Latif bin Abd al-Rahman, who was the father of both Ibrahim bin Abd al-Latif al-Sheikh and Muhammad bin Abd al-Latif al-Sheikh and the grandfather of Muhammad bin Ibrahim al-Sheikh, all three being from Riyadh. Muhammad bin Abdullah was in turn a teacher of several prominent religious scholars.[59]

All in all, religious scholars in Saudi Arabia formed a special class, members of which were related to one another either in a familial relationship or master–student relationship. As such, they could act as a special-interest group and, more significantly, protect their historical/traditional public roles in the judiciary and education. This was also possible because they had intensively participated in the foundation of the Kingdom of Saudi Arabia and, therefore, enjoyed a strong moral authority over the ruling Al Saud family. Over the course of modern sovereign state building in Saudi Arabia, this network was absorbed into the expanding state apparatus and its members, religious scholars, had become state employees.

This chapter shows that all the Gulf states were quite religious states from the 1950s to the 1980s. Yet, as claimed in the Introduction, the Muslim Brotherhood could still find them insufficiently religious: it could problematise, for example, the issuance of so many man-made laws or the insufficiency of religious classes in the public education system. The Brotherhood, however, remained non-oppositional in all Gulf countries in the first phase of modern state building. The next chapter discusses the circumstances that explain this.

56. He studied under Sulaiman bin Muqbil, Qarnas bin Abd al-Rahman, Abdullah bin Aba Batayn, Abd al-Rahman bin Hasan and the latter's son, Abd al-Latif bin Abd al-Rahman. Al-Bassam, *Ulama Najd*, v.6, pp. 150–9.
57. Al-Bassam, *Ulama Najd*, v.4, pp. 461–7 and al-Bassam, *Ulama Najd*, v.5, pp. 329–35.
58. Al-Bassam, *Ulama Najd*, v.4, pp. 70–3.
59. Such as Muhammad bin Abd al-Aziz al-Mane, see al-Bassam, *Ulama Najd*, v.6, pp. 100–13; Salih bin Uthman al-Qadi, see al-Bassam, *Ulama Najd*, v.2, pp. 517–20; Abdullah bin Muhammad bin Mane, see al-Bassam, *Ulama Najd*, v.4, pp. 482–5; Sulaiman bin Abd al-Rahman al-Amri, see al-Bassam, *Ulama Najd*, v.2, pp. 320–31; Ibrahim bin Hamad al-Jassir, see al-Bassam, *Ulama Najd*, v.1, pp. 277–93.

3

THE MUSLIM BROTHERHOOD IN THE GULF

The Brotherhood's expansion to the Gulf took place at a time when the Gulf states were expanding their state institutions. Because they had no prior experience, the states relied heavily on expatriate professionals from other Arab countries such as Egypt, Syria, Iraq and Palestine. Most of these professionals were inclined towards pan-Arab socialism. This approach would prove troubling because the Gulf states were facing not only a geopolitical challenge posed by pan-Arab socialist regimes that had come to power in other Arab countries, particularly Egypt, but also a domestic opposition that had adopted a discourse blended with the same ideology. In this domestic and regional context, the Muslim Brotherhood proved to be an acquiescent and loyal ally of the Gulf states. Most of the Brotherhood figures in the Gulf were foreigners who escaped persecution in their home countries at the hands of pan-Arab socialist regimes, not having the necessary social and cultural capital to be oppositional.

The Brotherhood's Trial

The Muslim Brotherhood originated in Egypt. But its founder, Hasan al-Banna, envisioned it as a transnational movement. Soon after its foundation, the Brotherhood sought to expand its activities. In 1935 the Consultative Council of the movement decided to expand the organisation beyond Egypt. In 1940 the Palestine and Islamic World Committee was established, which became the Section for the Liaison with the Islamic World in 1945.[1] According to Richard Mitchell, the Section 'was charged with: (1) spreading the message about Islam and the Brothers throughout the Muslim world . . . (2) studying the problems of the Islamic world . . . (3) organizing an annual meeting to be attended by leaders and representatives' of various Islamic movements in the Muslim world.[2]

At the time, Egypt was the centre of both religious and modern education in the Arab world. It had a highly developed modern education system, encompassing not only schools at all levels, including universities, but also vocational schools.[3] It was also home to an advanced religious education system, hosting, for example, the prestigious al-Azhar.

The Brotherhood greatly benefited from Egypt's status in its efforts to expand to other Arab countries. The Brotherhood approached and sought to recruit students who came to Egypt to pursue education, be it secular or religious, from other Arab and Islamic countries 'as potential missionaries for the cause after they returned to their respective countries'.[4] Egypt also exported professionals, especially teachers, in large numbers to other Arab countries, which needed professionals to build their own state institutions. Many Brotherhood members joined this migration in search of jobs and spread the Brotherhood organisation and ideology. The Brotherhood therefore expanded to other Arab countries, including Palestine, Lebanon, Syria, Iraq, Tunisia, Sudan, Yemen and Jordan.[5]

The problem was that the Brotherhood was not a strictly religious movement, which merely sought to make its followers more pious. 'The idea of the Muslim Brothers includes in it', al-Banna said, 'all categories of reform.' The movement was 'a Salafiyya message, a Sunni way, a Sufi truth, a political

---

1. El-Awaisi, *The Muslim Brothers and the Palestine Question 1928–1947*, p. 142.
2. Mitchell, *The Society of the Muslim Brothers*, pp. 172–3.
3. Matthews and Akrawi, *Education in Arab Countries of the Near East*.
4. Mitchell, *The Society of the Muslim Brothers*, pp. 172–3.
5. For the expansion of the Brotherhood into Syria, Lebanon and Palestine, see el-Awaisi, *The Muslim Brothers and the Palestine Question 1928–1947*; for Sudan, see el-Affendi, *Turabi's Revolution*; for Iraq, see al-Azimi, 'The Muslim Brotherhood: Genesis and development'.

organization, an athletic group, a cultural-educational union, an economy company, and a social idea'.⁶

Furthermore, rulers did not have, al-Banna held, any discretion over whether to follow the Brotherhood's programme or not. The prescriptions of Islam were not mere suggestions from God, whereby the implementation was left up to the discretion of Muslims, but rather definite legislation to be upheld in managing personal and public life. The rulers of Muslim countries, therefore, could not ignore Islam's prescriptions for public life. If they did, however, then Muslims were obliged to warn the rulers. If the latter still refused to abide by Islam, then Muslims would struggle until the rulers came to terms with Islam.

To this end, al-Banna stated, for example:

> We will direct our call to the leaders of the country: its notables, ministers, rulers, elders, delegates and political parties and invite them to follow our method. We will place our program in their hands and demand that they lead this Muslim country, the leader of the Islamic World, on the path of Islam with courage and without hesitation . . . If they respond to our call and adopt the path to this goal, we will support them. But if they resort to duplicity or evasion and hide behind false excuses and arguments, then we are at war with every leader, party chief or organization that does not work to support Islam and does not move to restore the rule and glory of Islam.⁷

The Muslim Brotherhood was therefore very much involved in domestic affairs, be it political or otherwise. If Islam had relevance in every aspect of life, this was the natural conclusion, as religion and politics were not distinct affairs for Muslims. 'If someone should ask you: "To what end is your appeal made?"' al-Banna once said, 'say: "We are calling you to Islam . . . government is part of it, and freedom is one of its religious duties. If someone should say to you: "This is politics!", say: "This is Islam, and we do not recognize such divisions."'⁸

---

6. Mitchell, *The Society of the Muslim Brothers*, p. 14.
7. Cited in Krämer, *Hasan al-Banna*, p. 52.
8. Al-Banna, *Five Tracts of Hasan Al-Banna (1906–1949)*, p. 37.

Having and promulgating such views, the Brotherhood was bound to clash with the equally ambitious but secular projects of state and nation building in the Arab world. The clash was harshest, and most violent, in Egypt, Iraq and Syria. Egypt led the way when Gamal Abdel Nasser, Egypt's new leader, violently cracked down on the Brotherhood and dissolved it after an assassination attempt on his life in 1954.[9] Abdel Nasser extended the crackdown on the Brotherhood into the Gaza Strip, which fell under Egyptian control after the 1948 war, and into Syria during its union with Egypt from 1958 to 1961.

The collapse of the union between Egypt and Syria brought some respite to the Brotherhood in Syria. But the the new secular, pan-Arab socialist Baath regime was no less hostile to the Brotherhood. The Brotherhood was itself eager to clash with the regime, which not only adopted a secular ideology, but was also dominated by the non-Sunni and heterodox Alawites, and engaged in a violent showdown which lasted throughout the 1970s and ended in 1982 with the brutal suppression of the movement. The fortunes of the Brotherhood were no brighter in Iraq. Soon after the Iraqi Baath Party came to power in 1968, it began a violent crackdown and succeeded in considerably reducing the movement's strength.

Successive waves of suppression in Egypt, Syria and Iraq led to the emigration of the Brothers to countries where the regimes were less hostile. Among those countries were the Arab Gulf states.

The Gulf States' Predicaments

The Gulf States welcomed the Muslim Brotherhood for their own reasons. In the 1950s Gulf rulers began to build their modern state institutions. The challenge was that they were ruling highly illiterate populations. Official statistics are lacking for the earlier years, but even after years of investment in education, 39 per cent of men were still illiterate in Kuwait in 1965. In the same year, 41 per cent of men could read and write, 10 per cent had a primary school degree, 6 per cent an intermediate school degree, 2 per cent a secondary school degree and 2 per cent a university degree.[10] The situation

---

9. Even before Gamal Abdel Nasser, the Brotherhood clashed with the state in Egypt and was dissolved by the government in 1948.
10. Sinclair, *Education in Kuwait, Bahrain and Qatar*, p. 48.

was no better in Saudi Arabia, Qatar and the UAE, as Kuwait had begun to invest in public education well before them. In the early 1970s literacy rates were reported as 55 per cent for Kuwait, 47 per cent for Bahrain, 33 per cent for Qatar, 33 per cent for Saudi Arabia and a mere 14 per cent for the UAE.[11]

To staff their expanding state schools, the rulers could not rely on the native populations and therefore had to import professionals from other countries. In the school year 1960–1, for example, only 4.7 per cent of primary school teachers in Kuwait were Kuwaitis and 4.45 per cent of primary school teachers in Qatar were Qataris. The same year, Bahrain fared much better than Kuwait and Qatar in supplying its primary school teachers from its own citizens: 78.3 per cent of primary school teachers in Bahrain were Bahrainis.[12] But at intermediate and secondary schools, Bahrain joined the other two. In the school year 1965–6, 1.5 per cent of these teachers in Bahrain were Bahrainis, 1.25 per cent of teachers in Kuwait were Kuwaitis and none were Qataris.[13]

When the Gulf states founded their national universities, they also had to rely on foreigners. In the school year 1977–8, for example, out of 33 professors, 32 associate professors, 11 readers and associate readers and 30 language teachers employed at Qatar University, none were Qatari citizens. Kuwait had a somewhat better record. In the school year 1975–6, 2 out of 116 professors, 6 out of 120 associate professors, 35 out of 115 readers and 2 out of 79 language teachers employed at Kuwait University were Kuwaiti citizens, making up 10.4 per cent of the total.[14]

Saudi Arabia also fared worse than Kuwait, but better than Kuwait and Qatar in supplying primary school teachers from within its own population: in the school year 1960–1, 52 per cent of primary school teachers were Saudi citizens. Saudi Arabia also fared better than all the others in supplying post-primary school teachers: in the school year 1969–70, 29.5 per cent of intermediate and secondary school teachers and 27.7 per cent of higher education teachers were Saudi citizens.[15]

---

11. Birks and Sinclair, *International Migration and Development in the Arab Region*.
12. Al-Misnad, *The Development of Modern Education in Bahrain, Kuwait and Qatar*, p. 122.
13. Al-Misnad, *The Development of Modern Education in Bahrain, Kuwait and Qatar*, p. 181.
14. Al-Misnad, *The Development of Modern Education in Bahrain, Kuwait and Qatar*, pp. 410–11.
15. Shukri, *Education, Man Power Needs and Socio-Economic Development in Saudi Arabia*, Appendix VII.

In order to staff their rapidly expanding state institutions, Gulf states brought in foreign labour in large numbers, naturally from other Arab countries, such as Egypt, Syria, Palestine, Lebanon and Iraq. Heavy reliance on these more educated professionals from other Arab countries would not have been troubling if the geopolitical context of the period, the 1950s and 1960s, were more friendly to the ruling Gulf families.

But it was not. It was in this period that successive pan-Arab socialist regimes came to power in other Arab countries.[16] It started in Egypt in 1952 when a group of officers calling themselves the Free Officers overthrew the monarchy and founded a republic in its stead. Egypt's Free Officers became a model for others, inspiring radical-revolutionary figures/parties elsewhere in the Arab world to take political power. In Syria, the Baath Party, a pan-Arab socialist party, came to dominate the government in 1957 and forged a union with Egypt: thus was founded the United Arab Republic in 1958. The union did not go as the Syrians hoped and collapsed in 1961. The Baath Party gained power again in 1963 in a successful coup staged by its members in the military. In Iraq a group of military officers, styling themselves after their Egyptian colleagues and calling themselves the Free Officers, overthrew the Hashemite monarchy in 1958 and founded a republic, ushering in a decade of extreme instability. The Baath Party came to power again a decade later. The next domino to fall was Yemen: in 1962 a military coup overthrew the monarchy and founded a republic: the royalists fought back, however, and the Yemen Civil War lasted until 1970. Lastly, the monarchy in Libya fell when a group of military officers, likewise calling themselves the Free Officers, took power, abolished the monarchy and founded a republic in 1969. There were also unsuccessful attempts: the revolution in Yemen spilled into Oman in the late 1960s, with the foundation of the Popular Front for the Liberation of the Occupied Arabian Gulf. The monarchy in Oman defeated the rebellion a decade later with military support from Iran and Britain.[17]

16. This ideology can be best assessed in Gamal Abdel Nasser's views, which are expressed in Abdel Nasser, *Egypt's Liberation*.
17. The Front was renamed in 1972 as the Popular Front for the Liberation of Oman and the Arabian Gulf, and renamed again in 1974 as the Popular Front for the Liberation of Oman. Oman had already been in civil war since the mid-1950s. For the first decade the rebellion against the ruling family was primarily tribal. Only in the late 1960s did the rebellion take a Marxist-Radical turn.

Among all the Arab countries where pan-Arab socialist regimes came to power, Egypt under the leadership of Gamal Abdel Nasser was the most disconcerting for the Gulf states. This was because after Abdel Nasser nationalised the Suez Canal in 1956 in defiance of Britain, he became a hero for the masses across the Arab world and relentlessly continued his anti-British rhetoric. For example, in 1964 he declared, 'We shall struggle unrelentingly until we rid the whole Arab nation of British imperialism, British occupation, British influence and British military bases.'[18]

Abdel Nasser's fiery anti-imperialist rhetoric had obvious ramifications for the Gulf states: at the time he wrote *Philosophy of the Revolution*, four of them, Bahrain, Kuwait, Qatar and the Trucial States (the future UAE), were directly under British protection. Equally critically, the oil companies operating in the Gulf states were either British- or American-owned. In Abdel Nasser's view, oil was one of the three sources of power the Arabs had that could be used in the 'united struggle'[19] against imperialism.

There was also the US. In the aftermath of the 1956 Suez Crisis, the US expressed its intention in the Eisenhower Doctrine that it would not leave the Middle East exposed to 'international communism'. As the Cold War engulfed the Middle East, the Gulf states sided with the US-led Western camp. Bahrain, Kuwait, Qatar and the Trucial States had no other choice, for they were under the protection of Britain and left their foreign policies in its hands. Even Kuwait, when it became independent in 1961, stayed under British protection until 1971, as neighbouring Iraq began to pose a direct threat.

As an independent state, Saudi Arabia could have pursued a neutral foreign policy, but did not and joined the US-led Western camp. Much more actively than others, Saudi Arabia opposed Egypt and therefore became a pivotal ally of the US in the Middle East. When the revolution broke out in Yemen, Saudi Arabia gave financial and logistical support to the royalists against the anti-royalists militarily supported by Egypt.

Abdel Nasser's anti-imperialist rhetoric was putting in question the very legitimacy of the Gulf rulers, who in Abdel Nasser's view were mere

---

18. Abdel Nasser, *Address by President Gamal Abdel Nasser at the International Labourers' Day Festivities May 1st, 1964*, p. 17.
19. Abdel Nasser, *Egypt's Liberation*, p. 66.

reactionaries allied with imperialism standing against Arab nationalism and unity. Abdel Nasser's socialism was also equally troubling for the Gulf states as it affected their political systems and domestic politics. The problem was twofold: first, monarchism as a political system was an inherently non-egalitarian system. Second, oil revenues were extremely unevenly distributed: especially initially, a ruling family would receive a large proportion of the total oil revenues through direct allocations, land purchases and lucrative government positions.[20]

More worryingly, the Gulf was not immune to the spread of Abdel Nasser's ideas among its peoples. In addition to books, journals and radio, there were two other channels through which pan-Arabism and socialism could be spread in the Gulf. First, the Gulf states had already sent a number of students to other Arab countries, especially to Egypt, to pursue higher education: during their stay these students might embrace pan-Arab socialism and spread the ideology when they returned. Second, lacking suitably qualified professionals, the Gulf states imported them from other Arab states: these professionals, especially teachers, might themselves be pan-Arab socialists and spread their ideology to their colleagues and students.

Through these channels, pan-Arab nationalism and socialism did indeed spread to the Gulf, finding adherents and sympathisers especially among the educated and the labourers in the oil industry. Even some members of the ruling families in the Gulf became sympathetic to pan-Arab nationalism, anti-imperialism and socialism. Not surprisingly, the opposition that first began as labour strikes in the oil industry in the late 1950s and early 1960s eventually adopted a discourse blending pan-Arabism and socialism.

The Muslim Brothers were among those who came to the Arab Gulf countries to staff state institutions. In fact, given that the Gulf states faced a geopolitical challenge from a pan-Arab socialist regime and a domestic opposition employing a pan-Arab socialist rhetoric, the Muslim Brothers were preferable, and even natural, allies. At a time when the Brothers were seeking safe havens, the Arab Gulf rulers welcomed them, employing them in the newly expanding state institutions.

20. See al-Kuwari, *Oil Revenue of the Arabian Gulf Emirates*.

The Brotherhood's Expansion to the Gulf

Even though the Gulf states had their own reasons to welcome the Muslim Brotherhood, the Gulf region's early exposure to Islamism facilitated the spread of the Brotherhood, especially in Kuwait and Bahrain. In terms of agency, therefore, Kuwait and Bahrain differed from the other Gulf states in that the local populations played a critical role from the beginning. In Qatar, the UAE and Saudi Arabia, however, the Arab expatriates, who worked in the expanding state institutions, played a critical role in introducing the Brotherhood's ideology and recruiting natives.

Kuwait and Bahrain: The Native-led Expansion

A Kuwaiti merchant, Abd al-Aziz Ali al-Mutawa, met Hasan al-Banna in Egypt in the mid-1940s and embraced his cause. This was an arranged meeting. According al-Zumai, Abd al-Aziz first met an Egyptian teacher working in Baghdad, who was a member of the Muslim Brotherhood. After meeting this teacher, Abd al-Aziz corresponded with and eventually met al-Banna in Egypt.[21] Abd al-Aziz sought to recruit other Kuwaitis into the movement. He first recruited his own brother, Abdullah Ali al-Mutawa, introducing him to al-Banna in Mecca during a pilgrimage.

Other Kuwaitis soon joined the movement, all from predominantly well-to-do families. In 1947 the Brotherhood had its first building in Kuwait and five years later officially founded Jamʻiyyat al-Irshad al-Islami (the Islamic Guidance Society).[22] A Kuwaiti religious scholar, Yusuf bin Isa al-Qinai, became the president of the society and Abd al-Aziz al-Mutawa its general supervisor. The society's raison d'être was typical of the Brotherhood and other Islamist movements. As described by Ahmad al-Shirbasi, an Egyptian member of the Brotherhood who was in Kuwait at the time, the society

---

21. Al-Zumai, *The Intellectual and Historical Development of the Islamic Movement in Kuwait*, pp. 69–70.
22. According to an IkhwanWiki article, the word 'Ikhwan' evoked bitter memories among Kuwaitis, for it was the name of the Wahhabi forces that attacked Kuwait in 1921. Therefore, Abd al-Aziz al-Mutawa asked Hasan al-Banna to name the Kuwaiti branch Jamʻiyyat al-Irshad al-Islami. Because Hasan al-Banna had died by 1952, this name must have already been in use long before the formal foundation of the Society. Mousa and Desouki, 'Tarikh al-Ikhwan al-Muslimun fi'l Kuwait'.

intended to 'spread Islamic culture among the new generation', to 'direct the nation according to its religion and its glorious history' and to 'show Islam as a creed and a way of life'.[23]

To this end, the society undertook a variety of initiatives.[24] It began to publish a magazine and founded a school, both named after the society: *al-Irshad Magazine* and al-Irshad School. The society was also fortunate to get an opportunity to broadcast its own programmes on the state-owned radio. The society's headquarters had a library, and a hall for lectures delivered by prominent religious figures and in which to hold meetings. In order to expand its membership among the workers, merchants and students, the society formed committees.[25]

In these efforts, the Kuwaiti Brothers received support from the main branch in Egypt. More experienced Brothers, such as Fadil al-Wartlani, who established the Brotherhood branch in Yemen, came to Kuwait and participated in meetings. The Brotherhood in Kuwait also benefited from the experience of those Arab expats who came to work there, such as Najib Jawfayel, Ahmad al-Shirbasi, Zuhdi Abu Al-Izz and Abd al-Aziz al-Sisi.

The Brotherhood in Kuwait made, therefore, a promising start and expanded its membership especially among students and merchants. The fact that the leadership came from well-to-do Kuwaiti families helped the society to recruit those from a similar socio-economic background. As al-Zumai observed, initially the society did not have members from the Shia, the Bedouins or poorer urban strata.[26]

Despite the relative homogeneity of the socio-economic background of its members, the Brotherhood was unable to maintain its unity. There was a growing generational gap between the leadership of the society and its student members. An internal dispute on how to respond to the suppression of the Brotherhood in Egypt resulted in Abd al-Aziz al-Mutawa's resignation

---

23. Cited in al-Mdaires, *Islamic Extremism in Kuwait*, p. 13.
24. For a detailed discussion, see al-Zumai, *The Intellectual and Historical Development of the Islamic Movement in Kuwait*, pp. 75–88.
25. For more details, see Freer, *Rentier Islamism*, pp. 49–50 and al-Mdaires, *Islamic Extremism in Kuwait*, pp. 11–17.
26. Al-Zumai, *The Intellectual and Historical Development of the Islamic Movement in Kuwait*, p. 73.

from the society in 1954. He was succeeded by a more elderly man from the same family, Abd al-Razzaq al-Salih al-Mutawa. Abd al-Aziz's departure weakened the movement in Kuwait, as others left the society with him.

This internal dispute and the subsequent departures could not have come at a worse time. Secular ideologies and movements were on the rise throughout the region. In particular, pan-Arab nationalism, represented by Gamal Abdel Nasser, had been gaining considerable ground among the Arab youth, undermining the appeal of religious ideologies and movements. Kuwait felt the impact.[27] Some Kuwaitis embraced it during their studies in Egypt, Lebanon and elsewhere in the Arab world. The leading Kuwaiti pan-Arab nationalist, Ahmad al-Khatib, for example, was introduced to the ideology during his studies in Beirut in the 1940s. Kuwait also received pan-Arab nationalist teachers, who inculcated the ideology in their students. Pan-Arab nationalism therefore gained adherents among the Kuwaiti youth.

As the Brotherhood weakened, pan-Arab nationalism strengthened. The results of the 1958 elections for the boards of various state departments are illustrative. While two leading pan-Arab nationalists, Jassim al-Qatami and Ahmad al-Khatib, received 325 and 251 votes respectively, two leading Brothers, Abdullah al-Mutawa and Muhammad al-Adsani, received 119 and 108 votes respectively.[28]

Egyptian–Syrian unification in 1958 further boosted pan-Arab nationalists in Kuwait. In February 1959 Ahmad al-Khatib led a massive demonstration celebrating the union and calling for Kuwait's participation. The regime reacted by expelling hundreds of Arab expatriates suspected of being involved in the demonstrations. The regime also closed down all clubs and societies, including the Brotherhood's al-Irshad. Despite these measures, the regime also sought to appease pan-Arab nationalists by taking some significant steps. In 1961 Kuwait became an independent state, which must have strongly appealed to anti-British nationalists. Immediately thereafter it became a member of the Arab League. At the end of the same year, Kuwait founded the Kuwait Fund for Arab Economic Development to provide loans to needy Arab states.

---

27. See al-Rashoud, *Modern Education and Arab Nationalism in Kuwait, 1911–1961*.
28. Al-Mdaires, *Islamic Extremism in Kuwait*, p. 17.

Yet these steps proved futile in undermining pan-Arab nationalism in Kuwait. The nationalists still won sixteen of the fifty seats in the first post-independence general council held in 1963. By contrast, none of the six Brothers who entered the elections won a seat in the parliament.[29] Sayyid Yusuf Sayyid Hashim al-Rifai, a candidate sympathetic to the Brotherhood in Kuwait, won a seat. However, his success was not due to the Brotherhood's popularity as his district was predominantly Shia.[30]

Nineteen sixty-three also witnessed some positive developments for the Brotherhood. First, the Kuwaiti brothers established a new organisation and called it Jam'iyyat al-Islah al-Ijtima'i (the Social Reform Society) or al-Islah Society. Even though some older figures became involved in the new organisation, new members joined and even assumed the presidency of the society. The first president, Yusuf al-Nafisi, was a new face. He was followed by Yusuf al-Hajji, then by an older figure, Abdullah Ali al-Mutawa. A figure sympathetic to the Brotherhood, Sayyid Yusuf al-Rifai, entered the cabinet as Minister of Posts, Telegraph and Telephone. Al-Rifai kept this ministry for two years then became Minister of State for Affairs of the Council of Ministers for a further two years.

Four years later, the Brotherhood received another boost. Egypt's defeat by Israel in 1967 dealt a heavy blow to the popularity of Gamal Abdel Nasser and the pan-Arab nationalism he represented. Three years after this defeat, Abdel Nasser died. Pan-Arab nationalism survived both Egypt's defeat and Abdel Nasser's death, as it continued to be upheld by the Baath Party in Syria and Iraq. But the movement had entered a period of decline elsewhere in the Arab world, paving the way for a period of religious revival.

The Brotherhood in Kuwait also experienced a similar revival, reflected in the transfer of the headquarters of al-Islah Society from a humble building to a modern one with a theatre, library, mosque and centre for various youth activities. It began to publish a newsletter, *al-Islah*, in 1965, which became a magazine, *al-Mujtama'*, in 1970. In the following years, *al-Mujtama'* became

---

29. They were Ahmad Baze al-Yassin, Abdullah al-Mutawa, Abd al-Aziz al-Qatayfi, Abd al-Rahman al-Umar, Muhammad al-Adsani and Abdullah Sultan al-Kulaib.
30. Both al-Zumai and Sami Awadh mention al-Rifai as a Brother. Al-Mdaires, on the other hand, calls him 'a supporter of the Brotherhood'. See al-Mdaires, *Islamic Extremism in Kuwait*, p. 20.

a major mouthpiece not only for the Kuwaiti Brothers but also for leading figures of the broader Islamist movement. Through al-Islah Society, the movement organised cultural and religious activities and reached out to diverse groups. For example, the movement founded its first Qur'an centre in 1968 and opened more of them over the following years.

Undertaking a variety of activities, the movement expanded its membership among a broader spectrum of classes in Kuwait, including notably the Bedouins. During this period a young generation of Kuwaitis, among whom were, for example, Ismail al-Shatti and Tariq al-Suwaidan, joined the movement and assumed leadership roles. Illustrating the Brotherhood's rising popularity among the youth, it succeeded in dominating the National Union of Kuwaiti Students from the late 1970s.[31] The Brothers also made similar advances in professional associations, dominating especially the teachers' associations.

The increasing popularity of the Brotherhood did not trouble the regime in Kuwait. In fact quite the opposite, as the regime was content for it to be happening at the expense of pan-Arab nationalism.[32] The regime even extended help to the Brotherhood, for example by financing some of its activities. The regime also made appointments of Brotherhood figures in the 1970s. For example, Ahmad Baze al-Yasin, a relative of Abd al-Aziz al-Mutawa and a member of al-Islah Society, was appointed to the board of the Central Bank of Kuwait as a member in 1970.[33] In 1976 the former president of al-Islah, Yusuf Jassim al-Hajji, entered the cabinet as Minister of Awqaf and Islamic Affairs and remained in post until 1981.[34] It is noteworthy that al-Islah Society collaborated with this ministry to run Qur'an courses in Kuwait. By 1980 the Society was running around sixty Qur'an centres in Kuwait.[35]

Bahrain was similar to Kuwait in that its first Muslim Brothers were local inhabitants, not Arab expatriates, as was the case in Qatar, the Trucial States and Saudi Arabia. It developed native Brothers earlier than other Gulf countries. It was also similar to Kuwait in that a school, called al-Hidayah, played

---

31. See the discussion in Freer, *Rentier Islamism*, p. 71.
32. Tétreault and al-Mughni, 'Gender, citizenship, and nationalism in Kuwait'.
33. Al-Bakri, 'Al-Sheikh Ahmad Baze' al-Yasin'.
34. Al-Kharafi, 'Yusuf Jassim Muhammad al-Hajji'.
35. Awadh, *Islamic Political Groups in Kuwait*, p. 191.

a critical role in preparing a receptive audience for the Brotherhood in Bahrain. Bahrain's first native Brother, Abd al-Rahman al-Jawdar, was a graduate of the school, as were many future members and sympathisers. Students of the school founded the Student Club in 1941. According to the Brotherhood movement's own encyclopedia, this club was the nucleus of what became the Brotherhood's first organisation in the Gulf, al-Islah Club.[36]

By the early 1940s, Bahrain had become host to a number of teachers from Egypt,[37] some of whom were probably members of the Brotherhood and may have introduced their students to the Brotherhood. Abd al-Rahman al-Jawdar was possibly one of those students and among the founders of the Student Club. Lacking higher education at home, Bahrain sent students to other Arab countries. The first group went to Beirut in the late 1920s. By the 1940s Bahrain was also sending students to Egypt. Al-Jawdar was one of them. During his stay in Egypt from 1944 to 1946, al-Jawdar met Hasan al-Banna, participating in and witnessing first-hand Brotherhood activities.[38]

Bahrain was in desperate need of qualified personnel to fill its expanding state institutions. Native Bahrainis were in particularly high demand. Coming from an established Sunni family from Bahrain and being among the few educated Bahrainis, Abd al-Rahman al-Jawdar easily found a position in the Ministry of Education on his return and began to work as a teacher in the Ministry. Soon afterwards, in 1948, he played a role in transforming the Student Club into al-Islah Club.

Al-Hidayah School was originally founded on the initiative of a powerful political figure, Abdullah bin Isa Al Khalifa, the son of Bahrain's ruler, and financed by donations from powerful Bahraini political figures and leading merchants. The school was situated in Muharraq, near the ruler's residence, and therefore attracted predominantly the sons of well-to-do Sunni families. Having access to the school through teachers and alumni, the Brotherhood could continue to recruit students. A report completed by

36. See 'Tarikh al-Ihwan al-Muslimun fi'l Bahrain'.
37. In 1944 the number of teachers from Egypt was twelve. There were two teachers from Syria and twelve from Lebanon. See Qubain, 'Social classes and tensions in Bahrain', p. 279.
38. Al-Shahabi, 'Al-Ikhwan al-Muslimun fi'l Bahrain Tahwilat al-'Uqud al-Sab'a'. Abdullah al-Aqil also confirms this. Al-Aqil, 'Al-Akh al-Da'iyya 'Abd al-Rahman 'Ali al-Jawdar (Abu Ahmad)'.

Britain's political resident in Bahrain in December 1949 attested that al-Islah Club, which was also based in Muharraq, had around 120 members, the majority of them students.[39]

The Brotherhood's most valuable recruit in this period was Isa bin Muhammad Al Khalifa, a member of Bahrain's ruling family. Born in 1938, Isa bin Muhammad was the grandson of Abdullah bin Isa, who founded al-Hidayah School and served as Bahrain's Minister of Education for decades. Isa bin Muhammad also studied at al-Hidayah, then moved to Egypt and studied at Helwan Secondary School, graduating in 1956. He then enrolled at Cairo University and graduated in 1962 with a degree in law. During his stay in Egypt, Isa bin Muhammad met with the Brothers at a time when the latter were experiencing hardships in Egypt. He even befriended the family members of Sayyid Qutb, who was hanged by the regime in 1966, and helped the Brothers hide.[40] He returned to Bahrain after graduating and assumed the presidency of al-Islah Club in 1963, a post he would keep until his death in 2015.

Through their members and sympathisers among the well-to-do Sunni families of Bahrain, who were the ruling family's prime allies against the Shias who constituted the majority in the country, the Brotherhood had wide access to the ruling family. A religious event organised by al-Islah Club in 1956, for example, was attended by the crown prince and future ruler of Bahrain, Isa bin Salman, the future prime minister, Khalifa bin Salman, and Abdullah bin Isa, the long-standing Minister of Education and grandfather of Isa bin Muhammad. At the end of the event, Isa bin Salman even made a considerable donation to the club.[41]

The relationship between the Brotherhood and the regime in Bahrain was thus organic. It was also strategic. In the mid-1950s the regime faced a serious domestic disturbance. As the most exploited group, the Shias had often been a source of disturbance, but now the regime faced not only the Shias but

39. 'File 35/7 Agitation for Constitutional Reforms in Bahrain.'
40. Al-Hamad, 'Isa bin Muhammed min al-Islah ila al-Islah'.
41. The Brotherhood's magazine in Bahrain, *al-Islah Magazine*, published a picture of Isa bin Salman walking to the event along with leading figures of al-Islah Society, including Abd al-Rahman al-Jawdar. See al-Sheikh, 'Li Mihat min Hayat al-Ustadh Qasim Yusuf al-Sheikh', p. 26.

also the Sunnis. The latter had been undergoing a period of political awakening, as evidenced by the growing number of clubs in Bahrain. Most notable among them was the Aruba Club or Arabism Club. The Club was founded by Shias but also attracted Sunnis.

Speaking of the impact of these clubs on the Bahrainis, Charles Belgrave, the ruler's British advisor, said in the early 1950s, 'Bahrain was quiet. Yet I was aware of a new, indefinable feeling of an emerging political consciousness. One sign of this was the increasingly important part which the Arab clubs played in the lives of the educated young men.'[42]

What triggered the disturbance was a fight between Shias and Sunnis at a Shia religious festival in 1953. After this incident, a Sunni crowd attacked Shia villages, injuring some Shias. The Shias responded by attacking the Sunnis. The country was on the verge of a serious sectarian conflict. Fortunately the country escaped this thanks to the decade-old work of some clubs to transcend sectarianism on the island. Even though sectarian disputes occasionally erupted in Bahrain, Sunnis and Shias cooperated in their opposition to the ruling family. A public meeting held in October 1954 and attended by both Sunnis and Shias resulted in a number of demands being sent to the ruler, the most important of which was the formation of a legislative council. The meeting also formed a Higher Executive Committee, which consisted of four Sunnis and four Shias.

Enjoying great popularity among the Shias and the Sunnis, the Committee, which later came to be called the Committee for National Unity, confronted the regime for the next two years and even succeeded in gaining concessions. For example, the regime agreed to the formation of consultative councils for some state departments. It even announced that it would terminate the service of the ruler's favourite advisor, Charles Belgrave. However, any gains the Committee had made were in vain, as the regime dissolved it in 1956, jailing its leading figures and closing down all private newspapers.[43]

During this period of disturbance, al-Islah Club was invited to join the opposition, but its leadership remained loyal to the regime. The Club's pro-regime stance must have been disappointing those who supported the

---

42. Belgrave, *Personal Column*, p. 144.
43. For a discussion of this period, see Rumaihi, *Bahrain*; Khuri, *Tribe and State in Bahrain*.

Committee and joined the opposition. Complicating the situation further was al-Islah's connection to the Muslim Brotherhood in Egypt, for Egypt's Abdel Nasser, who turned against the Brotherhood in 1954, was becoming a national hero in Bahrain as well. During some of the street protests, al-Islah Club was even stoned by protesters, further cementing the Brotherhood's pro-regime stance in Bahrain.

However, such closeness to the regime became a burden for the Brotherhood as it seriously limited its appeal among the Bahraini masses. Among the Shias the Brotherhood didn't have much appeal anyway. But it also lost its appeal especially among educated Sunnis, who came increasingly to embrace popular pan-Arab nationalism represented by Abdel Nasser and then the Baath Party in Syria and Iraq.[44]

In fact, a member of al-Islah Club, Qasim Yusuf al-Sheikh, also acknowledged the negative impact of the whole episode on the fortunes of the Brotherhood in Bahrain. He argued that the Club could not recruit new members and had even lost some of its existing members. He also added that participation in the Club's activities had decreased noticeably. Some of those who attended did so clandestinely in order not to attract attention.[45]

The Club survived, but only on paper. Fuad Khuri claimed that due to the high number of members lost in the mid-1950s, the Club became 'almost defunct'.[46] It was also absent from the first elections held in 1973, after Bahrain gained independence in 1971. As it came to be known, the religious bloc consisted only of Shia religious figures and activists. Abd al-Rahman al-Jawdar contested the elections, but failed to be elected.[47]

Despite this setback, the Brotherhood's activities continued in Bahrain. Individuals played critical roles. In addition to working in the Ministry of Education, first as a teacher and then principal, Abd al-Rahman al-Jawdar continued to expand the library he founded in the 1950s and turned it into a major centre for Islamist literature in Bahrain. He also kept his ties with the broader Muslim Brotherhood movement. He became, for example, a member of the Brotherhood-dominated, Saudi-funded Muslim World League. In the

---

44. See al-Mdaires, *Islamic Extremism in Kuwait*.
45. Al-Sheikh, 'Li Mihat min Hayat al-Ustad Qasim Yusuf al-Sheikh', p. 25.
46. Khuri, *Tribe and State in Bahrain*, p. 174.
47. 'The Brotherhood in Bahrain.'

1980s he also became a member of the Kuwait-based Hay'at al-Khayriyya al-Islamiyya al-'Alamiyya (International Islamic Charity Organization). Which was headed by Yusuf al-Hajji, a member of the Brotherhood in Kuwait.[48]

Meanwhile, Isa bin Muhammad Al Khalifa, the president of al-Islah Club, entered the Ministry of Justice as a judge and eventually rose to the top, serving as Minister of Justice, Islamic Affairs and Endowments in 1974–5 and as Minister of Labour and Social Affairs in 1976. This was the period during which Bahrain gave fellowships to hundreds of students to pursue university education in other countries, both Arab and non-Arab. Using his political influence, Isa bin Muhammad secured fellowships for students sympathetic to the Brotherhood.[49] It is likely the Brotherhood did not leave these students on their own in the countries where they studied, and involved them in their activities. For example, Abdullah al-Aqil acknowledged that those who went to Kuwait were in touch with and even involved in the activities of the Brotherhood's al-Islah Society.[50]

The late 1970s gave the Brotherhood in Bahrain a new lease of life. By then, pan-Arab nationalism was no longer as serious a threat as it had been in the 1950s and 1960s. But the Iranian Revolution of 1979 gave birth to another threat, which increased Shia political activism.

Qatar, the UAE and Saudi Arabia: The Expatriates-led Expansion

Unlike Kuwait and Bahrain, Qatar, the UAE and Saudi Arabia became home to the Muslim Brotherhood via those Arabs who arrived to work in the expanding state institutions, especially education.

In Qatar, the first serious initiative to build a modern educational system came in the early 1950s. The ruler, Sheikh Ali bin Abdullah Al Thani, formed a committee to organise education, appointing a wealthy merchant and his close confidant, Qasim Darwish, as its head. Qasim Darwish went to Egypt and sought the advice of Muhib al-Din al-Khatib. Qasim Darwish was a student of Qatar's former religious judge, Muhammad bin Abd al-Aziz al-Mana, as was another committee member, Abdullah bin Turki al-Subae. Hence, it

---

48. See Jinahi, ''Abd al-Rahman al-Jawdar'. See also al-Aqil, 'Al-Akh al-Da'iyya 'Abd al-Rahman 'Ali al-Jawdar (Abu Ahmad)'.
49. Al-Shahabi, 'Al-Ikhwan al Muslimun fi'l Bahrain Tahwilat al-'Uqud al-Sab'a'.
50. Al-Aqil, 'Mubarak Rashid al-Khatir al-Mu'arikh al-Adib'.

is likely that both were familiar with the Islamist literature, to which Muhib al-Din al-Khatib was a contributor. Al-Khatib was also a populariser of this literature as the owner of a press. Though he was not a member of the Muslim Brotherhood, he had a close friendship with al-Banna, on whose request he edited the first issues of the Brotherhood journal. It was therefore not surprising that on al-Khatib's recommendation, Darwish recruited a Muslim Brother, Abd al-Badi Saqr, to serve as Qatar's Director of Education.[51] Saqr remained in this post from 1954 to 1957 and was instrumental in bringing more pro-Brotherhood teachers to Qatar, such as Hasan al-Mayarji, Abd al-Halim al-Shaqqa, Izz al-Din Ibrahim, Muhammad al-Shafai, Abd al-Latif Makki, Kamal Naji and Ali Shahatah.[52]

Yet Saqr, intentionally or not, placed himself and the Brotherhood on the side of Sheikh Ali and his merchant allies in the growing conflict with some leading members of the ruling Al Thani family, including Sheikh Khalifa bin Hamad Al Thani and his allies from major Qatari families, both workers and merchants.[53] To appease the opposition, Sheikh Ali dismissed Abd al-Badi Saqr from the Directorate of Education, but appointed him as his cultural advisor. Saqr later founded and became the Director of the Public Library.[54]

When Saqr was dismissed, a pan-Arabist, Abdullah Abd al-Daim, was appointed as Director of Education. He occupied the post for just one year and then left Qatar. During his appointment, Abd al-Daim established a branch of the Arab Socialist Baath Party, which remained active even after his departure. In 1963 the branch joined others in the reform movement, which were also critical of the ruling family.[55] However, following the reform movement of 1963, pan-Arab nationalism in Qatar seems to have ceased.

---

51. See Kobaisi, *The Development of Education in Qatar, 1950–1977*, p. 122; Ghazal, 'Power, Arabism and Islam in the writings of Muhib al-Din al-Khatib'.
52. For this period I have relied on al-Qaradawi, 'D. Hasan al-Ma'ayarji.
53. The rivalry between the two was due to the succession issue. Sheikh Khalifa's father, Hamad, was the designated successor to Sheikh Abdullah, Sheikh Ali's father and the previous ruler. But because Hamad died in 1948, Ali succeeded his father.
54. He was expelled from Qatar in 1972, when Sheikh Khalifa became the ruler of Qatar. See Kobaisi, *The Development of Education in Qatar, 1950–1977*, p. 125.
55. See al-Mdaires, 'The Arab Ba'th Socialist Party and the Gulf Society'.

It seems that some Brothers left Qatar during the directorate of Abd al-Daim. Yusuf al-Qaradawi mentions two of them: Hasan al-Mayarji, who went on to study agriculture in Germany, and Izz al-Din Ibrahim, who studied literature in the UK, both receiving PhDs in their respective fields. In the 1970s al-Mayarji returned to Qatar and worked at Qatar University. In the 1960s other Brothers came to Qatar, such as Muhammad Mustafa al-Azami, Abd al-Muiz al-Sattar, Ahmad al-Isal and Yusuf al-Qaradawi.[56] A pro-Brotherhood figure, Kamal Naji, even became the Director of Education in 1964, a position he held until 1979.[57]

Qatar established its first state university in 1977. Yusuf al-Qaradawi became the founding Dean of the College of Shariah at Qatar University, a position he held until 1990. Hasan al-Mayarji worked in the Center for Scientific and Applied Research at Qatar University.[58] Two other friends of Yusuf al-Qaradawi also worked at the College of Shariah at Qatar University: Abd al-Azim al-Dib served as the Chair of the Department of Principles of Jurisprudence and Hasan Abd al-Zahir as the Chair of the Department of Da'wah.[59]

The Brotherhood did not face any ideologically hostile groups in Qatar once pan-Arabism dissipated in the mid-1960s. However, this is not to suggest that the Brothers worked in an ideological vacuum. Qatar is the only Muslim country, other than Saudi Arabia, where the ruling family openly adheres to Wahhabism.[60] Since the 1910s the country had imported religious scholars from Saudi Arabia. Muhammad bin Abd al-Aziz al-Mana has been mentioned already. Serving as Qatar's religious judge from the 1910s to the

---

56. See Qaradawi, 'D. Hasan al-Ma'ayarji. For a discussion on the roles these and some other names played in Qatar, see Freer, *Rentier Islamism*, pp. 57–9.
57. The Director of Education worked under the Minister of Education. Naji stayed in Qatar after his tenure ended in 1979 and for a long time served as the Director of the Centre for Muslim Contribution to the Civilisation. Yusuf al-Qaradawi served on the board of trustees of the Centre, which was founded in 1983. The Centre is now part of the Qatar Faculty of Islamic Studies.
58. Al-Qaradawi does not give a specific date as to the employment of Hasan al-Mayarji at Qatar University but it is probably before 1984. Hasan al-Mayarji died in Qatar in 2008.
59. Both Abd al-Azim al-Dib and Hasan al-Zahir died in Qatar in 2010. See "Abd al-'Azim al-Dib . . . al-'Alim al-Muhaqqiq'; 'Al-Sheikh Hasan 'Abd al-Zahir'.
60. This adherence came in the early twentieth century during the reign of Sheikh Jassim bin Muhammed (r. 1878–1913).

late 1930s, al-Mana also taught at least three figures who played critical roles in the political development of Qatar: Abdullah bin Zaid al-Mahmoud, who served as the Chief of Shariah Courts, Abdullah bin Turki al-Subae, a member of the educational committee established in 1952/3 who later served as the Director of Religious Affairs in the Ministry of Education, and Abdullah bin Ibrahim al-Ansari, who served as the Director of Religious Affairs and Director of Rural Affairs in the Ministry of Education.[61] When the Brothers came to Qatar in the 1950s, they had to work with these figures, with whom they had cordial relations in large part because of the ideological affinity between Salafi-Wahhabism and the Brotherhood.

In Qatar, in short, the Brotherhood found a perfect environment to operate. Yet to what extent the movement expanded its membership base among the local population is disputable.[62] For example, the Brotherhood established its local branch in Qatar in 1975 thanks to the coming of age of figures like Jassim Sultan,[63] who studied in Egypt in the early 1970s and witnessed first-hand the movement's rebirth there. But Jassim Sultan admitted that the branch was 'just collaboration, a simple thing. Only one page described the organization, and no one knows where that paper is.'[64]

Like oil, the Brotherhood came to the UAE comparatively late, which began to initiate its modern state institutions in earnest in the late 1960s during the reign of Sheikh Zayed, who replaced his brother in 1966.[65]

---

61. Kobaisi, *The Development of Education in Qatar 1950–1977*, p. 35.
62. Courtney Freer admits that the Brotherhood became an amorphous group in Qatar and has not developed a structured organisation. However, she still claims that the movement was politically influential, despite the evidence she provides to prove her claim being highly problematic. See Başkan, 'Book review'. I am of the same opinion as David Roberts, that the Brotherhood has not penetrated deeply into Qatari society. See Roberts, 'Qatar and the Muslim Brotherhood'. Also see Roberts, 'Qatar and the Brotherhood'.
63. Jassim Sultan was born in 1953 and studied medicine in Egypt. Upon his return, he led the establishment of the local branch in Qatar. Ashour, 'Tajrabat al-Ikhwan al-Muslimin fi Qatar', p. 189.
64. Cited in Freer, *Rentier Islamism*, p. 61.
65. Sheikh Shakhbut's downfall is attributed to his resistance to spending oil revenues. For more detail, see Rabi, 'Oil, politics and tribal rulers in eastern Arabia'.

Emirates including Sharjah, Dubai, Ras al-Khaimah and Ajman opened their first modern schools in the 1950s. However, these were primary schools and operated under continued financial stress. They could not serve as a stable channel of penetration for the Brotherhood. However, the UAE's early modern schools did receive financial and logistical support from Kuwait and Qatar. The Brotherhood's presence in the public educational systems of these two countries must have helped it to expand into the UAE.[66] A prominent Syrian Muslim Brother, Adnan Saad al-Din, was the supervisor of the Qatari educational mission to the UAE.[67]

As mentioned previously, Abd al-Badi Saqr was a cultural advisor to Sheikh Ali and was also close to his son, Sheikh Ahmad, who became the ruler in 1960. Sheikh Ahmad was son-in-law of the enigmatic ruler of Dubai, Sheikh Rashid bin Said al-Maktoum. Abd al-Ghaffar Hussain, Chairman of the Emirates Human Rights Association, argues that Abd al-Badi Saqr was personally involved in the formation of the Qatari educational mission to the UAE and opened a school and a public library in Dubai, bringing people to the UAE who were affiliated with the Brotherhood. Yusuf al-Qaradawi himself was involved in the activities organised in the public library, as he regularly visited the UAE.[68]

In the late 1960s the Brotherhood found a higher-level connection in the UAE. A long-time friend and comrade of Yusuf al-Qaradawi, Izz al-Din Ibrahim, who had worked in Qatar in the 1950s, settled in the UAE in 1968 and became a cultural advisor to Sheikh Zayed bin Sultan Al Nahyan, the ruler of Abu Dhabi and later the first president of the UAE. As a cultural advisor, Izz

---

66. In the early twentieth century, the Trucial States had some modern schools opened and financed by merchants. However, these schools did not survive the collapse of the pearling industry in the 1930s.
67. Al-Qaradawi mentions Adnan Saad al-Din in his account of his travels to the UAE. During this visit, al-Qaradawi also met Sharjah's ruler, Saqr bin Sultan, Dubai's ruler, Rashid bin Said, and Ajman's ruler, Rashid bin Humaid. Adnan Saad al-Din was present at al-Qaradawi's meeting with Saqr bin Sultan. See al-Qaradawi, 'Al-'Awdat ila Qatar ba'da al-I'tiqal'.
68. Husain, 'Al-Ikhwan al-Muslimun fi'l Imaraat'.

al-Din Ibrahim administered Sheikh Zayed's charity works across the world and ran cultural programmes.[69]

There was also another channel for the Brotherhood to enter the UAE. Due to the late development of higher educational institutions, Emiratis had travelled abroad and pursued higher education elsewhere, including Egypt, Kuwait, Qatar and other Arab countries. During their studies abroad, some of them became affiliated with the Muslim Brotherhood and embraced its ideology.

The religious institute in Qatar, directed by Yusuf al-Qaradawi, had, for example, two Emirati students, Said Abdullah Salman and Muhammad Abd al-Rahman al-Bakir.[70] These two students' careers are illustrative of the opportunities the Brotherhood-affiliated figures found in the UAE. Said Abdullah Salman entered the first post-independence cabinet, formed in December 1971, as the Minister of Housing and Urban Planning and kept this post until March 1977. Said Salman spent the next two years in Paris as the UAE Ambassador to France and the Euro region and then assumed the critical post of Minister of Education and Youth in 1979. During his ministry, Said Abdullah also assumed the post of Chancellor of the United Arab Emirates University,

69. Izz al-Din Ibrahim was born in Cairo in 1928. He studied Arabic literature at the University of King Fuad I (now Cairo University), during which time he also became a member of the Muslim Brotherhood. In the 1950s he left Egypt and worked in Syria, Qatar and Saudi Arabia, and finally settled in the UAE. He had a master's degree in education and psychology from Ain al-Shams University and a doctorate in literature from the University of London, awarded in 1963. He died in 2010. See al-Antably and Desouki, 'Al-Sheikh 'Izz al-Din Ibrahim'; 'Scholar who left cultural mark on the Emirates'.
70. Yusuf al-Qaradawi became the Director of the Religious Institute in 1961. He mentions Said Abdullah Salman among the graduates of the school. Since the school had not been long established before al-Qaradawi's appointment, Said Abdullah Salman must have studied there in the early 1960s. The Religious Institute in Qatar was at the level of high school. After graduation, Said Abdullah Salman probably went to Egypt and pursued a college-level degree. However, I could not confirm this through the available biographical sources. Without mentioning any specific name, al-Qaradawi says that many graduates of the school went to Egypt to study, most of them in al-Azhar and some in Dar al-'Ulum. See al-Qaradawi, 'Bi Rouz al-Ma'had al-Dini'.

the UAE's only university, founded in 1977.⁷¹ The Vice Chancellor was also a known name: Izz al-Din Ibrahim, who served for four years from 1977.⁷² Muhammad Abd al-Rahman al Bakir, who was also Yusuf al-Qaradawi's student at the Religious Institute in Qatar, entered the cabinet in 1977 as Minister of Justice and Awqaf.⁷³

Meanwhile, in 1974 the Brotherhood had established their own association in the UAE, called Jam'iyyat al-Islah wa'l-Tawjih al-Ijtima'i, (the Society of Reform and Social Counselling), named after the Brotherhood association in Kuwait. Among the founders of the Society in Ras al-Khaimah was a member of the royal family, Sultan bin Kayid Al Qasimi, who later became its Chairman. Seven years later, in 1981, Al Qasimi assumed the critical position of Director of the Department of Curricula and Textbooks in the Ministry of Education.⁷⁴

The Society received a generous start-up grant from Sheikh Rashid bin Said Al Maktoum, the ruler of Dubai and the vice president of the UAE. Sheikh Rashid not only donated to the Society's headquarters in Dubai, but also financially helped it to establish two other branches in the emirates of Ras al-Khaimah and Fujairah. In 1978 al-Islah Society began to publish its first journal, *al-Islah Journal*, an important new channel by which to spread its message.⁷⁵

However, while the Brothers worked alongside ideologically aligned figures in Qatar, they faced competition from ideologically opposed, even hostile, figures, the pan-Arabists, in the UAE.⁷⁶ One such figure was Sheikh Sultan

71. For a brief discussion of Said Salman's management of the university, see Fyfe, *Wealth and Power*, pp. 323–5.
72. Another graduate of the Religious Institute, Shahib Abdullah al-Marzuqi, became Secretary General of the UAE University. See al-Qaradawi, *Ibn al-Qaryah wa'l-Kuttab*, p. 371.
73. After graduating from the Religious Institute, Muhammad al-Bakir probably went to Egypt and studied at al-Azhar. The name of Muhammad Abd al-Rahman al-Bakir appears among the participants of the second meeting of Azhar graduates organised by the World Association for al-Azhar Graduates, which was founded in 2006 in Egypt. See the list of participants at http://www.waag-azhar.org/second_moltaka_05.aspx.
74. Born in 1958 in Ras al-Khaimah, Sultan bin Kayid Al Qasimi belonged to the ruling family of Ras al-Khaimah.
75. Al-Nuqaidan, 'Al-Ikhwan al-Muslimun fi'l Imarat al-Tamaddad wa'l Inhisar'.
76. As mentioned previously, Qatar also attracted pan-Arabists, though pan-Arab nationalism seems to have run its course in Qatar by the mid-1960s.

bin Muhammad Al Qasimi, the ruler of Sharjah (1972–present), who was strongly sympathetic towards Gamal Abdel Nasser, the towering figure of pan-Arab nationalism.[77] Sheikh Sultan was also a close friend of two pan-Arabist brothers, Taryam Umran Taryam and Abdullah Umran Taryam.[78] The brothers were from Sharjah and studied with Sheikh Sultan in the same primary and secondary schools in Sharjah and Kuwait. Attracted to the idea of creating pan-Arab unity, Sheikh Sultan and Taryam Umran even briefly joined the Baath Party during their stay in Kuwait. In particular, Taryam was, in the words of Sheikh Sultan, 'a fanatical supporter of Gamal Abdel Nasser'.[79]

Like Sheikh Sultan, Taryam and Abdullah went to Egypt and graduated from the University of Cairo. On their return in 1970, the brothers established a newspaper, *al-Khaleej*, Abdullah serving as its Editor in Chief. The newspaper was closed down in 1973 because of financial difficulties.[80] In the meantime, Taryam became ambassador to Egypt and the Arab League in 1971, a position he held until 1977.[81] When he returned to the UAE in 1977, Taryam became the Speaker of the Federal National Council until 1981. His younger brother, Abdullah, became Minister of Justice in the first post-independence UAE government formed in December 1971. In the same government, Sheikh Sultan was the Minister of Education. In January 1972, Sheikh Sultan became

---

77. Sheikh Sultan was in Egypt, studying agriculture in Cairo University, when Nasser resigned after defeat in the 1967 war against Israel. He describes his feelings on hearing the news of Nasser's resignation: 'Masses of people poured into the streets. The sun disappeared on that day and we entered darkness, as all the street lights were turned off. I couldn't go anywhere because of the crowds of people filling the streets, so I sat on a wooden bench on the pavement of Al-Gazira Street . . . I was overcome by emotion, which inspired me to make up a poem.' Sheikh Sultan failed some of his courses that semester because of, he claims, his psychological state at that time. See Ali, Pridham and Hroub (eds), *My Early Life*, pp. 242–5.
78. I thank Aysha Abdullah Taryam for the biographical information about her father and uncle.
79. Ali, Pridham and Hroub (eds), *My Early Life*, p. 156.
80. Cass, 'Newspaper archiving in the UAE'.
81. Information about the UAE cabinets can be found in al-Abed, Vine and al-Jabali (eds), *Chronicle of Progress*.

the ruler of Sharjah, vacating the post of Minister of Education in May the same year. In his place, Abdullah Taryam became the Minister of Education, leaving the position of Minister of Justice.[82] Abdullah kept this position until 1979, when he was replaced by a Muslim Brother, Said Salman. From 1980, the Taryam brothers resumed publication of their pan-Arabist *al-Khaleej* newspaper, which served as a harsh critic of the Brotherhood.[83]

This is important, I believe. The presence of pan-Arabists, represented by such figures as Sheikh Sultan and the Taryam brothers, created an ideologically tense and competitive context in which the Brothers would benefit from more organisational strength and intra-group solidarity. Therefore, the Brothers in the UAE developed more organisational capacity and in-group solidarity than their colleagues in Qatar.

Lastly, the Brotherhood also found a welcoming environment in Saudi Arabia in the 1950s. Like all the other Arab Gulf countries, Saudi Arabia lacked the necessary human capital to staff its expanding state institutions and therefore imported professionals from other Arab countries. Among the imported professionals were many members of the Brotherhood.

Possibly the first Brother who arrived to work in Saudi Arabia was Mana bin Khalil al-Qattan. Born in 1925 in Egypt, al-Qattan studied at al-Azhar. While he was still a student, he joined the Muslim Brotherhood and was involved in the movement's activities. On graduation in the early 1950s, he worked in Egypt for a while and in 1953 went to Saudi Arabia to teach at a religious school. After five years, he began to work at a more advanced school, the College of Shari'a in Riyadh, which became the nucleus of what later became the Imam Muhammad bin Saud University. In the following years, al-Qattan gradually rose through the hierarchy and became the head of graduate studies.

---

82. Abdullah Umran also pursued higher education and received his doctorate in Arabic and Islamic studies from the University of Exeter in 1986. In 1990 Abdullah Umran Taryam re-entered the cabinet as Minister of Justice and kept the post until 2003. His older brother Taryam died in 2002. I thank Aysha Taryam for the biographical information. See also 'The man behind UAE's first newspaper'.
83. See the discussion in Fyfe, *Wealth and Power*, pp. 320–6.

Around the same time Saudi Arabia and other Gulf states initiated their modern state-building projects, the Brotherhood fell out with the new regime in Egypt, led by the popular Gamal Abdel Nasser, enduring a period of suppression, called mihna in the Brotherhood literature. The Brotherhood members found refuge in Saudi Arabia and other Gulf states. In her memoirs, Zainab al-Ghazali mentions Said Ramadan, Mustafa al-Alim, Kamil al-Sharif, Muhammad al-Ashmawi and Fathi al-Khawli among those who escaped to Saudi Arabia.[84]

Said Ramadan, Hasan al-Banna's son-in-law, did not stay in Saudi Arabia, however. He moved first to Pakistan and then to Switzerland, where he settled and founded the Brotherhood's first organisation in Europe.[85] Fathi Ahmad al-Khawli, on the other hand, stayed in Saudi Arabia. Born in 1922, al-Khawli studied at Dar al-'Ulum and the Institute of Education at 'Ain Shams University. After working in Egypt for a while, he moved to Saudi Arabia after Abdel Nasser's suppression of the Brotherhood started. Al-Khawli found a job in Saudi Arabia, first working as a teacher at the Institute of Teachers in Riyadh and then in the College of Education and Law in Mecca.[86]

Starting in the late 1950s, the suppression of the Brotherhood expanded to other Arab countries, such as Syria and Iraq. Successive waves of suppression drove the Brothers in these countries to seek refuge in Saudi Arabia. Among them were several luminaries of the Brotherhood movement. Abd al-Fattah Abu Ghudda was one of them. Born in Aleppo in the late 1910s, Abu Ghudda studied at al-Azhar in Egypt and met Hasan al-Banna. On returning to Syria, he joined the Brotherhood, led there by Mustafa al-Sibai. Abu Ghudda was jailed in 1966 for eleven months for his opposition to the Baath Party, and exiled to Saudi Arabia.[87] He settled in Saudi Arabia, teaching at the College of Shariah at the Imam Muhammad bin Saud University, and spent most of the rest of his life in the kingdom until his death in 1997.

Muhammad Mahmud al-Sawwaf was from Iraq and had a similar experience. Born in the mid-1910s in Mosul, he studied at al-Azhar, met Hasan

---

84. Al-Ghazali, *Return of the Pharaoh*, p. 15. Al-Ghazali claims these figures were planning to take revenge and kill Abdel Nasser.
85. See Johnson, *A Mosque in Munich*.
86. 'Al-Sheikh Fathi al-Khawli . . . Romouz al- 'Atai'.
87. Moubayed, Sami, *Steel and Silk: Men and Women who Shaped Syria 1900–2000* (Seattle: Cune Press, 2006), pp. 129–30.

al-Banna and joined the Muslim Brotherhood. When he returned to Iraq, al-Sawwaf became the general guide of the Brotherhood. At the same time, he took up a teaching position at the College of Shariah in Baghdad. When a military coup overthrew the monarchy in 1958, al-Sawwaf opposed the new government and was imprisoned. He left Iraq after his release from jail in 1959 and settled in Saudi Arabia. He remained in Saudi Arabia for decades, teaching at the College of Shariah and Islamic Studies in Mecca. He spent his last years in Turkey and died there in 1992. However, he was buried in Mecca.[88]

Muhammad Qutb was another luminary of the Brotherhood who settled in Saudi Arabia. Born in Egypt in the late 1920s, Qutb first studied English literature at Fuad University (later called Cairo University) and then psychology and education. His more prominent brother, Sayyid Qutb, a staunch critic of Gamal Abdel Nasser, was arrested and eventually executed in 1966. Muhammad Qutb also suffered at the hands of the regime. He was jailed a number of times, the last from 1966 until 1972. After his release, he left Egypt and settled in Saudi Arabia. He taught at King Abd al-Aziz University and then Umm al-Qura University in Medina. Qutb spent the rest of his life in Saudi Arabia, until his death in 2014 in Mecca.

Many others who left their home countries and settled in Saudi Arabia, contributing to its modern state building, can be added to this list.[89]

Saudi Arabia also had another motive for welcoming the Brotherhood. The kingdom was in geopolitical rivalry with Egypt, a rivalry that had begun in the late 1950s. Egypt propagated pan-Arab nationalism. To counter this, Saudi Arabia turned to pan-Islamism. Saudi Arabia established a radio station, Sawt al-Islam, and founded an Islamic university in Medina to replicate Egypt's Sawt al-Arab and al-Azhar respectively. In order to compensate for the popularity of Gamal Abdel Nasser in the Arab world, Saudi Arabia sought to improve its ties with religious groups across the Muslim world, for which it founded Rabitat al-'Alam al-Islami (the Muslim World League) in 1962.

In the midst of this escalating rivalry, Saudi Arabia extended its help to the Brothers. The Brotherhood was the most transnational religious movement

---

88. 'Muhammad Mahmoud al-Sawwaf . . . Ra'ed al-Harakat al-Islamiyya fi'l 'Iraq'.
89. See Lacroix, *Awakening Islam*, ch. 2. A lengthier list is available in al-Utaibi, 'Al-Ikhwan al-Muslimun wa'l Sa'udiyya, al-Hijrah wa'l 'Alaqah'. This later study does not provide any information about the whereabouts of the Brothers in Saudi Arabia.

of the period, having branches, members and sympathisers across the Muslim world. It could therefore provide critical help in counter-mobilising conservative Muslims. Furthermore, the Brotherhood had every reason to hate Gamal Abdel Nasser, due to the persecution its members had faced under his regime.

Of the twenty-one members of the constituent assembly of the Muslim World League, for example, three were Brotherhood figures: Said Ramadan, Kamel al-Sharif and Muhammad Mahmud al-Sawwaf. The Brothers also took part in various councils of the League. For example, a number of Brothers became members of al-Majlis al-A'la al-'Alami l'il-Masajid (the World Supreme Council of Mosques), founded in 1976: Abd al-Majid Zinjani from Yemen, Kamil al-Sharif from Jordan and Abdullah al-Mutawa from Kuwait.[90] Saudi Arabia also founded al-Nadwat al-'Alemiyya li'l Shabab al-Islami (the World Assembly of Muslim Youth), in 1972. The founder of this organisation was a Brother from Egypt, Kamal Halwabi, who later declared that he had left the movement. Yet, during the period when he served as the organisation's Executive Director, he was definitely part of the movement. Many other Brotherhood figures were involved in this organisation: Muhammad Mehdi Akif, the future general guide of the Brotherhood in Egypt, Juma Amin Abd al-Aziz from Egypt, Abdullah al-Aqil from Iraq-Kuwait and Nizar Ahmad al-Sabbagh from Syria are just a few examples.[91]

Involvement in these Saudi Arabia-founded and -financed institutions helped the Brotherhood expand its global reach. But it is difficult to assess the extent to which this involvement helped the Brotherhood to expand in Saudi Arabia. There was indeed a sizeable expatriate Brotherhood community inside Saudi Arabia and Mana al-Qattan acted as its leader. But it is difficult to speak of it as an organised group. Given their foreign status, the expatriate Brothers who settled in Saudi Arabia understandably had to act cautiously and remained reluctant to engage in any organised activity. The state was also apprehensive that the Brothers could organise and recruit inside

---

90. See al-Aqil, 'Ta'rif bi Rabitat al-'Alem al-Islami'.
91. Biographical information about these names can be found at http://www.ikhwanwiki.com under the section Al-I'lam al-Harekat al-Islami.

the Kingdom. This is evident in that it has never officially authorised the establishment of a formal Muslim Brotherhood branch or organisation inside its territory.[92]

Yet there still emerged in Saudi Arabia a native Brotherhood movement. This was inescapable perhaps, given the critical role some expatriate Brothers came to play in shaping the Saudi educational system, especially from the 1970s. It is important to note that Mana al-Qattan was a member of the committee that prepared the prime document that set out Saudi Arabia's national education policy in 1970. This document had a view of Islam along the lines the Brotherhood had suggested, and more critically, added Islamic Culture as a subject to be taught in all years of higher education. In designing this course and preparing textbooks for it, the Brotherhood figures played leading roles.[93]

Through their influence on the educational system, therefore, the expatriate Brothers indirectly helped the emergence of a native Brotherhood movement in Saudi Arabia. Yet this movement did not operate as an official organisation, as it did in other Gulf states. Therefore, it remained prone to division. The Brotherhood in Saudi Arabia eventually came to encompass three different groups.[94] The largest and most influential group was Ikhwan al-Hijaz, as its founding members such as Muhammad Umar Zubair came predominantly from the western region of Hijaz. The group also expanded into the eastern region of Hasa, recruiting from there two of its most famous figures, Awad al-Qarni and Said al-Ghamdi.

Another group was Ikhwan al-Riyadh, as its members were predominantly drawn from the College of Shariah in Riyadh, where Mana al-Qattan was teaching. The group's successive leaders, Hamad al-Sulaifih, Abdullah al-Turki and Saud al-Funaisan, were all al-Qattan's students and were all originally from Najd.

---

92. A Turkish student who studied religious sciences in a Saudi University. A Turkish student who studied religious sciences in a Saudi University in the early 1980s told me that the Brotherhood was not active on the campus in terms of recruitment. He also added that the Saudi regime was not tolerant towards any group activity. This vigilance might be because of the notorious Juhaiman al-Otaibi case.
93. See the discussion in Lacroix, *Awakening Islam*, pp. 46–7. See also footnote 48 at p. 290.
94. I follow al-Utaibi, 'Al-Ikhwan al-Muslimun wa'l Sa'udiyya, al-Hijrah wa'l 'Alaqah'. Lacroix, *Awakening Islam*, divides the three groups into four by further dividing Ikhwan al-Riyadh into two sub-groups.

The last group was Ikhwan al-Zubair, as its members were originally from the southern Iraqi town of Zubair, where a number of families from Najd were present. In the early 1950s, Zubair became home to a local branch of the Muslim Brotherhood. The movement survived many trials, starting with the 1958 military coup. As the regime began a full-frontal attack in the early 1970s, the Brotherhood in Iraq disintegrated. As repeated before in Egypt and Syria, the members migrated elsewhere, including to Saudi Arabia.[95] Those who escaped to Saudi Arabia formed Ikhwan al-Zubair, led by Saad al-Faqih, the son of Rashid al-Faqih, the founder of the Brotherhood branch in Zubair.[96]

The Brotherhood's ideational influence cannot be restricted to these groups only. What came to be known as Soururism was another Brotherhood-inspired group that originated in Saudi Arabia. The group was named after its intellectual and spiritual architect, Muhammad Sourur Zein al-Abidin. Muhammad Sourur was originally a Syrian Muslim Brother who left Syria in the mid-1960s and became a mathematics teacher in Buraidah, Najd, in Saudi Arabia. During his stay he influenced the thinking of a number of Saudi students, including Salman al-Awdah. Muhammad Sourur left Saudi Arabia in the early 1970s but his students formed a distinct religious group, called Soururis, and expanded their influence in the Kingdom.

As of the late 1970s, therefore, the Muslim Brotherhood was present in all five Gulf countries. The Gulf states welcomed the movement, for they had faced similar challenges in the 1950s and 1960s. In the domestic and regional context of the 1950s and 1960s, the Gulf states found in the Muslim Brotherhood an acquiescent and loyal ally. However, this was about to change in some, if not all, of the Gulf countries.

---

95. Abdullah bin Aqil al-Aqil was one of those Zubairis who settled. Abdullah bin Aqil al-Aqil was one of those Zubairis who settled in Kuwait. He studied at al-Azhar, worked in Zubair and then settled in Kuwait. While in Kuwait, he worked in different ministries. He was a member of the World Assembly of Muslim Youth. See 'Al-Mustashar 'Abdullah al-'Aqil'.
96. Lacroix, *Awakening Islam*, p. 66. For more on Saad al-Faqih, see Fandy, *Saudi Arabia and the Politics of Dissent*, ch. 5.

4

MODERN SOVEREIGN STATE BUILDING IN THE GULF: FROM THE 1980S TO THE 2000S

The Gulf rulers set out to build their modern state institutions in the 1950s. By the late 1970s, they had laid the foundations of their modern states. Saudi Arabia had been an independent state all along. By the late 1970s, Bahrain, Kuwait, Qatar and the UAE were also fully independent and sovereign states. In the following decades, Gulf rulers worked to improve the overall quality and efficiency of their state institutions. This chapter aims to show that their efforts from the 1980s to the 2000s did not change state–religion relations in any fundamental way. If there was a new element, however, it was that the Gulf states began to emphasise their religious credentials in clearer and stronger terms.

Improving Legal Systems

By the late 1970s, the Gulf States had already passed a number of laws, but these were promulgated rather on an ad hoc basis and often copied from those of other Arab countries. Especially Bahrain, Qatar and the UAE rushed to pass some laws in the wake their independence to fill any legal vacuums caused by the closure of the British courts. In the early 1980s new laws had to be passed to cover matters that were not covered by the existing laws; the existing laws had to be revised to eliminate contradictions and inconsistencies. Moreover, the Islamic Shariah, to which Shariah judges referred in cases referred to them, had still to be codified.

By the late 1970s, Saudi Arabia had already made considerable progress in building up its legal system.[1] Yet its efforts had brought more disorder than order, as the legal system now had multiple bodies acting as courts, such as the Shariah courts, the Board of Grievances and other special administrative committees. Saudi Arabia continued to pass news laws in such diverse fields as media, culture, commerce, economics, investment, education, municipal services, agriculture, tourism, health, etc. As Saudi Arabia issued new laws it faced the question of which competent authority would apply these laws over and over again. In large part due to the intransigence of the Shariah courts, the new laws remained outside their jurisdiction. Therefore Saudi Arabia either established new administrative committees or granted the authority to apply them to the Board of Grievances. In addition to the previous laws put under its jurisdiction, the Board, for example, became the competent judicial authority for the 1973 Civil Pension Law, the 1975 Law of Misappropriation of Public Funds, the 1976 Civil Service Law,[2] the 1984 Law of Commercial Trademark and the 1987 Law that regulated private hospitals and clinics, and more critically assumed the functions of the Commercial Dispute Committees.

As the Board's responsibilities expanded, it also underwent reorganisation through the 1982 Law of the Board of Grievances and the 1989 Rules of Procedure of the Board of Grievances. These two laws organised the Board into three tiers: First Instance Circuits, Appellate Circuits and Board of Appeal. The laws also tied the Board directly to the king as an independent body outside the Ministry of Justice, running in parallel to the Shariah courts.[3]

By the mid-2000s, the legal system in Saudi Arabia was still not unified, with multiple judicial authorities such as the Shariah courts, the Board of Grievances and special administrative committees. Saudi Arabia therefore implemented another major reorganisation of its legal system. First, the kingdom established more specialised courts in 2005. Second, and more importantly, it passed two critical laws, the Law of Judiciary and the Law of Board of Grievances, which repealed the 1975 Law of Judiciary and the 1982 Law

1. For the broader set of reforms Saudi Arabia has undertaken in this period, see Kechichian, *Legal and Political Reforms in Saudi Arabia*.
2. Ansary, 'Update: A brief of overview of the Saudi Arabian legal system'.
3. Al-Jarbou, 'The role of traditionalists and modernists on the development of the Saudi legal system'.

of Board of Grievances. The Law of Judiciary restricted the jurisdiction of the Supreme Judicial Council to some administrative roles and in its stead created the High Court as the highest court in the Kingdom. Courts of Appeal constituted the second tier in the legal system. The First-Degree Courts constituted the lowest tier with six types of court: General Courts, Criminal Courts, Personal Status Courts, Labour Courts, Commercial Courts and Enforcement Courts.

With this reorganisation, Saudi Arabia introduced a major overhaul in its judicial system, initiating a transfer to the Shariah courts of some major jurisdictions that arose due to the new laws, but granted to several special administrative committees and the Board of Grievances. As a result of the new reorganisation the jurisdiction of the Board of Grievances became more restricted to administrative cases. However, the envisioned transfer of jurisdiction was complex and could not be achieved overnight, so for years to come the Board continued to adjudicate on certain commercial and penal cases.

Saudi Arabia also reorganised the Board of Grievances in 2007. The Law of the Board of Grievances introduced the same structure of the Shariah courts to Saudi Arabia's administrative court system, which came to comprise the Administrative Judicial Council with administrative roles and three-tier courts, the Administrative Highest Court, Administrative Courts of Appeal and Administrative Courts.[4]

In the last three decades Saudi Arabia has considerably improved its legal system by issuing new laws and creating a more specialised court system. In a significant step, for example, it issued the Law of Criminal Procedure in 2001.[5] But Saudi Arabia has not passed any law codified from the Islamic Shariah, even though some attempts have been made. In 2007 and 2008, for example, it published an anthology of judicial decisions taken by the Supreme Judicial Council so that judges could become familiar with 'the judgments handed down by the kingdom's various courts'.[6] It was hoped that judges would over time standardise their judgments. Saudi Arabia took a more serious step in 2010 when the Committee of the Grand Senior Religious Scholars, the Kingdom's highest religious

---

4. Ansary, 'Update: A brief of overview of the Saudi Arabian legal system'. I also benefited from Yargı, *Suudi Arabistan'ın Yargı Sistemi*.
5. Saudi Arabia's Royal Decreee M/39 of 2001.
6. Mouline, *Clerics of Islam*, p. 168.

authority, issued a fatwa sanctifying the codification. Despite the support of the highest religious authority in the Kingdom, these steps did not produce any immediate tangible outcome.

Other Gulf states also worked to improve their legal systems, passing new laws, amending old ones and reorganising their court systems. In terms of legislation, Kuwait was the frontrunner: it took a major step in 1977 and established four committees to amend the existing laws and draft new laws. Thanks to the efforts of these committees, Kuwait passed a number of new laws, including the 1980 Civil Law, which repealed all previous relevant laws such as the Ottoman *Majalla* and the 1961 Tort Law. In the same year, Kuwait also passed a new Commercial Law, which repealed the 1961 Commercial Law, and a new Civil Procedure Law, which repealed the 1960 Civil Procedure Law. Most significantly, in 1984 Kuwait passed the Personal Status Law to regulate those matters to which the Islamic Shariah most pertained, such as personal status, marriage, inheritance and child custody. The significance of this law is that for another two decades Kuwait would remain the only Gulf state with a codified law covering these matters.

Bahrain also passed a number of significant laws, such as the Commercial Law in 1987, the Law of Evidence in Civil and Commercial Matters in 1996, the Civil Law in 2001, the Commercial Companies Law in 2001, which repealed the 1975 Law of Commercial Companies, the Criminal Procedure Law in 2002, which repealed the 1966 Law of Criminal Procedure, and the Labour Law in 2012, which supplemented or repealed the 1976 Labour Law for the private sector. Bahrain also took a step towards codifying the Islamic Shariah in 2009, passing the Family Law for Sunnis. Bahrain has yet to pass a similar law for Shias in the country.

Qatar also took steps to improve its legal system by passing new laws and amending the existing ones, intensifying its efforts in the 1990s and 2000s: it passed, for example, the Civil and Commercial Procedure Law in 1990 and amended the Penal Law in 1994, the Criminal Procedure Law in 1995, the Law of Commercial Companies in 1998 and the Criminal Procedure Law again in 1998 and 2003. In 2004 Qatar passed the Criminal Procedure Law, the Civil Law, the Labour Law and the Penal Law, which repealed the 1971 Criminal Procedure Law, the 1971 Law of Civil and Commercial Articles, the 1962 Labour Law and the 1971 Penal Law respectively. More significantly,

Qatar passed the Family Law in 2005, thus codifying the Islamic Shariah's rulings on the subject.

The UAE also passed a number of significant laws starting in the 1980s: it passed, for example, the Law of Labour Relations in 1980, the Law of Commercial Companies in 1984, the Law of Civil Transactions in 1985, the Penal Law in 1987, the Criminal Procedure Law and the Civil Procedure Law in 1992 and the Law of Commercial Transactions in 1993. Moving towards codifying the principles of the Islamic Shariah, in 2005 the UAE passed the Personal Status Law.

The extent to which Gulf states incorporated rulings of the Islamic Shariah into these laws requires a more systematic and thorough analysis, an analysis that is beyond this author's capacity. Yet it is still possible to get a sense. As discussed above, Bahrain, Kuwait, Qatar and the UAE codified the rulings of the Islamic Shariah pertaining to such matters as personal status, marriage and inheritance. The only exception is that Bahrain still has to pass a Family Law for Shias. Kuwait's Personal Status Law explicitly specifies its source as the Maliki School of jurisprudence.[7] Qatar's Family Law is likewise explicit in specifying that it applies the Hanbali School of jurisprudence.[8] Both the UAE's Personal Status Law and Bahrain's Family Law are less explicit: while the UAE's law states that its rules are derived from the Islamic jurisprudence, Bahrain's law is silent. Yet both the UAE's law and Bahrain's law direct judges as to what to do in the absence of a ruling in their laws. The UAE's law refers judges first to the Maliki School of jurisprudence, then to the Hanbali School, then to the Shafi School and finally to the Hanafi School. Bahrain's law is slightly different, referring judges to the Maliki School first, then to other Sunni schools of jurisprudence with no specific order and finally to the general principles of the Islamic Law.[9] It must be added, however, that Bahrain, Kuwait, Qatar and the UAE apply their personal status or family laws only to those who follow the particular schools from which they derive

---

7. See Article 346 of Kuwait's Personal Status Law. The Maliki School of Jurisprudence is one of the four dominant schools of jurisprudence in Sunni Islam. The others are Hanafi, Shafi and Hanbali.
8. See Article 4 of Qatar's Family Law.
9. See Article 2 of the UAE's Personal Status Law.

their laws. Non-Muslims and Muslims of other schools can opt for laws of their own choice.[10]

Gulf states have also passed civil laws, another field of law on which the Islamic Shariah has certain rulings. With no exceptions, the Civil Laws of Gulf states recognise the Islamic Shariah as a source of ruling in the absence of a specific ruling in the law. Both Qatar's Civil Law and the UAE's Civil Law, for example, direct judges to adjudicate first according to the Islamic Shariah and then, in the absence of a ruling from the Shariah, according to customs.[11] The only difference between the two is that the UAE's law specifies the Hanbali School of jurisprudence as the first school to be consulted. Qatar's law makes no such a specification. Bahrain, on the other hand, differs from Qatar and the UAE in that its Civil Law directs judges to decide first according to customs and in their absence according to the Islamic Shariah. When it first passed its Civil Law in 1980, Kuwait also recognised customs before the Islamic Shariah as a source of law in the absence of a specific ruling in the law. However, in 1996 it amended its Civil Law and put the Islamic Shariah before customs.[12]

The Islamic Shariah also informed the Penal Laws of Bahrain, Kuwait, Qatar and the UAE. Article 1 of the UAE's 1987 Penal Law, for example, stated that rulings of the Islamic Shariah should apply *Hudud* (literally meaning borders, limits), *Qisas* (retaliation) and *Diyah* (blood money). It is worth noting that *Hudud* crimes are those cited in, with punishments fixed by, the Qur'an. *Qisas*, on the other hand, refers to crimes for which the victim can demand retaliation in kind. *Diyah* is financial compensation demanded in the case of unintentional crimes. Yet the law did not specify what exactly these crimes were.[13]

---

10. Saudi Arabia does not have a codified family law. All personal matters are under the jurisdiction of the Shariah courts, which generally apply the rulings of the Hanbali school of jurisprudence and are therefore regulated by the Islamic law.
11. Article 1 of Qatar's Law No. 22 of 2004 and Article 1 of the UAE's Federal Law, No. 5 of 1985.
12. Article 1 of Bahrain's Legislative Decree No. 19 of 2001 and Article 2 of Kuwait's Law No. 67 of 1980.
13. See al-Muhairi, 'Islamisation and modernization within the UAE penal law'; Al-Muhairi, 'The Islamisation of laws in the UAE'.

Qatar's 2004 Penal Law was similar to the UAE's Penal Law, in that its first article stated that the rulings of the Islamic Shariah would apply *Hudud*, *Qisas* and *Diyah*. Unlike the UAE Penal Law, however, Qatar's Penal Law listed six specific *Hudud* offences. Neither Kuwait's Penal Law nor Bahrain's Penal Law made specific reference to *Hudud*, *Qisas* or *Diyah*.

However, all four Penal Laws criminalised and specified penalties for certain acts that were considered great sins in the Islamic Shariah. All, for example, declared blasphemy as a crime and set a penalty for it. Qatar's Penal Law criminalised and specified penalties for 'insulting the Divine Being', 'offending, misinterpreting or violating the Holy Quran', 'offending the Islamic religion or any of its rites and dictates', 'cursing any of the divine religions' and 'insulting any of the prophets'.[14] The UAE Penal Law also criminalised and specified a penalty for blasphemy, described as crimes offending 'any of the Islamic sacred beliefs or rites', insulting 'any of the divine recognized religions', offending 'the sacred beliefs or rites prescribed by other religions', religions considered divine in the Islamic faith, opposing or vilifying 'the foundations or teachings on which is based the Muslim religion' and offending Islam.[15] Kuwait's Penal Law also criminalised and set a penalty for broadcasting 'views that ridicule, contempt or belittle the religion or any religious school, whether this is to challenge its beliefs, or practices, or teachings'.[16] Bahrain's Penal Law also criminalised and set a penalty for offending 'by any method of expression against one of the recognized religious sects or ridicul[ing] the rituals', publicly insulting 'a symbol or a person being glorified or considered sacred to members of a particular sect' and imitating 'in public a ritual or ceremony with the intention of ridiculing it'.[17]

To improve their legal systems, Bahrain, Kuwait, Qatar and the UAE also reorganised their court systems. By the late 1970s, Kuwait already had a two-tier court system. In 1990 it introduced a three-tier system. At the lowest level were the Courts of First Instance, comprising specialised circuits for

---

14. Article 256 of Qatar's Law No. 11 of 2004.
15. Title Five of the UAE's Federal Law No. 3 of 1987.
16. Article 111 of Kuwait's Law No. 16 of 1960.
17. Article 309 and Article 310 of Bahrain's Law No. 15 of 1976.

civil, commercial, personal status and penal cases. The Courts of Appeal constituted the second tier in the system and the Court of Cassation the highest level, as the final court of appeal.[18]

In 1987 Qatar passed a law, contrary to the general trend in the Gulf states, that tied the presidency of the Shariah courts directly to the ruler. However, this proved to be temporary. Qatar reorganised its judiciary again in 1993 and put the presidency under the Ministry of Justice. Below the presidency was a two-tier court system: the Grand Shariah Court, which functioned as an appellate court, and the petty Shariah Court.[19] Finally, in 2003, Qatar took a major step in unifying its court system and established a three-tier court system similar to that of Kuwait: the Courts of First Instance constituted the first tier, the Court of Appeal the second and the Court of Cassation the third. The courts came to have specialised circuits for different types of cases, such as *Hudud* and retribution cases, criminal, civil and commercial matters, family issues, inheritance and administrative disputes.

The UAE also took steps in the reorganisation of its judiciary. By the late 1970s, it had already created a court system at the federal level comprising the Federal Courts of First Instance, the Federal Courts of Appeal and the Federal Supreme Court. Four emirates – Abu Dhabi, Sharjah, Ajman and Fujairah – transferred the jurisdiction of their local secular courts to the federal court system, keeping their Shariah courts outside the system.[20] In 1992 the UAE took a major step and reorganised its federal court system. The new system had three-tiers like that of Kuwait. Each emirate in the federal system came to have the Courts of First Instance, the Federal Courts of Appeal and the Federal Courts of Cassation. The courts had specialised circuits for different types of cases, such as personal status cases, criminal cases and civil cases. The Federal Supreme Court continued to exist, functioning as the final court of appeal at the federal level. However, the unification of the judiciary envisioned by the constitution is still not complete in the UAE. In 1991 Umm al-Qawain joined the four emirates and transferred the jurisdiction of its local

---

18. Khedr, 'Update: Overview of the Kuwait legal system'.
19. Hamzeh, 'Qatar'.
20. See al-Muhairi, 'The development of the UAE legal system and unification with the judicial system'.

courts to the federal courts. The two remaining emirates, Dubai and Ras al-Khaimah, have stayed outside the federal court system. In the mid-2000s Abu Dhabi joined Dubai and Ras al-Khaimah by opting out of the system. Therefore, in addition to the federal court system in Sharjah, Ajman, Umm al-Qawain and Fujairah, the UAE also kept local legal systems with court structures quite similar to the federal court system.

Bahrain also took steps to reorganise its judiciary, having already established a judicial system formed of two types of court: civil courts and Shariah courts. In 1989 it established Courts of Cassation for civil courts as the final court of appeal, thus adding a third tier. In 1999 Bahrain extended this organisation to its Shariah courts and reorganised both Sunni and Shia courts into a three-tier structure of Junior Shariah Court, Senior Shariah Court and High Shariah Court of Appeal.

All four Gulf states reorganised their courts in similar ways. Most critically, they have incorporated Shariah courts and restricted their jurisdictions to personal matters that the Islamic Shariah regulates in most detail, such as marriage, divorce, child custody and inheritance. However, Shariah courts, especially in Qatar and the UAE, might still look into other cases, especially criminal ones. This is because the Penal Laws of both Qatar and the UAE did not set any specific penalty for certain *Hudud* crimes, such as apostasy. Hence, one can argue that in both Qatar and the UAE, judges are autonomous in being able to interpret the relevant rulings of the Islamic Shariah. Because such an interpretation necessitated expertise in Islamic Law, Shariah courts might intervene in those crimes and have some jurisdiction over cases of *Hudud*, *Qisas* and *Diyah*. It is interesting to note that the UAE passed a law in 1996 specifying that the Shariah courts had jurisdiction over *Qisas* and *Diyah*, excluding *Hudud* crimes.[21] In Qatar, if a crime is deemed a religious crime, it might be submitted to the Shariah courts.

Even if the Shariah courts have jurisdiction over some crimes in Qatar and the UAE, they do not have the same prominence in the legal system as the Shariah courts have in Saudi Arabia. In the kingdom, the Shariah courts are the courts with general jurisdiction. That the Board of Grievances expanded

---

21. The UAE's Federal Law No. 3 of 1996, on the jurisdiction of Shariah courts in examining some crimes.

its jurisdiction should not hide the fact that it also had to comply with the Islamic Shariah. The High Administrative Court also reviews appeals on the ground of 'violation of provisions of Sharia'.[22] Even though the Board of Grievances has developed outside the Shariah courts, it has employed judges who go through the same religious education as Shariah court judges. In fact, the 1982 Law of the Board of Grievances stated that the Board judges must also have degrees from Shariah colleges, like Shariah court judges.[23]

To put it in another way, religious scholars in Saudi Arabia have kept their dominant roles in the expanding Saudi legal system. It is illustrative that all Ministers of Justice in Saudi Arabia have so far been religious scholars.[24] In other Gulf states, religious scholars have never been in such a position of authority and influence. Needless to say, because religious scholars occupied such high positions in Saudi Arabia they had successfully resisted the codification of the Islamic Shariah.[25] Not surprisingly, the resistance of Shia scholars in Bahrain has also constituted a serious impediment to the codification of the Family Law of the Shias.

Expanding Public Education

In addition to investing in their legal systems, the Gulf states also invested in their public education systems. By the late 1970s, they had made quite remarkable progress in extending educational opportunities to their citizens. In 1978, for example, Bahrain enrolled 75.1 per cent of its population aged 5–19 years, Kuwait 65.7 per cent, the UAE 64.3 per cent, Qatar 52.1 per cent and Saudi Arabia 34.5 per cent. For comparison, the same year Bahrain, Kuwait, the UAE and Qatar had higher figures than Egypt, the Arab state with the longest history of modern education, which enrolled 43.8 per cent of its 5–19 population.[26]

---

22. Article 11 of Saudi Arabia's Royal Decree No. M/78 of 2007.
23. Article 37-d of the 1975 Judiciary Law and Article 11-d of the 1982 Law of the Board of Grievances.
24. Religious scholars also served in other capacities, such as members and presidents of the Advisory Council and advisors to kings. I will shortly mention their roles in education. See Mouline, *Clerics of Islam*, p. 195.
25. Vogel, *Islamic Law and the Legal System*.
26. Al-Misnad, *The Development of Modern Education in Bahrain, Kuwait and Qatar*, p. 134.

But further progress still needed to be made. The Gulf states had to open more schools so that they could enrol higher percentages of their school-age populations. While doing so, they also had to correct an imbalance they all had in their educational systems to a varying degree: more primary schools than intermediate and secondary schools. In recent decades the Gulf states have worked to correct this imbalance by opening more intermediate and secondary level schools and encouraging private initiatives.

In 1979 Kuwait primary schools made up 46.4 per cent of all schools (168 primary schools, 128 intermediate schools, 66 secondary schools),[27] but over two decades later, in 2002, only 39.2 per cent of all schools (182 primary schools, 164 intermediate schools and 118 secondary schools).[28] In the UAE, primary schools made up 83.6 per cent of all schools (185 primary schools and 44 non-primary schools) in 1978,[29] but in 2002 51.7 per cent (221 primary schools and 206 intermediate and secondary schools).[30] Bahrain, Qatar and Saudi Arabia also corrected the imbalance in their educational systems: in Saudi Arabia, primary schools made up 74.5 per cent of all schools in 1979, but 57.9 per cent in 2000.[31] In Bahrain, primary school classrooms made up 64.2 per cent of all school classrooms in 1979, but 55.4 per cent in 1999.[32] In Qatar, primary schools made up 69.4 per cent of all schools in 1978, but 47.3 per cent in 2005.[33]

These efforts paid off, as can be observed in the changes in the literacy rate among populations aged sixty-five and older. Kuwait's figure increased from 12.95 per cent in 1975 to 69.55 per cent in 2015; Bahrain's figure increased from 12.76 per cent in 1980 to 49.28 per cent in 2010; Qatar's figure increased from 24.11 per cent in 1985 to 78.91 per cent in 2014; Saudi Arabia's figure increased from 13.13 per cent in 1992 to 51.39 per cent

27. Kuwait Annual UNESCO Report 1981.
28. Kuwait Annual UNESCO Report 2001.
29. The UAE Annual UNESCO Report 1981.
30. The UAE Annual UNESCO Report 2004.
31. Saudi Arabia Annual UNESCO Report 1981 and Saudi Arabia Annual UNESCO Report 2001.
32. Bahrain Report 1981 and Bahrain Report 2001.
33. Qatar Annual UNESCO Report 1979 and Qatar Annual UNESCO Report 2008.

in 2013; the UAE's figure increased from 8.75 per cent in 1975 to 42.07 per cent in 2005.³⁴

In the same period, the Gulf states also invested in higher education. In the early 1980s, Saudi Arabia had seven universities under the Ministry of Higher Education, in Riyadh in Najd, Jeddah, Mecca and Medina in the Hijaz, and Dhahran and Hofuf in the Eastern Region. Through the 1980s Saudi Arabia expanded the capacity of these universities. Starting in the mid-2000s, however, the kingdom began to open new universities, establishing twenty-one in the next ten years.³⁵

Other Gulf states also invested in higher education. In the early 1980s, Kuwait, Qatar and the UAE had their national universities – University of Kuwait, Qatar University and the UAE University – respectively. In 1986 Bahrain merged the College of Science, Literature and Education and the Gulf Polytechnic College and founded Bahrain University. Like Saudi Arabia, the UAE also opened new state universities to make higher education more accessible, founding the Higher Colleges of Technology in 1988 and Zayed University in 1998. Because Kuwait, Qatar and Bahrain have concentrated populations, they didn't open new state universities but instead expanded the capacity of their national universities. All the Gulf states also expanded higher education by allowing private and semi-private initiatives to establish higher-education institutions. Especially noteworthy is that Kuwait, Qatar and the UAE have campuses of some prominent US and European universities, such as the American University in Kuwait, Georgetown University and several others in Qatar, New York University in Abu Dhabi and the American University in Sharjah.

As for religion in the public education system, the Gulf states have not made any fundamental departures from their earlier policies. They have made some changes in the composition of courses in their curriculums, but have kept religious courses with slight changes in the titles of the courses and the number of class hours. Saudi Arabia, however, not only taught more diverse courses in religion, but also devoted more class hours to them. In the 2010s, for example, Saudi Arabia's primary schools taught the Qur'an across Grades

---

34. These figures are from UNESCO's Country Profiles.
35. Saudi Arabia Annual UNESCO Report 2008.

1–4, Proper Recitation of the Qur'an across Grades 5–6, Islamic Theology and Islamic Jurisprudence across all grades, and the Prophetic Traditions and the Biography of the Prophet across Grades 4–6; intermediate schools taught the Qur'an, the Qur'an Exegesis, Islamic Theology, Islamic Jurisprudence and Islamic Traditions across all grades; secondary schools taught the Qur'an, the Qur'an Exegesis, the Prophetic Traditions, the Islamic Theology and the Islamic Jurisprudence across all grades and sections. In the 2010s, other Gulf states offered fewer religious classes: Kuwait taught two religious courses titled Islamic Education and the Holy Qur'an; Bahrain, Qatar and the UAE taught only one religious course titled Islamic Education.

Saudi Arabia also differed from the other Gulf states in that it devoted more class hours to religious courses: for example, nine class hours across Grades 1–3 and Grades 5–6 and ten at Grade 4 in its primary schools; eight class hours across all grades in its intermediate schools; and five class hours at Grade 1, eight at Grade 2 and five in the scientific track and five at Grade 1, nine at Grade 2 and twelve in the literature track of its secondary schools. In primary schools these classes made up around 30 per cent of the total weekly class hours across Grades 1–4 and around 27 per cent across Grades 5–6; in intermediate schools they made up around 22 per cent across all grades; in secondary schools they made up around 14 per cent at Grade 1, around 22 per cent at Grade 2 and around 14 at Grade 3 in the scientific track and around 14 per cent at Grade 1, around 27 per cent at Grade 2 and around 36 per cent at Grade 3 in the literature track.[36]

Other Gulf states devoted fewer class hours: Qatar devoted to its religious class four hours across all grades; the UAE devoted three hours across all grades; Kuwait devoted four hours across Grades 1–5 in primary schools, three hours in intermediate schools and two hours in secondary schools; Bahrain devoted three hours in primary schools and two hours in intermediate schools.[37] These classes made up between 6 and 13 per cent of the total class hours.

---

36. I based my calculations on the 2012–13 class plans issued by the Saudi Ministry of Education.
37. Bahrain's Ministry of Education adopts a different reporting process for grades 10–12, allocating four credit hours in the industrial and technical track and eight credit hours in all other tracks.

In addition to teaching religion in their ordinary schools, the Gulf states also had religious schools, which devoted more class hours to religious subjects than ordinary schools. In the mid- 1970s, Saudi Arabia had thirty-six operating as part of the Imam Muhammad bin Saud University. Over the next four decades the kingdom established another thirty religious schools, spread across the country. Kuwait also established new religious schools: in 1975 it had three but forty years later there were nine. Bahrain and Qatar both had one religious school by the late 1970s and have not established any more. The UAE had four religious schools in 1978 and still had four in the early 2000s.

The Gulf states have also kept higher institutions of religious education. By the late 1970s Saudi Arabia had two religious universities, the Muhammad bin Saud University in Riyadh and the Islamic University in Medina, and a number of Shariah colleges in other regions. In 1981 the College of Shariah in Mecca became Saudi Arabia's third religious university and was named Umm al-Qura University. These universities have remained Saudi Arabia's prime religious universities. However, Saudi Arabia also established colleges teaching the Islamic Shariah in most of its old and newly founded universities, either as Colleges of Shariah and Law (Regulations) or Colleges of Shariah and Fundamentals of Religion.[38]

Other Gulf states did not have specifically religious universities, but instead established religious colleges or programmes within their national universities. In the late 1970s Qatar University already had the College of Shariah, Law and Islamic Studies; Kuwait University had the College of Law and Shariah; and the UAE University had the College of Law and Shariah. Bahrain had a Department of Arabic and Islamic Studies in the University College. These states have not since then disestablished these colleges or programmes, but have introduced some changes. Both Qatar University and Kuwait University have Colleges of Shariah and Islamic Studies; the UAE University has a Department of Shariah and Islamic Studies as part of its

---

38. For example, Taif University, Jazan University, al-Jouf University, Hail University and Tabouk University have Colleges of Shariah and Law; King Khalid University and Najran University have Colleges of Shariah and Fundamentals of Religion; Qassim University has a College of Shariah and Islamic Studies.

College of Law; and Bahrain University incorporated the Department of Arabic and Islamic Studies as part of its College of Arts. In addition, the UAE gained two more higher institutions of religious education: the Muhammad bin Saud University's campus in Ras al-Khaimah and the University of Sharjah's College of Shariah and Islamic Studies.

It is worth pointing out that Kuwait University, Qatar University and the UAE University had originally established colleges that combined Law and Shariah. This fact alone illustrates the extent to which state laws and the Islamic Shariah complemented one another. Yet the issuance of more state laws and the concomitant decreasing scope of the jurisdiction of the Shariah courts necessitated the establishment of separate Colleges of Law. Kuwait led the way, establishing a separate College of Law at Kuwait University in 1981 and turning the College of Shariah into the separate College of Shariah and Islamic Studies. Qatar took the same step more than two decades later and in 2006 established the College of Law at Qatar University, a separate from the College of Shariah and Islamic Studies. The UAE, on the other hand, transformed the College of Law and Shariah at UAE University into the College of Law and created within that the Department of Shariah and Islamic Studies. Bahrain did not have a college joining law and the Islamic Shariah. It therefore established a College of Law at Bahrain University in 2002.

In the expanding field of education, religious scholars in Saudi Arabia could not keep their historical dominance. For example, after Hasan al-Sheikh, a religious scholar, stepped down as the Minister of Education in 1975, his replacement was not another religious scholar, but Abd al-Aziz al-Khuwaitir, who studied History and Philosophy in Egypt and the UK. Al-Khuwaitir served as the Minister of Education until 1995. Since then, no religious scholar has served as the Minister of Education in Saudi Arabia. The only consolation religious scholars might have felt came from the fact that al-Khuwaitir graduated from a religious school in Mecca and the two successive ministers, Muhammad al-Rashid and Abdullah al-Ubeid, graduated from Imam Muhammad bin Saud University, both having a bachelor's degree in Arabic studies. However, both went on to pursue their doctorates in the US. Until the death of Hasan al-Sheikh in 1987, a religious scholar had at least served as the Minister of Higher Education. But since him no religious scholar has held the post: al-Sheikh was succeeded by al-Khuwaitir, who was replaced four years later by Khalid bin Muhammad al-Anqari. Serving for twenty-three years until 2014, al-Anqari had a PhD from the University of Florida.[39] An even bigger loss for religious scholars in Saudi Arabia was the presidency of Girls' Education, which had usually been under the administration of a religious scholar and kept outside the Ministry of Education since its foundation in 1960, but transferred to the Ministry of Education in 2002. However, this did not amount to a total purge of religious scholars from the Ministry of Education and Ministry of Higher Education, as many graduates of Islamic universities and Colleges of Shariah continued to find employment in both ministries as teachers and administrators.

Intruding into Religious Services

In the same period, the Gulf states also moved to impose some measure of control over mosques, where the most pious undertake their daily prayers at least five times a day and also congregate once a week to attend the Friday prayer. Like some other states in the Muslim world, such as Egypt and Turkey, the Gulf states have imposed a certain measure of supervision over mosques. Saudi Arabia was the first, establishing the Ministry of Hajj, Umrah and Endowments in 1961, primarily tasked with overseeing the pilgrimages (hajj) and religious visitations (umrah) to Mecca and Medina. But it was also given authority to oversee pious endowments (awqaf) and thus to supervise mosques financed by them. In 1972 Saudi Arabia took a more significant step and issued the Law of Prayer Leaders (imams), Callers to Prayer (muezzins) and Servants of Mosques, in which it specified the criteria for religious personnel in mosques and tasked the Ministry with implementing the law.[40] There was another major reorganisation in 1993: supervision of endowments was removed from the Ministry and the new Ministry of Awqaf, Islamic Affairs and Islamic Call (Da'wah) and Guidance was established, which thus became the authority responsible for both endowments and mosques. As its name

---

39. Khalid al-Sabti succeeded al-Anqari as the Minister of Higher Education: he had a BA and PhD in Computer Science from King Saud University and Syracuse University respectively. Al-Sabti's tenure was short, ending in 2015. No one replaced him, as the Ministry of Higher Education merged with the Ministry of Education the same year.
40. Saudi Arabia's Regulation No. M/1 of 1392H.

suggests, this new Ministry also became responsible for proselytisation. The Ministry's website counts among its objectives, 'calling the people to Islam'.

Other Gulf states developed similar ministries. Even prior to their independence they moved to supervise endowments: Bahrain, for example, established the Department of Endowments for both Sunni and Shia endowments in the 1920s. Kuwait established its own department to oversee endowments in 1949. Qatar tasked the presidency of Shariah courts with the supervision of endowments until 1993.[41] After their independence, the Gulf states established the relevant ministries: Kuwait and Qatar each established a Ministry of Endowments and Islamic Affairs, and the UAE and Bahrain a Ministry of Justice, Islamic Affairs and Endowments. In a further move, the UAE divided its Ministry into the Ministry of Justice and the General Authority of Islamic Affairs and Endowments. Bahrain retains its Ministry of Justice, Islamic Affairs and Endowments.

Tracking different paths, all the Gulf states, however, have eventually assumed the same religious tasks: expanding beyond the supervision of endowments and mosques, they also came to regulate the affairs of mosques and work to spread the message of Islam.

The 1993 law that established the Ministry of Endowments and Islamic Affairs in Qatar, for example, tasked the Ministry 'to establish, administer and supervise over mosques to ensure their discharge of their mission in the most perfect manner'.[42] The law also tasked the Ministry 'to disseminate the Islamic Call (Da'wah)' and 'to spread the Islamic culture and develop religious awareness using all suitable means'.[43] The ruler similarly tasked the Ministry of Endowments and Islamic Affairs in Kuwait not only to preserve 'the interests of endowments' and guide them in accordance with the rulings of the Islamic Shariah, but also to supervise and take care of mosques, and even provide religious scholars and servants in order for 'the discharge of their mission in the most perfect manner'.[44] Likewise, the decree tasked the

41. See Hamed, *Islamic Religion in Qatar during the Twentieth Century*, ch. 5.
42. Article 2 of Qatar's Law No. 9 of 1993.
43. Article 2 of Qatar's Law No. 9 of 1993.
44. Article 1 and Article 2.2 of Kuwait Ruler Decree of 1979 about the Ministry of Endowments and Islamic Affairs.

Ministry with 'spreading the Islamic Call (Da'wah) with various means inside and outside and reviving the Islamic Heritage'.[45] The UAE's federal law that defined the jurisdiction of the Ministry of Justice, Islamic Affairs and Endowments in 1974 likewise tasked it to 'manage and supervise the mosques to achieve the message thereof as best as possible'. It also tasked the Ministry with the revival and spread of Islamic heritage, demonstration of 'the Islamic values', spreading 'the Islamic culture'[46] and developing religious awareness.[47]

Saudi Arabia also continued to keep the religious police during this period.[48] In 1980 the kingdom issued a statute for the force, which defined the religious police as an independent organisation and put it directly under the Council of Ministers. The statute outlined certain basic principles concerning the structure, personnel and duties of the religious police. The statute mandated the religious police, for example, 'to guide and advise people to observe the religious duties prescribed by Islamic Law', and critically, 'to make them carry out these duties'. It also tasked the force to prevent 'commission of things which are unlawful and prohibited by Islamic Law, and observance of bad traditions or abominable innovations' and authorised the force 'to take the measures and impose the penalties listed' in the statute and 'apprehend and interrogate people who commit unlawful actions, are accused of doing so, or are negligent of the obligations set by Islamic Law'.[49]

Six years later, the presidency of the religious police issued more detailed by-laws, which further detailed the religious police's authority, relations with other state authorities, especially the regular police, and certain procedures to be followed by the force.[50] For example, the by-laws tasked the religious police to make sure that prayer 'is performed in mosques at the times set for it in Islamic Law, and to urge people to hasten in answering its call'.

---

45. Article 2.3 of Kuwait Ruler Decree of 1979 about the Ministry of Endowments and Islamic Affairs.
46. Article 3 of the UAE Federal Law No. 1 of 1974.
47. Article 3 of the UAE Federal Law No. 1 of 1974.
48. For a detailed discussion, see Mouline, *The Clerics of Islam*, ch. 8.
49. Article 9 and Article 11 of the Regulation. An English translation of the regulation is available in al-Hedaithy, *Modernization and Islam in Saudi Arabia*, Appendix E.
50. An English translation of the by-laws is available in al-Hedaithy, *Modernization and Islam in Saudi Arabia*, Appendix G.

The religious police was also tasked to 'make sure that stores are closed and no sales take place at prayer time'[51] and by-laws also authorised the force to watch public places to enforce sex-segregation and prevent behaviours that would be against public morality.[52]

Yet the religious police was not merely an executive body. It was also a judicial body, not only investigating crimes in its jurisdiction but issuing verdicts and punishments. It could, for example, decide 'to discipline the offender by whipping to a maximum of fifteen lashes or by imprisonment to a maximum of three days'.[53] However, the 2002 Law of Criminal Procedure took this judicial authority away from the religious police and granted it to the Shariah courts.[54]

The issuance of the statute and the by-laws imposed more order on the religious police. In the 1980s and 1990s, Saudi Arabia also worked to create a more professional and efficient religious police force, and to this end increased its budget from 18.8 million rials in 1970 to 242.4 million rials in 1994, even though the size of the religious police only increased from less than 3,000 in 1970 to around 4,500 in 1994. In judging the effectiveness of the religious police, it is also important to note that it had the right to demand additional manpower from the regular police in carrying out its duties.[55] With its powers to supervise and enforce public morality, the religious police continued to be one of the distinguishing features of Saudi Arabia.

Emphasising Religious Credentials

Saudi Arabia had always distinguished itself in strongly and clearly emphasising its religious credentials. During this period, other Gulf states also began to emphasise their religious credentials. This can be seen in what they claimed as their educational objectives.

---

51. Article 1-B in Section 1 of the by-laws, available in al-Hedaithy, *Modernization and Islam in Saudi Arabia*, Appendix G.
52. Actual punishment could only be implemented once the provincial governor approved it. See Article 1-C in Section 1 of the by-laws.
53. Article 61 and Article 62 of the by-laws.
54. The religious police continued to investigate matters that fell under its jurisdiction: Article 26 of Saudi Arabia's 2001 Law of Criminal Procedure.
55. Figures are from Mouline, *The Clerics of Islam*, ch. 8.

Saudi Arabia was also the frontrunner in this regard. In 1970 the kingdom issued its Education Policy and stated in its very first article, 'Education policy in the Kingdom of Saudi Arabia emanates from Islam'. This first section outlined the general principles on which Saudi education was based. These principles covered some well-known religious propositions and beliefs. The first principle, for example, was a restatement of the faith 'in Allah as the Lord, in Islam as the religion, and Muhammad, may Allah's blessings and peace be upon him, as the Prophet'. The second principle presented Islam as a perfect blueprint 'for humanity and life'; the third stated a religious view of this life, which was a stage in which 'the Muslim spends his energy for the infinite life in the next life'; the fourth presented 'the Mohammedan message' as 'the most powerful path' to pursue 'a virtuous life'; the fifth was once again about 'the message of Islam's Prophet', claiming that it 'aims to realize dignity in this world and happiness in the after world'.[56]

Like Saudi Arabia, other Gulf states also began to emphasise the importance of Islam in their education policies, but later than the Kingdom. Until the 1980s the reports other Gulf states submitted to UNESCO were statements of facts. In its report submitted in 1971, Kuwait made a rare reference to religion, stating that the religious course, Islamic Education, 'aimed to inculcate Islamic spirit and ideals in students'.[57] In 1979 it laid much stronger emphasis on religion, counting among the aims of education the creation of 'the good national who believes in . . . Islamic values and ideals, and models his behaviour and relations with God and people accordingly', and 'promoting the individual's religious and moral values in the light of the teaching of Islamic ethics'.[58] A decade later, Kuwait stated, 'education in Kuwait stems from the nature of the Muslim, Arabian Gulf and Kuwaiti society . . . it aims at implanting faith in the principles of Islam in the students, introducing them to their Islamic, Arabic legacy . . . establishing the feeling of belonging to Kuwait, the Arabian fatherland as well as the Islamic world'. Even at

---

56. The document lists a total of twenty-six similar principles from Article 2 to Article 27. The Education Policy Document is available in Arabic on a variety of online platforms, for example at http://www.almekbel.net/PolicyofKsa.pdf.
57. Kuwait Annual UNESCO Report 1971, p. 4.
58. Kuwait Annual UNESCO Report 1979, pp. 5–6.

kindergarten level, Kuwait pursued a religious aim: education at this stage, the report said, 'aims at implanting Islamic faith in the minds of the children'. At higher levels of education too, Kuwait pursued a religious aim: students were 'to acquire the various aspects of knowledge, attitudes, and skills relevant to the basics of the religion of Islam' at primary school level, 'to acquire those aspects of knowledge, attitudes and skills related to the facts of Islam' at the intermediate level, and 'to acquire the knowledge, attitudes and skills related to correct understanding of Islamic faith'. Furthermore, education would encourage students 'to practise the teaching of Islam in their levels'.[59]

Qatar's reports to UNESCO had also been statements of facts until the 1980s, any policy objective being rather technical in nature. In an early reference to Islam, Qatar, for example, stated in its 1976 report, 'education should provide their cadres with scientific and technological abilities, cultural consciousness, absorption of the experimental methodologies and technologies of the age, and combine them with inculcating the moral ideals and Islamic values so as to be effective means of reconstructing their society'.[60] Five years later, in its 1981 report, Qatar stated, however, 'Education in Qatar aims at bringing up a generation believing in God, proud of Islam, adherent to its teachings.' In elaborating this objective, the Ministry stated that education aimed to provide religious and moral education 'through inculcating faith in the oneness of Allah Almighty, thus creating a feeling of piety and obedience to all ordinance revealed by Allah' and 'through the application of Islamic ideals and values in everyday life as a direct impact of including such values in the content of education'.[61]

In its 1986 report, Qatar further specified the objectives of education at different stages: education aimed 'to bring up children on the basis of the sublime principles of Islam' at the primary stage, 'to prepare students to live in an Islamic society' at the intermediate level and 'to help students formulate a rational philosophy for their life based upon the genuine Islamic and Arab values' at the secondary stage.[62]

---

59. Kuwait Annual UNESCO Report 1989, pp. 20–3.
60. Qatar Annual UNESCO Report 1977, p. 15.
61. Ministry of Education, *Development of Education in Qatar, 1979/80–1980/81*, p. 4.
62. Qatar Annual UNESCO Report 1986, pp. 6–7.

Until the late 1970s, Bahrain's reports to UNESCO had also been statements of facts and any expressed policy objectives were more technical in nature. Bahrain expressed any religious objective for the first time in its 1981 report, stating among its educational objectives, 'to prepare the individual to be a devout Moslem'.[63] Four years later, in its 1986 report, Bahrain cited among the objectives of education the inculcation of 'the Islamic faith, emphasizing its role in the integration of the individual personality, the unity of the family and society and its co-operation, and showing the Islamic role as a comprehensive way of life suitable for any place and time and its ability to cope with the demands of time', and of 'the pride in belonging to the Arab and Islamic nations'.[64]

The increasing emphasis put on religion in education policy is most evident in the UAE's changing discourse. In its 1981 report the UAE counted among the goals of education 'realization of the democracy of education to all pupils', 'realization of the productivity of education' and 'realization of integration of efforts among all institutions, formal and non-formal, that are concerned with education in the countries'.[65] However, in its 1984 report the UAE stated that its educational policy was based 'on Islamic models'.[66] In its 1992 report, the UAE was unequivocal in its emphasis on religion in its education policy, stating among its educational objectives, 'forming and deepening faith in God and recognition of the principles of Islam: its noble spiritual values and the fundamentals of sound Islamic behaviour' and 'acquiring and developing social behaviour adopted from Islamic ethics and morals'.[67]

As mentioned above, Saudi Arabia issued its education policy earlier than the others. As I will claim shortly, while Bahrain, Kuwait, Qatar and the UAE put more emphasis on religion in their educational policies in the newly emerging geopolitical context, Saudi Arabia did so well before that context came into existence. Still, Saudi Arabia must have been driven to make a similar case. An opportunity arose in 1992 when it issued the Basic Regulation

---

63. Bahrain Annual UNESCO Report 1981, p. 2.
64. Cited in the Bahrain Annual UNESCO Report 1986, p. 2.
65. UAE Annual UNESCO Report 1981, p. 3.
66. UAE Annual UNESCO Report 1984, p. 1.
67. UAE Annual UNESCO Report 1992, pp. 1–2.

for Governance[68] in place of a constitution. The first article in the Regulation is unequivocal in stating the Kingdom's religious character: 'the Kingdom of Saudi Arabia is an Islamic Arab state with full sovereignty. Its religion is Islam and its constitution is the Book of Allah and the Traditions of his Messenger, may Allah's blessings and peace be upon him.' The second article recognises Islam's two religious holidays as official holidays of Saudi Arabia. The fifth and sixth articles specify that the ruler has to rule and the citizens pledge allegiance to the ruler on the basis of the Qur'an and the Prophetic Traditions. Even though the fifth article states that the system of governance is monarchical, the seventh article states that the system derives its authority, read as its legitimacy, from the Qur'an and the Prophetic Traditions, which, the article restates, 'govern this Regulation and all the regulations of the state'. The eighth article states, once again, that governance shall be based on justice, consultation and equality, adding in accordance with the Islamic Shariah.

The Basic Regulation repeats religious terms such as Allah, the Book of Allah, the Prophetic Traditions, the Islamic Shariah: in total it mentions Allah eleven times, Islam or Islamic nineteen times, the Qur'an and the Prophetic Traditions five times, and the Islamic Shariah nineteen times. The Basic Regulation confirms the indisputably religious character of the Saudi state, leaving no doubt that it is bound by Islam's Holy Book, the Prophetic traditions and the rulings derived from them.

This chapter has shown that in the post-1979 period, the Gulf states did not change their relations with religion in any fundamental way. They made some adjustments and introduced some reforms, but overall kept their relations with religion cordial. Saudi Arabia continued to be different from the others in that it continued to apply the Islamic Shariah in a more comprehensive way, retaining the Shariah courts as the main courts, teaching more religion in its public education system and running a separate police force to enforce public morality. Yet in this period all the Gulf states began to emphasise their religious credentials more clearly and strongly. They did this for a reason: the changing geopolitical context. In this new geopolitical environment, state–Muslim Brotherhood relations also changed.

68. In Arabic it is called al-Nizam al-Asasi li'l Hukm, not the Constitution or al-Dustur.

5

GULF STATES' DIVERGING ATTITUDES TOWARDS THE MUSLIM BROTHERHOOD

In the 1970s the conditions that had led all the Gulf states to adopt a friendly attitude towards the Muslim Brotherhood began to disappear. New conditions and more pressing concerns began to shake state–Muslim Brotherhood relations. In this new geopolitical context, the Brotherhood became oppositional in Kuwait, the UAE and Saudi Arabia. Here I will discuss how the context changed, and then turn to the change in state–Muslim Brotherhood relations.

The Changing Regional Context

The geopolitical challenge Egypt posed to the Gulf states weakened after Egypt's humiliating defeat in the 1967 war with Israel. In this war Egypt lost not only Sinai and its oilfields, but also its prestige and claims to the leadership of the Arab world. Egypt also withdrew from Yemen and even began to court the Arab monarchies. Three years after the defeat, Abdel Nasser died a broken man.

The defeat also discredited pan-Arab socialism as a means of political and economic development and seriously undermined its appeal across the broader Arab world and in the Gulf. Its adherents, be it Nasserites or Baathists, continued to be active and part of the political spectrum, but they would no longer pose the most serious opposition to the rulers across the Muslim world. In place of secular ideology groups, religion and religious groups began to surge.

This was a region-wide development that swept across the Muslim world. Even though Egypt's defeat in 1967 was a watershed event, it was just one of the manifestations that secular-nationalist ideologies had failed to deliver on their promises of political and economic development. Whatever its exact causes, the religious resurgence shaped the context within which the Gulf states have continued to evolve.

It was within this context that the fortunes of the Muslim Brotherhood improved, even in Egypt where the movement had been under severe repression in the 1960s. At the beginning of his tenure as president, Anwar Sadat, Abdel Nasser's successor, sought to rehabilitate the Brotherhood and released those Brothers from jail. He also helped to create a national environment which was much more conducive to the growth of the Brotherhood. Over the following decades the Brotherhood benefited from this environment and set out to become a major socio-political force in Egypt. But this religious revivalism was not peculiar to Egypt. In the 1970s the Muslim Brotherhood also flourished in the Gulf.

By the late 1970s a new regional context was in place as religious movements surged across the Arab and Muslim worlds. The 1979 revolution in Iran marked the beginning of the new era, with multiple and still lingering consequences. First, the revolution had a geopolitical consequence. Prior to 1979, Iran's potential as a security risk in the Arabian Gulf had been limited at least since the beginning of the 19th century. Iran had been preoccupied with its own survival against Britain and Russia well into the 1950s. Until 1971, Britain had maintained a military presence in the Gulf. Iran only became a source of concern after Britain left. It had, for example, laid claim to Bahrain, although it eventually came to accept it as a fully independent state in 1971. It also invaded three tiny islands in the Gulf that belonged to the UAE.

However, other than these two incidents, Iran had not posed a serious threat to the Arabian Gulf states through the 1970s. On the contrary, the US relied on it, along with Saudi Arabia, as one of the pillars of stability and security in the Gulf. Iran had even supported Saudi Arabia against Egypt in Yemen in the 1970s and been instrumental in the suppression of the Dhofari rebellion in Oman in the 1970s.

With the revolution in 1979, everything changed. The revolution toppled a pro-US monarchical regime and, even more critically, replaced it with an extremely anti-US, radical regime led by a religious scholar, Ruhullah Khomeini. The new regime became a serious concern for all states in the Middle East but particularly for the Arabian Gulf states, because it openly sought to export the revolution to other countries and even established in 1981 the Office of Liberation Movements to realise this objective. Even though Iran closed this office in 1986,[1] it sought ways to expand its sphere of influence throughout the Middle East by nurturing ties with both Sunni and Shia sub-state actors. Ebbing and flowing, the geopolitical challenge Iran posed to the Arabian Gulf states shaped the regional context within which state–Brotherhood relations in the Gulf evolved in the decades after the revolution.

The 1979 revolution also had other consequences. One still-lingering consequence was that it generated a new political activism among Shia populations, especially in three countries: Saudi Arabia, Kuwait and Bahrain.[2] In all three, the Shia population took part in street protests and demonstrations in support of the revolution. In Kuwait and Bahrain, Khomeini's personal representatives were actively involved. In both cases, the regimes expelled them and sought ways to quell the protests. In Saudi Arabia, the protests were even larger, with some demonstrators carrying Khomeini's picture and shouting pro-Iran slogans. The regime resorted to force to quell the protests. Some Shias were killed, hundreds were wounded and arrested, and hundreds fled the country. Like the geopolitical challenge Iran posed, Shia political activism also ebbed and flowed, but has remained an issue in all three countries.

Another important consequence of the Iranian revolution was that it inspired and emboldened religious movements across the Muslim world,[3] for the revolution represented Islam's triumph over its secular rivals, the only case of a religious mass mobilisation overthrowing a pro-West secular regime. The revolution could therefore serve as a model to be replicated elsewhere. The Muslim Brotherhood embraced the revolution with 'unqualified enthusiasm and unconditional euphoria'.[4] A magazine of the Muslim Brotherhood in

---

1. Marschall, *Iran's Persian Gulf Policy*, p. 30.
2. For a detailed discussion of Shia political activism after the revolution, see Louër, *Transnational Shia Politics*.
3. See Matthee, 'The Egyptian opposition on the Iranian revolution'; Sivan, 'Sunni radicalism in the Middle East and the Iranian revolution'.
4. Matthee, 'The Egyptian opposition on the Iranian revolution', p. 263.

Egypt, *al-Mukhtar al-Islami*, for example, conducted an interview with the leader of the revolution, Ruhullah Khomeini, in its July 1979 issue. The same year a member of the Egyptian Brotherhood also published a book, tellingly entitled *Khomeini: The Islamic Solution and the Alternative*.

Other branches of the Brotherhood were also jubilant about the Iranian revolution. Some sent delegations to Iran to congratulate the leaders. Even from Syria, where the Brotherhood had been anti-Shia, a prominent Brother, Said Hawwa, visited Iran and met Ruhullah Khomeini, most likely 'to elicit Tehran's support and patronage against' the Baath regime the Brotherhood had been fighting.[5] Hawwa, and the Syrian Brotherhood, were disappointed, however, as Iran and Syria forged closer ties, signing a number of critical treaties in 1982, the year the Baath regime violently crushed the Brotherhood in the city of Hama.

With the start of the Iran–Iraq war in 1980, and Iran's growing alliance with the Baath regime in Syria, the Egyptian Brotherhood lost its early enthusiasm and adopted a more ambivalent attitude towards the Iranian revolution. Yet the revolution had already inspired and emboldened the Muslim Brotherhood into more political activism. In this new context, state–Muslim Brotherhood relations changed in the Gulf.

Changing Attitudes towards the Muslim Brotherhood: Kuwait, the UAE and Saudi Arabia

State–Muslim Brotherhood relations began to change first in Kuwait and the UAE and then in Saudi Arabia. In all three cases, the Brotherhood became less acquiescent and more oppositional.

As discussed previously, the Muslim Brotherhood had flourished in Kuwait throughout the 1970s.[6] The Iranian revolution in 1979 turned out to be another blessing for the Brotherhood in Kuwait. The revolution, which brought to power a group of Shia clerics, emboldened and energised Shias in Kuwait and had a similar effect in Iraq, Saudi Arabia and Bahrain.[7] To counter this challenge, the regime in Kuwait sought to empower Islamist groups even

---

5. Haykel, 'Jihadis and the Shia', p. 206. Also see Abdelnasse, 'Islamic organizations in Egypt and the Iranian revolution of 1979'.
6. Also see the discussion in Freer, *Rentier Islamism*, pp. 70–4.
7. Louër, *Transnational Shia Politics*.

more. Even though a member of the Brotherhood, Yusuf al-Hajji was dismissed from the Ministry of Endowments and Islamic Affairs in 1981, he was appointed as the president of an important, newly founded, semi-public charity organisation, Bayt al-Zakat (the Alms House), in 1982. Four years later, he was appointed to the newly founded International Islamic Charity Organization, Hay'at al-Khariyya al-Islamiyya al-'Alamiyya. In another appointment, Ahmad Baze al-Yasin became the president of Bayt al-Tamwil al-Kuwait (the Kuwait Finance House), which was owned by major public institutions.

Even though the Brotherhood in Kuwait began to face a rival Islamist group, the Salafis, organised under Jam'iyyat Ihya' al-Turath al-Islami (the Islamic Heritage Revival Society), founded in 1981, it still flourished:[8] for example, the number of Qur'an centres al-Islah Society ran increased to around four hundred by the end of the decade.[9] The Brotherhood also came to dominate the workers' union in the 1980s. In fact, when the Brotherhood established its dominance over the unions in the oil sector, the editor of its journal, *al-Mujtama'*, reported, 'finally the stronghold of the left fell'.[10] The Brotherhood also expanded its control over most of the cooperatives.

The Brotherhood in Kuwait had always sent charities to other Muslim countries. The Brotherhood was committed especially to the Palestinian cause. In order to carry out more charity activities abroad, it established another organisation in 1984 as an affiliate of al-Islah Society: Lajnat al-Da'wah al-Islamiyya (the Islamic Call Committee). Until 1991 the Committee devoted its activities to Pakistan and Afghanistan, which had been the centres of Islamist charity activities all over the Muslim world because of the ongoing jihad against the Soviet Union.

However, for the regime in Kuwait there was a downside to the increasing activities of the Brotherhood, whose members became more emboldened. Even before the 1979 Iranian revolution, the Brothers had shown signs of this. When Anwar Sadat, president of Egypt, visited Israel, al-Islah Society dropped its usual non-political silence and issued an inflammatory statement criticising not only Sadat but also, implicitly, the regime in Kuwait for the

---

8. See the discussion in al-Mdaires, *Islamic Extremism in Kuwait*, ch. 5.
9. Al-Mdaires, *Islamic Extremism in Kuwait*, p. 19.
10. Cited in al-Mdaires, *Islamic Extremism in Kuwait*, p. 135.

latter's silence. The Society also called on the regime to finance those states that 'prepare truly for war'.[11]

After the 1979 revolution the Brotherhood became even more daring. Abdullah al-Nafisi, by then the Brotherhood's leading thinker in Kuwait, wrote in *al-Mujtama'* in 1981: 'The Islamic movement is in a state of war with its enemies. The most significant principles of war are to determine the real enemy and gather groupings against it to avoid dispersion and dissipation.' Al-Nafisi asked 'who the real and present enemy of the Islamic movement is' and then declared, 'the actual enemy of the Islamic movement is the ruling regimes as they are apparent groupings that we see day and night. They are the obstacles against the Islamic call.'[12]

In tandem with this increasingly emboldened discourse, the Brotherhood in Kuwait became increasingly politicised. In 1981 a few Brothers ran for office and eventually made it into the parliament.[13] Even though they could not Islamise all the country's laws or amend the constitution so that it recognised the Islamic law as the – rather than a – source of law, they did succeed in, for example, banning the consumption of alcohol in certain places such as embassies.

In the 1985 elections, nine Brothers competed, and four made it into parliament: Hamoud al-Rumi, Abd al-Aziz Abd al-Latif al-Mutawa, Abdullah al-Nafisi and Mubarak Fahad al-Duwaylah.[14] The Brotherhood deputies began to take an increasingly confrontational attitude towards the regime, supporting parliamentary inquiries into corruption cases involving high-ranking figures. When the ruler of Kuwait dissolved parliament in 1986, the Brotherhood joined other political groups in opposing the move.[15]

---

11. Cited in a US diplomatic cable from Kuwait. See 'Kuwaiti react to Sadat visit, Gok silent, but Kuwaitis love it confidential'.
12. Cited in Awadh, *Islamic Political Groups in Kuwait*, pp. 192–3.
13. According to Michael Herb's Kuwait Political Database, only one Brother, Muhammad al-Adsani, entered the parliament in 1981. According to Awadh, *Islamic Political Groups in Kuwait*, p. 185, two Brothers entered parliament that year: Hammoud al-Rumi and Aysah Majid al-Shahin.
14. Awadh, *Islamic Political Groups in Kuwait*, p. 186, does not mention Abd al-Aziz Abd al-Latif al-Mutawa among the Brothers who won seats in the parliament in the 1985 election.
15. See the discussion in Freer, *Rentier Islamism*, pp. 76–7.

In retaliation, the regime did not wage a full attack on the Brotherhood, but instead sought to silence the most vocal Brotherhood-affiliated dissidents, arresting, for example, Abdullah al-Nafisi. The regime's move against the Brotherhood remained limited, however, as the latter had not deployed all its resources and by and large its members refrained from attending street demonstrations against the regime.

This period of controlled tension between the regime and the Brotherhood in Kuwait came to an unexpected end in the summer of 1990, when Iraq occupied Kuwait for six months. The invasion provided an opportunity for the Brotherhood. Having a relatively developed grassroots organisation, the Brotherhood was actively involved in providing social services, distributing food and medicine to the Kuwaitis who had not fled the country. The Brotherhood considerably improved its social standing and image, especially among the youth.[16]

The invasion also posed a challenge for the Brotherhood, as the attitude of the broader Muslim Brotherhood movement to the invasion was disappointing for the Kuwaitis. The immediate reaction of the transnational office of the Brotherhood based in Egypt was to denounce the invasion. But this changed when Saudi Arabia invited the US and other foreign countries to help defend its territories and to expel Iraq from Kuwait. Now the transnational office called for the expulsion of foreign forces from Muslim territories. Other branches of the broader Muslim Brotherhood movement, however, sent confusing signals: while the Lebanese and Iraqi branches called for the liberation of Kuwait by any means, others opposed any foreign intervention.[17]

A delegation of Brotherhood leaders went to Iraq to meet Saddam Hussein and, problematically, seemed to support the invasion. Appalled by the attitude of the broader Muslim Brotherhood movement, Ismail al-Shatti, a leading figure of the Brotherhood in Kuwait, called for the secession of the Kuwaiti branch from the broader movement. However, there were opposing views within the movement and hence, secession was averted. But relations were certainly to weaken in the coming years.

16. Tétreault, *Stories of Democracy*, p. 95. Also see Freer, *Rentier Islamism*, pp. 78–81.
17. Awadh, *Islamic Political Groups in Kuwait*, pp. 197–8.

During the invasion the regime, now in exile, announced that it would restore the constitution after the liberation. Five months after the liberation, in June 1991, the regime indeed announced that parliamentary elections would be held in October 1992. As Kuwait prepared for post-liberation transition, the Muslim Brotherhood formed a political front in late March 1991 called the Harakat al-Dusturiyya al-Islamiyya (the Islamic Constitutional Movement, or ICM), Harakat al-Dusturiyya al-Islamiyya. Jassim Muhalhel became the ICM's president and Isa al-Shahin its official spokesperson.

The Brotherhood in Kuwait thus had activities in two separate organisations. Through al-Islah Society and its affiliate, the Islamic Call Committee, the Brotherhood continued to engage in social and cultural activities both in Kuwait and abroad. Through the ICM, the Brotherhood continued to engage in politics.

This dual structure helped the Brothers overcome a dilemma they had faced all along. The Brotherhood in Kuwait had first developed among the merchants. The first brother in Kuwait, Abd al-Aziz al-Mutawa, was a merchant. The Brotherhood continued to have members among the merchants and the businessmen who had sought to keep good relations with the regime, which distributed oil wealth. Yet the Brotherhood also expanded among the professional classes, who had a freer hand in taking a more confrontational attitude towards the regime. The establishment of the ICM alleviated the problem. Al-Islah Society, led by Abdullah al-Mutawa, a merchant-businessman, could continue to keep cordial relations with the regime. The ICM, on the other hand, could be more flexible, taking pro-regime or oppositional positions depending on the circumstances.

The Brotherhood's objective, whether through al-Islah Society or the ICM, was to Islamicise the constitution and laws of Kuwait. This was not new. The Brothers in Kuwait had long held that the constitution and laws were not in full accordance with the Islamic Shariah. In return for their loyalty in the 1970s, they had expected the regime in Kuwait to make the necessary changes. For example, they pressed for an amendment of Article 2 of the constitution, which recognised the Islamic Shariah as *a* source of law. For the Brothers this was not enough: the Islamic law must be *the* source of law in Kuwait. But their efforts proved in vain as the Shariah had remained only a source of law into the 1980s.

One of the ICM's priorities was to make this amendment. The call was renewed after the liberation. Abdullah al-Mutawa, then the president of al-Islah Society, suggested making the Islamic law 'the only and main source of legislation', not 'a source of legislation'.[18] Article 2 was not the only article, however, that, the Brothers believed conflicted with the Islamic Shariah. According to the ICM's president, Jassim Muhalhal, Articles 157 and 6 also transgressed the Islamic law:

> Article 157 indicates that the laws are only applicable if the Amir [the ruler] of the country endorses them. Then there is Article 6, concerning the issue of sovereignty; this article comments upon the subject of the sovereignty of the Council and the sovereignty of the Amir of the country, yet does not mention the sovereignty of God . . . even though sovereignty belongs, first and foremost to God.[19]

Even before the elections were held, the regime in Kuwait positively responded to the Brotherhood's call to Islamicise the laws. To this end, the ruler established a higher consultative committee to make recommendations regarding how to enforce the Islamic law in Kuwait.[20] Some Brothers sat on this committee. In the 1992 elections, the ICM officially endorsed seven Kuwaiti Brothers and some twenty candidates from other groups.[21] Five of the Brothers and another ten ICM-backed candidates entered the parliament in the elections.[22] The post-election cabinet also reflected the rising popularity of the Brotherhood: a figure backed by the ICM, Abdullah Rashid al-Hajri, became the Minister of Commerce and Industry and a Kuwaiti Brother, Jaman al-Azemy, became the Minister of Endowments and Islamic

---

18. Cited in Ghabra, 'Balancing state and society', p. 63.
19. Cited in Awadh, *Islamic Political Groups in Kuwait*, pp. 188–90.
20. Ghabra, 'Balancing state and society', p. 64.
21. These are Hammoud al-Rumi, Nasir al-Sana, Mubarak al-Dawaylah, Jammal al-Kandary, Muhammad al-Beseyri and Jaman al-Azami. Michael Herb's Kuwait Political Database mentions the first five figures only and adds to them five others: Jarallah al-Jarallah, who is described as close to the Brotherhood, Saad al-Ajmi, Adil al-Subeih, Abd al-Aziz al-Mutawwa and Falah al-Mutairi.
22. Tétreault, *Stories of Democracy*, Appendix 6.1. According to the Kuwait Political Database, ten Brotherhood-affiliated candidates ran in the elections, only four of them winning seats.

Affairs. In 1993 the Brotherhood-backed Muhammad al-Shaye was elected to head the influential Municipal Board.

Seeking to capitalise on the popularity it enjoyed, the ICM was able to pass in parliament a proposal that amended Article 2 of the constitution with the support of other groups. But the ruler of Kuwait vetoed the amendment. The Brotherhood, along with the Salafis, also passed a proposal in the mid-1990s that segregated the sexes at Kuwait University. Segregation was to be implemented over a period of five years.[23]

The regime in Kuwait began to perceive the Brotherhood's popularity as a potential threat from the late 1980s. More popular owing to its activities during the invasion, the Brotherhood posed a serious challenge in the post-liberation period. As also happened in Saudi Arabia and the UAE, the regime in Kuwait finally took preventive measures against the Brotherhood in the mid-1990s. First, Abdullah al-Hajri and Jaman al-Azemy were dismissed from their ministerial positions in a 1994 cabinet reshuffle. Likewise, Muhammad al-Shaye was dismissed from his post on the Municipal Board. In 1996 the regime imposed stricter controls on the Brotherhood's financial resources, such as regulating the collection of alms in the mosques. The regime also dissolved consumer cooperatives, through which the Brotherhood had distributed food and medicine during the Iraqi invasion. In taking these measures, the regime could in part rely on the acquiescence of secular groups in Kuwait, who themselves had become worried about the Islamist camp's plans for the country.

Yet with these measures, the regime sought to tame the Brotherhood rather than completely destroy it.[24] In fact, after the 1996 elections, in which six Brothers won seats in the parliament,[25] the regime even appointed a figure close to the Brotherhood as a minister. Abdullah Rashid al-Hajri, who was endorsed by the ICM in the 1992 elections, became Minister of State for

---

23. Ghabra, 'Balancing state and society', p. 66; Also see Tétreault, *Stories of Democracy*, ch. 7.
24. In the 1990s the state and the Muslim Brotherhood also disagreed on the expansion of women's political rights in Kuwait. See al-Mughni, *Women in Kuwait*; Al-Mughni, 'The rise of Islamic feminism in Kuwait'.
25. This is according to the Kuwait Political Database. According to Tétreault, *Stories of Democracy*, pp. 177–81, eight Brothers competed in the election, six of them winning seats.

Housing.[26] In 1998 the regime made another gesture to the Brotherhood, appointing a Brother, Adil Khalid al-Subeih, as Minister of Health, who also served as the acting Minister of Education and Higher Education. Al-Subeih survived the cabinet reshuffles of 1999 and 2001: he served as the Minister of State for Housing and Minister of Electricity and Water from 1999 to 2001, becoming the Minister of Oil in 2001 and leaving the latter post in 2002.

However, as it rehabilitated its relations with the regime, the Brotherhood began to face setbacks in its electoral fortunes in the late 1990s. In the 1999 elections, four Brothers won seats in the parliament, even though thirteen competed in the elections.[27] In cooperation with other Islamists, the Brotherhood members passed another law that made segregation in higher educational institutions mandatory after Kuwait University failed to implement the previously prescribed law. The Brotherhood also succeeded in blocking legislation initiated by the ruler of Kuwait that gave women the right to vote.

But these successes did not help the Brotherhood in future elections. In 2003 only two Brothers made it into the parliament, even though eleven competed in the elections. This electoral failure triggered a leadership change in the ICM in 2003, the much younger Badir al-Nashi replacing Isa Majid al-Shahin as General Secretary.

The change in leadership might not have been motivated by this electoral defeat, however. The defeat came in the aftermath of the 9/11 attacks, in which the US became a victim of international terrorism led by al-Qaeda. In this period the US had not only invaded two countries it accused of supporting al-Qaeda, but also initiated an extensive campaign to trace financial sources of international terrorism. Al-Islah Society, and especially its affiliate, the Islamic Call Committee, were put under surveillance as the latter had engaged in some charities in places where al-Qaeda and its affiliates had operated, such as Chechnya and Central Asia. In fact, on the request of France, the UN added the Committee to its terrorist finance list. In January 2009 the

---

26. Both Tétreault and the Kuwait Political Database cite Abdullah al-Hajri among the Brothers who won seats in the parliament in the 1996 election.
27. According to Tétreault, *Stories of Democracy*, pp. 230–2, six Brothers won seats in the parliament in the 1999 election.

US also added the Committee to its list of organisations assisting or sponsoring support for terrorist acts.

Al-Islah Society also came under scrutiny. Fortunately for the Society, the US Embassy in Kuwait concluded in a cable, 'given the apparent lack of evidence on SRS [Social Reform Society] Kuwait complicity in terrorist finance ... we would not recommend the designation of the parent SRS operation in Kuwait at this stage'.[28] Yet the US continued to pressure the regime in Kuwait to scrutinise the charity's activities. To appease the US, Kuwait founded a special office, Charity Oversight and Supervision, within the Ministry of Social Affairs and Labour.

In this environment, the Brotherhood engaged in image-polishing activities. With a new and young leadership, the ICM could do this more persuasively. In the ensuing years, the ICM began to soften some of its policy stances. It continued to call for the implementation of the Islamic Shariah but it began to emphasise gradualism and voluntarism in the achievement of this objective.[29] The new ICM leader, Badir al-Nashi, declared in 2004 that he was not against women's rights and announced the ICM would consider its position on the matter. Yet the Brothers maintained their reservations. For example, even though Naser al-Sane, one of the Brothers who won a seat in the 2003 elections, spoke positively of women's rights, he also asked the government to be careful so that women did not undermine the traditions with any new rights.[30]

Al-Nashi likewise was concerned. He boasted that when the law granting women political rights came to the parliament, the ICM could add the phrase, 'according to the stipulations of sharia'. He explained, 'the aim of this addition was to ensure that the law did not violate the Islamic identity of Kuwaiti society. For example, there should be separate polling places for men and women, as well as a law criminalizing the abuse by women of the right to vote.'[31]

The change in leadership and a relative moderation in policy stances worked positively for the Brotherhood. In early 2006 a Brother, Ismail

28. 'Terrorist finance.'
29. Brown and Hamzawy, *Between Religion and Politics*.
30. Jamal, *Of Empires and Citizens*, p. 97.
31. Hamzawy, 'Interview with Dr Badr al Nashi, President of the Islamic Constitutional Movement'.

al-Shatti, entered the cabinet first as the Minister of Communications. A few months later he became the Minister of State for Affairs of the Council of Ministers and Deputy Prime Minister. More importantly, the Brotherhood increased its presence in parliament. In the elections in late 2006, Brotherhood candidates won six seats. To further expand its voter base, especially among women, the ICM established an office for women. It also worked on a law proposal that would expand women's social rights.

However, this approach did not pay off in the succeeding elections, as the Brotherhood continued to lose seats. The next election was held in 2008, after the ruler of Kuwait had dissolved the parliament. Nine Brothers competed but only four of them made it into parliament. This parliament was also dissolved a year later. In the 2009 elections, seven Brothers competed and only two of them won seats.

Nathan Brown and Amr Hamzawy claimed that the ICM's unstable political stances prior to the elections 'confused voters . . . In 2006, it stood strongly in the opposition. In the 2008 balloting, it posed as a movement above the fray. In 2009, it entered the campaign having brought on the elections by resigning suddenly from the government and launching strong criticisms against those with whom it had just sat.'[32] Holding itself responsible for the defeat, claimed Ikhwanweb.com, the official portal of the broader Muslim Brotherhood movement, the whole political bureau of the ICM, including Badir al-Nashi, submitted their resignations.[33]

State–Muslim Brotherhood relations also changed in the UAE. As outlined in Chapter 3, 1979 to 1983 were the golden years of the Brotherhood in the UAE. Two ministers were in the cabinet and many others were in influential posts in the education system. During these years the future leaders of the Brotherhood in the UAE, such as Muhammad al-Rukn and Muhammad al-Siddiqi, studied at the UAE University.[34]

---

32. See Brown and Hamzawy, *Between Religion and Politics*, p. 118.
33. 'HADAS political bureau resigns.'
34. Hasan al-Diqqi, one of the founders of al-Islah Society in the UAE also studied at the UAE University during this period. However, al-Diqqi withdrew from the Brotherhood in the late 1990s and adopted a more Salafi-orientated position. See Gümüşlüoğlu and Kurşun, 'Katar Krizi, Birleşik Arap Emirlikleri İhvan'ı ve Kilit Bir İsim'.

The Brotherhood's dominance did not go uncontested, however, as pan-Arabists continued their opposition in their newspapers such as *al-Khaleej*, owned by the Taryam Brothers. One critic, for example, asserted that the UAE University was no longer 'an Arab Islamic university' and had become 'purely an Islamic one' under Said Salman's management.[35] In another instance, *al-Khaleej* accused the Minister of Education of enforcing a curriculum that 'gave priority to the Islamic element in education'. The minister, *al-Khaleej* charged, had abolished 'national history and society as subjects' and even banned 'the daily flag-saluting ceremony as "idolatrous"'.[36]

This opposition paid off and three prominent Brothers, Said Salman, Muhammad Abd al-Rahman and Sultan bin Kayid, were dismissed from their positions in 1983.[37] A member of the Abu Dhabi ruling family and an Oxford graduate, Nahyan bin Mubarak Al Nahyan was appointed the new Chancellor of the UAE University. He served until 1990, when he became the Minister of Higher Education.

Under the leadership of Nahyan Al Nahyan, the UAE set out to reform its higher education, with the ultimate objective of expanding English as a medium of education. To this end, the UAE University started a foundation programme in 1988 so that students could improve their English, mathematics and Arabic before they moved to more advanced academic programmes. The UAE founded the Higher Colleges of Technology in 1988 and Zayed University in 1998, both under the leadership of Nahyan Al Nahyan. Most programmes were taught in English.

The UAE also targeted the rest of the state school system: Ahmad Humaid al-Tayer, who replaced Said Salman as the Minister of Education, not only transferred some twenty officials from the Curriculum Department to other posts, but also set out to reform the state schools' curriculum, which would

---

35. This critic was one of the six professors fired by Said Salman, the Minister of Education and the Chancellor of the University. See the discussion in Fyfe, *Wealth and Power*, p. 324.
36. Cited in ibid., p. 325.
37. After 1983, Said Abdullah Salman continued his studies in France and received a doctorate in law and humanities from the University of Paris II in 1986. In 1988 Said Abdullah became the founding President of Ajman University of Science and Technology, a position he still holds. See al-Sha'ir, 'D. Sa'id Salman Masirat 'Atirah fi khidmat al-'ilm wa'l mujtama".

promote 'a national as well as an Islamic allegiance'.[38] The overall impact of these steps was, intentionally or not, to decrease the 'Arab-Islamic' elements in education at all levels,[39] thus undermining the dominance of the Brothers in their influence on the educational system.

The Brothers fought to stop the transformation. For example, they portrayed the foundation programme as a plan to corrupt the 'morals and beliefs' of the students. The foundation courses would be a 'nest of depravity', in which 'foreign teachers would teach girls dancing and revolting against the morals and traditions of the society'.[40] Beyond the foundation programme, however, the Brotherhood in the UAE was concerned with broader issues, some strictly religious, such as the sale of alcohol, and some political, such as corruption in government spending.[41]

The Brotherhood's opposition failed to bring any substantial change in the UAE's overall direction. Illustrating the declining fortunes of the Brotherhood in the UAE, the Brothers' arch-rival, Abdullah Umran Taryam, was installed in 1990 as the Minister of Justice. A somewhat more radical act against the Brotherhood came in 1994 after the visit of Egyptian president Hosni Mubarak to the UAE. At that time Mubarak was waging his own fight against the Muslim Brotherhood and it is likely he accused the Emirati Muslim Brothers of supporting the Egyptian Muslim Brotherhood. However, it is difficult to confirm the link. But a year later the UAE disbanded the administrative council of al-Islah Society, forbidding the society to undertake any activity abroad and putting all branches of the Society under the supervision of the Ministry of Social Affairs.

This was undoubtedly a significant blow against the Emirati Muslim Brothers. But it was not a fatal one. The confederal system in the UAE greatly helped the Brothers escape the assault. Ras al-Khaimah's ruler, Sheikh Saqr bin Muhammad Al Qasimi, put al-Islah Society's branch in Ras al-Khaimah under his protection. In 1996, for example, he refused to hand over to the federal

---

38. Cited in Fyfe, *Wealth and power*, p. 327.
39. See Findlow, 'Higher education and linguistic dualism in the Arab Gulf' and Findlow, 'International networking in the United Arab Emirates higher-education system'.
40. Al-Nuqaidan, 'Al-Ikhwan al-Muslimun fi'l Imarat al-Tamaddad wa'l Inhisar', p. 116.
41. See the discussion in Freer, *Rentier Islamism*, pp. 99–103.

authorities a leading Emirati Muslim Brother, Muhammad al-Mansuri, even though an arrest warrant had been issued.[42] It is worth noting that al-Islah Society's Chairman in Ras al-Khaimah was a member of the ruling family, Sultan bin Kayid al-Qassimi.

However, it must be emphasised that the UAE did not intend to deal a fatal blow to the Brotherhood in the UAE. The UAE was ambivalent about what to do about the Brothers, rather than hostile towards them. The state even hoped that at some point reconciliation would be possible. To this end, for example, the crown prince of Abu Dhabi, Muhammad bin Zayed Al Nahyan, met with three leaders of the Brotherhood. However, this meeting did not bring about any substantial changes in relations.[43] The UAE rulers continued to suspect the Brothers. A cable sent from the US Embassy in Abu Dhabi argued, for example, that 'Sheikh Muhammad bin Zayed and his brothers Hamdan and Hazza rarely fail to tell high-level USG [the government of the US] interlocutors about the threat to stability posed by the "Muslim Brotherhood"'. The same cable even claimed that Muhammad bin Zayed, the crown prince of Abu Dhabi had said, 'we are having a (cultural) war with the "Muslim Brotherhood" in this country'.[44]

Throughout the 2000s the UAE acted in line with this thinking. The Brothers continued to find employment in state institutions, but not in critical state positions. There were also sporadic acts. Muhammad Al-Rukn, a leading figure in the Brotherhood in the UAE and a professor of law at the UAE University, was put on 'permanent sabbatical' in 2002 and 'banned from lecturing, publishing articles in UAE newspapers, and granting interviews to UAE journalists without prior government permission'.[45] In 2002 ninety expatriate Arab teachers were forced to retire or reassigned to non-teaching jobs.[46] In 2007 some eighty teachers were reassigned from the Ministry of Education to other ministries even though they were UAE citizens. According to two of the teachers, a cable reported, they were reassigned to 'marginal' jobs because

42. See the discussion in Freer, *Rentier Islamism*, pp. 99–103.
43. Al-Nuqaidan, 'Al-Ikhwan al-Muslimun fi'l Imarat al-Tamaddad wa'l-Inhisar'. See also Freer, *Rentier Islamism*, ch. 6.
44. 'UAE minimizing influence of Islamist extremists.'
45. 'UAE activist attempts to open independent human rights NGO.'
46. 'UAE activist attempts to open independent human rights NGO.'

they were members of al-Islah Society.⁴⁷ The same cable reported the Minister of Cabinet Affairs as saying that the UAE was facing an Islamist threat 'that stemmed from the late seventies and early eighties when an Islamist served as Minister of Education [Saed Abdullah Salman] and brought a number of religious conservatives into the Educational apparatus'.⁴⁸

During the same period, the Brotherhood in the UAE also developed its oppositional discourse, emphasising the rule of law, demanding respect for human rights, calling for expansion of political participation and criticising corruption and other political malpractices. This change in emphasis is best illustrated in the person of Muhammad Al-Rukn, for whom the institutionalisation of the 'rule of law' in the country was a crucial tool for the achievement of democratic, economic and social justice. Al-Rukn claimed that the federal UAE constitution recognised the political and civil rights of all UAE citizens but was either bypassed by the national security measures adopted by the regime or non-supported by the necessary laws. By the beginning of the Arab Spring, therefore, the Brotherhood's discourse as propagated by figures like Muhammed Al-Rukn became not purely religious but also political. In the development of this discourse the Brothers were not alone, but were joined by other intellectuals and academics who necessarily did not belong to the movement.⁴⁹

State–Muslim Brotherhood relations also changed in Saudi Arabia. Nineteen seventy-nine was truly dramatic and tumultuous for Saudi Arabia as it witnessed not only the Iranian revolution but also the Juhayman al-Utaybi incident in Mecca. Both events questioned the religious legitimacy of the ruling family. The leader of the Iranian revolution, Ruhullah Khomeini, was particularly harsh about Saudi Arabia and often criticised its ruling family, Al Saud. For Khomeini, the US was the 'great Satan' and Saudi Arabia was its puppet. Khomeini targeted not just Saudi Arabia's alliance with the US, but also criticised and insulted its ruling family, its clerics and its understanding

---

47. 'Ministry of Education dismissed eighty-three Emirati teachers.'
48. 'Ministry of Education dismissed eighty-three Emirati teachers.'
49. See al-Zoby and Başkan, 'Discourse of oppositionality in the Arab Spring'. This change in the Brotherhood's discourse in the UAE was not a disconnected instance, but rather part of the broader changes the Brotherhood and other Islamist groups in the region adopted. See, for example, Baker, *Islam without Fear*; Bayat, *Making Islam Democratic*.

of religion. Reflecting his view of Al Saud family, Khomeini declared in his testament written in 1983:

> Malik Fahd [the king of Saudi Arabia] spends enormous sums of people's wealth on publishing the Holy Qur'an and propagating an anti-Qur'anic religion, that is this totally baseless and superstitious religion of Wahhabism, and leads the uninformed and unaware peoples to the superpowers whilst they exploit the beloved Islam and the Holy Qur'an to destroy both Islam and the Qur'an.

Khomeini expressed this hatred in the clearest way possible: 'Al Saud, these traitors to the greatest Divine Sanctuary, upon whom be the maledictions of Allah and His Angels.'[50]

The Juhayman al-Utaybi incident was home-grown. Juhayman al-Utaybi was the leader of a group that took over the Grand Mosque in Mecca and held it for a number of weeks with the pilgrims inside. Al-Utaybi questioned Al Saud's fitness to rule on several grounds, such as the family's failure to wage religious wars and its alliance with foreigners. He also criticised Wahhabi religious scholars for supporting the family.

In response to both events, the regime in Saudi Arabia took measures seeking to boost its religious legitimacy. To this end, it became more supportive of the Muslim Brotherhood-inspired Sahwa movement. With the regime's continued support, the Sahwa movement began to direct its criticisms against secular groups that had benefited from state largess in the 1970s.[51]

A dissertation written by a leading Sahwa figure, Safar al-Hawali, was emblematic of the attacks on secular groups and religious scholars. Written under the supervision of a well-known Brotherhood figure, Muhammad al-Qutb, the dissertation stated that Islam, which was supposed to regulate all fields of human life, had receded into irrelevance, to which secular groups had contributed.[52] Awad al-Qarni's book, *al-Hadatha fi Mizan al-Islam* (Modernity on the Scale of Islam), and Said al-Ghamdi's various lectures, both from

---

50. Cited in Marschall, *Iran's Persian Gulf Policy*, p. 48.
51. See the discussion in Lacroix, *Awakening Islam*, ch. 4.
52. For a detailed discussion, see Lav, *Radical Islam and the Revival of Medieval Theology*, ch. 4

the same period, likewise targeted secular groups 'and accused them of undermining the Islamic foundations of Saudi society'.[53]

It was difficult to guess whether the Sahwa movement would eventually direct its criticisms against Al Saud's regime and the Wahhabi religious scholars. It certainly criticised the latter but its criticisms either remained implicit or were made in private circles. Only after Iraq's invasion of Kuwait in August 1990 did the Sahwa movement become publicly critical.

The triggering event was Saudi Arabia's invitation to the US to defend its territories against a possible Iraqi attack and to expel Iraq from Kuwait. Within six months, half a million American soldiers were stationed in the territories of Saudi Arabia. Even though the Saudi regime secured the support of high-ranking Wahhabi religious scholars, it could not escape the criticism raised both abroad and at home. A delegation of leading Muslim Brothers, Hasan al-Turabi of Sudan, Rashid al-Ghannushi from Tunisia, Muhammad Abd al-Rahman Khalifa from Jordan and Abd al-Majid al-Zindani from Yemen, joined by an Islamist party leader, Necmettin Erbakan from Turkey, first visited Saudi Arabia and then Iraq. Their statement at the conclusion of their visit to Iraq was supportive of Saddam Hussein: it praised his steadfastness and condemned foreign forces whose objective was to 'destroy the Iraqi military forces in order to serve the Zionist scheme and to enable Israel to absorb citizens from the Soviet Union so it can strike against the intifada'.[54]

More troublesome was that the Sahwa movement began to criticise the regime in Saudi Arabia for relying on and creating an alliance with the US: leading figures such as Awad al-Qarni, Safar al-Hawali and Salman al-Awdah devoted their lectures and sermons to this cause, their speeches being recorded on tape and then distributed throughout the Kingdom. The 1991 incident when some forty Saudi women drove their cars in Riyadh, Saudi Arabia's support for the peace talks between Palestine and Israel, and what came to be known as the Liberal Petition, which demanded a diminished role for religious scholars in Saudi Arabia, further galvanised the Sahwa leaders.

All this culminated in an unprecedented development. Shortly after Kuwait was liberated, a number of Sahwa leaders penned a letter of demands

---

53. Fandy, *Saudi Arabia and the Politics of Dissent*, p. 48.
54. Cited in Pargeter, *The Muslim Brotherhood*, p. 121.

from the Saudi regime. This was circulated throughout the country and gained the signatures of more than four hundred mostly religious figures. It was submitted to the king in May 1991. A year later, in July 1992, 107 religious figures signed a document known as the Memorandum of Advice, forty pages detailing their demands, and submitted it to the King.

Both the letter and the Memorandum demanded total Islamisation in Saudi Arabia, from laws to the legal system, from the economy to international relations. As such, they reflected the Brotherhood's view of Islam as a total religion. Both documents were critical of the place afforded to religion in the political system of Saudi Arabia. The Kingdom's reliance on the US was just one problem. For example, religious scholars had a minimal role in the running of the state and had no independence from the regime. Second, not all the laws of Saudi Arabia conformed to the Islamic law, which should have regulated all sorts of relations, individual, societal and international. Accordingly, the country had a dual court system, religious and secular, which needed to be corrected. Both documents also asked for a more Islamic foreign policy: Saudi Arabia had 'to support all Islamic states and groups and to cut off the kingdom's relations with states hostile to Islam', such as the US.[55]

The regime reacted to the demands. Immediately after the letter was submitted, all signatories were detained and interrogated. Some were even held in jail temporarily. Unable to stem the tide of criticism, the regime began to implement a more comprehensive counter-campaign, such as firing university professors and mosque preachers who were critical of the regime and jailing the more outspoken leaders of the movement. The regime also received the support of high-ranking religious scholars and mobilised other anti-Sahwa religious groups to counter the Sahwa movement. By 1995 the Sahwa challenge to the regime in Saudi Arabia was basically over. Some of the leading figures, such as Safar al-Hawali, Awad al-Qarni and Salman al-Awdah, were in jail; others, such as Saad al-Faqih and Muhammad al-Massari, escaped from Saudi Arabia and settled elsewhere.[56]

---

55. See Fandy, *Saudi Arabia and the Politics of Dissent*, p. 59. See a lengthier discussion of the letter and the memorandum at pp. 50–60 in the same source.
56. See Teitelbaum, *Holier than Thou*.

Beyond the ideological incompatibility, what might also have driven the Sahwa movement into opposition against the regime in Saudi Arabia is debatable. A plausible explanation[57] is that, unlike other Gulf states, Saudi Arabia had a native class of religious scholars. Over the course of modern state building Saudi Arabia had extensively employed them in staffing its expanding religious, educational and judicial institutions. As discussed in Chapter 1, this class originated in Najd and drew its members from this region's largest tribes. When the kingdom expanded and came to control such regions as Hasa, Hijaz and Asir, the Wahhabi religious scholars from Najd continued to dominate the religious field, formed the upper levels of this class and controlled the top echelons of the religious component of the political system and the state in Saudi Arabia.

There might have been exceptions, but the opposition figures who had been inspired by or affiliated with the Brotherhood in Saudi Arabia came predominantly from regions such as Hijaz or Hasa, and therefore might not have shared much hope in any upward mobility in either the secular or religious components of the political system given the dominance of religious figures from Najd.

There were Brotherhood figures who came from Najd, too. Whether they were involved in the Sahwa opposition depended on their ideological orientation and relative position in the system. Salman al-Awdah, for example, came from the Najd region and received his education at Imam Muhammad bin Saud University in Riyadh. But when he took part in the Sahwa opposition he was merely a teacher in his native town, Buraidah. Abdullah al-Turki was also from Najd; he studied at the Shariah College in Riyadh, which later became Imam Muhammad bin Saud University. Al-Turki was also a student of a famous Brotherhood figure, Mana al-Qattan. But, unlike al-Awdah, al-Turki was quickly promoted: soon after he received his doctorate in 1972, he became the Provost of Imam Muhammad bin Saud University in 1975 and later became its president. Even after the Sahwa opposition became public, al-Turki continued to be promoted and in 1995 became the Minister of Islamic Affairs and Waqfs. Having also served in the Muslim World League and contributed greatly to the Brotherhood's activities in Europe, al-Turki became the

---

57. For a lengthier discussion, see Lacroix, *Awakening Islam*.

General Secretary of the Muslim World League in 2000, a post he had held until 2016. But the age difference between al-Awdah and al-Turki must be noted. The prospect of upward mobility was lower in the 1990s than it was in the 1970s. Therefore, al-Turki had better opportunities than al-Awdah.

Having successfully dealt with the Sahwa challenge, Saudi Arabia began to face an even more formidable opposition in the second half of the 1990s, in the person of Osama bin Laden. Born in Jeddah in 1957 into a wealthy business family originally from Yemen, Osama bin Laden passed through the Saudi educational system and was influenced by the Brotherhood ideology. In the early 1980s, he embraced the Afghan cause or religious war, jihad, against the invading Soviet Union, a cause both the US and Saudi Arabia supported. By the end of the decade, Osama bin Laden was the leading figure of those Arabs who participated in the Afghan jihad, bringing them into one organisation, al-Qaeda.

After a transitional period during which he left Afghanistan and initially settled in Saudi Arabia then eventually in Sudan, Osama bin Laden first became critical of Saudi Arabia. In 1994, after he was stripped of his citizenship, bin Laden expressed his support for the then ongoing Sahwa opposition and even established a separate organisation to this end. Bin Laden eventually selected the US as his prime enemy. In 1996 he declared religious war against Americans in Saudi Arabia. In 1998 he extended this to all Americans: he announced that killing any American was an individual religious duty for every Muslim 'who can do it in any country in which it is possible to do it'.[58]

Al-Qaeda undertook increasingly daring and lethal attacks on US targets, but all outside the States. It eventually hit the US at home on 11 September 2001, killing and wounding thousands of civilians.

Al-Qaeda also posed security challenges to Saudi Arabia, undertaking, for example, two lethal attacks against Americans inside the kingdom in 1995 and 1996. But its targeting of the US was also troubling for Saudi Arabia. Particularly, the monstrous 9/11 attacks raised the question of Saudi Arabia's role in the whole al-Qaeda phenomenon, as fifteen of the nineteen militants who undertook the attacks were citizens of Saudi Arabia, and Osama bin Laden, the leader of al-Qaeda, was an ex-Saudi citizen.

---

58. See World Islamic Front, 'Jihad Against Jews and Crusaders'.

In the aftermath of the 9/11 attacks, Saudi Arabia faced harsh criticism from Washington, DC and other world capitals.[59] A briefing from the influential US-based RAND Corporation think tank, for example, submitted to a top Pentagon advisory board, described Saudi Arabia as 'the kernel of evil, the prime mover, the most dangerous opponent in the Middle East'. Being a major supporter of terrorism, the briefing suggested, Saudi Arabia was an enemy of the US.[60] A task force of the reputable Council on Foreign Relations likewise raised harsh criticisms, concluding, for example, 'for years, individuals and charities based in Saudi Arabia have been the most important source of funds for Al-Qaeda. And for years, Saudi officials have turned a blind eye to this problem.'[61]

Saudi Arabia's strategy to counter the challenge al-Qaeda had unleashed was multi-pronged. It first sought to rehabilitate the Sahwa movement. By the end of the 1990s the regime had released almost all Sahwa figures from jail. In return the regime expected them not to engage in any political activism critical of the regime and thus respect the division of labour between the religious scholars and the rulers. In the words of Madawi al-Rasheed,

> After almost a decade of confrontation, Sahwis and the state reached a modus vivendi. Sahwis accepted the old schism between the secular state and the religious coterie. They retreated into their educational programmes, thus socialising society into Islam while leaving politics to the government. Today they concentrate on healing society and its ills . . . they blame society's ignorance, tribalism, corruption, regionalism, opportunism and other negative traits for social problems . . . Sahwis have moved from blaming the regime for the ills of society to blaming society itself, as a way out of a dilemma. Reforming society is today an alternative to reforming the state.[62]

By rehabilitating the Sahwa leaders, the regime aimed to diminish the attractiveness of al-Qaeda among Saudi Arabia's youth. This strategy partly

---

59. See Peterson, 'Saudi–American relations after 11 September 2001'; Bahgat, 'Saudi Arabia and the war on terrorism'; Ottaway, 'The king and us'.
60. Ricks, 'Briefing depicted Saudis as enemies'.
61. Cited in Gause III, *The International Relations of the Persian Gulf*, p. 145.
62. Al-Rasheed, *Contesting the Saudi State*, p. 96.

worked. A religious group grew out of the Sahwa movement and embraced the message of al-Qaeda, even forming a branch of al-Qaeda known as Al-Qaeda in the Arabian Peninsula. But the group didn't flourish. Saudi Arabia also garnered the support of leading Sahwa figures such as Safar al-Hawali and Salman al-Awdah, who denounced violence in the name of religion.[63]

The regime needed the help of these figures to counter al-Qaeda even more after two leading and respected members of the official religious establishment, Abd al-Aziz bin Baz, the Grand Mufti, and Muhammad al-Uthaymin, a member of the Committee of Senior Religious Scholars, died in 1999 and 2001 respectively. They left such a vacuum in the religious field that the official Wahhabi scholars could not fill it.[64]

This was an opportunity that the leading Sahwa figures had long been looking for. They would be technically independent since they would not occupy any official position. Yet they would act from a position of great religious authority and, more importantly, were to be treated as such by the regime.

Part of Saudi Arabia's strategy to counter the criticisms that linked it to international terrorism was to 'absolve the regime and its Wahhabi foundation from any responsibility'.[65] Instead, the Muslim Brotherhood and its ideology were presented as the culprit. In the best-known case, Prince Nayef, who was by then Minister of Interior of Saudi Arabia, said: 'All our problems come from the Muslim Brotherhood. We have given too much support to this group . . . The Muslim Brotherhood has destroyed the Arab world', and added: 'Whenever they got into difficulty or found their freedom restricted in their own countries, Brotherhood activists found refuge in the Kingdom which protected their lives . . . But they later turned against the Kingdom.'[66]

Prince Nayef was not alone. Many others both inside and outside Saudi Arabia accused the Muslim Brotherhood and its ideology of inspiring domestic and international terrorism. A Wikileaks document on the meetings the US Commission on International Religious Freedom held in Saudi Arabia noted that two high-ranking Saudi officials, the Assistant Minister of Foreign

---

63. See the discussion in al-Rasheed, *Contesting the Saudi State*, pp. 83–6.
64. Al-Rasheed, *Contesting the Saudi State*, p.81.
65. Al-Rasheed, *Contesting the Saudi State*, p.80.
66. 'Naif say Muslim Brotherhood cause of most Arab problems.'

Affairs and the Minister of Culture and Information, likewise blamed the Brotherhood for perpetuating 'intolerant and hateful thoughts and ideas'[67] in the country. Another Wikileaks document mentioned a Vice Dean for Academic Research at Imam Muhammad University telling his guests from the US Embassy in Riyadh that the Brotherhood figures who escaped from Egypt and settled in Saudi Arabia had educated 'the current generation of radical fundamentalists'.[68]

International media also linked international terrorism to the Brotherhood ideology. An article published in the *Guardian*, for example, called Sayyid Qutb, who inspired the Brotherhood in Saudi Arabia, 'the father of modern Islamist fundamentalism' and even claimed, 'the most useful insights into the shaping of Bin Laden may lie not in the rugged mountains of Afghanistan, or the rampant materialism of 1970s Saudi Arabia, but the biography of a long dead Egyptian fundamentalist scholar called Sayyid Qutb'.[69]

In order to ward off increasing criticism both at home and abroad and to prove their innocence, the leading figures of the Sahwa movement accepted the role the regime expected them to play, to denounce violence in the name of religion. In May 2003, for example, immediately after an al-Qaeda attack inside Saudi Arabia, a number of Sahwa figures condemned the attacks and called the perpetrators 'ignorant and misguided young men'.[70] The Sahwa figures continued to issue similar statements in the succeeding years and played a critical role in de-legitimising al-Qaeda, thus contributing to the weakening of al-Qaeda's branch in Saudi Arabia.[71] A Wikileaks cable penned by the US Ambassador to Riyadh, Ford Fraker, noted, for example, that Saudi Arabia's Ministry of Interior considered two Sahwa figures, Safar al-Hawali and Salman al-Awdah, 'instrumental' in the 'War of Ideas' the Ministry was waging to discredit al-Qaeda.[72]

---

67. 'May 27–June 5, 2007 visit by US Commission on International Religious Freedom to Saudi Arabia.'
68. 'Ambassador's dinner with "Enlightened Conservative" religious figures.'
69. Irwin, 'Is this the man who inspired Bin Laden?'
70. Al-Rasheed, *Contesting the Saudi State*, p. 83.
71. See Ansary, 'Combatting extremism'. See also Lacroix, *Awakening Islam*; Al-Rasheed, *Contesting the Saudi State*.
72. 'Terrorist finance: Designation of five Saudis.'

Throughout the 2000s the leading Sahwa figures walked a tightrope. On the one hand they distanced themselves from al-Qaeda-led international jihadism and worked to dissociate themselves from it. On the other hand they were not too subservient to the regime of which they had been previously so critical. At the same time, they avoided a total confrontation with the regime. To this end they carefully chose the topics on which to express their opinions, speaking more unreservedly, for example, about international developments than domestic issues.[73]

Maintaining Friendly Attitudes towards the Muslim Brotherhood: Bahrain and Qatar

The Muslim Brotherhood has not become oppositional in Bahrain. This is in large part because, among all the Gulf states, Bahrain was particularly exposed to the 1979 Iranian revolution. The revolution and Khomeini's fiery rhetoric generated a new political activism among the Shia population in Bahrain, where they constituted the majority and saw themselves as the original inhabitants of the island, with the Sunnis as the usurpers.[74] The whole regional context was also worrisome for the regime in Bahrain, as the Shias in Kuwait and Saudi Arabia also went onto the streets in protest.

In response to the emboldened Shias, Bahrain sought to consolidate its support base among the Sunnis and to this end encouraged the Islamist groups, not only the Muslim Brothers but also the Salafis. Even before the Iranian revolution, the Brotherhood's al-Islah Club began to recover its vibrancy. In 1975, for example, it opened its first Qur'an learning centre. In 1980 the club was renamed and became Jam'iyyat al-Islah (the Reform Society) or al-Islah Society. As the old headquarters became unsuitable for the needs of the Society, in 1983 the Brothers opened a new and more spacious building, with sport facilities and lecture halls. Reflecting the regime's support of the Society, the opening ceremony was held under the auspices of the ruler of Bahrain, Isa bin Salman Al Khalifa. Moreover, the ceremony was attended by the ruler, the crown prince and future king, Hamad bin Isa, and the prime minister, Khalifa bin Salman. A number of prominent Islamist figures from the Gulf

---

73. See al-Rasheed, *Contesting the Saudi State*, ch. 2.
74. See Louër, *Transnational Shia Politics*.

also attended the opening. One of them was Yusuf al-Qaradawi, a prominent Brotherhood figure, originally from Egypt, but a naturalised citizen of Qatar.[75] Recollecting the event, al-Qaradawi described it as 'a wedding day for Bahrain' and reported that he congratulated the king for what he had done for the Islamic mission.[76]

Over the next three decades al-Islah Society expanded its activities and membership base. It organised lectures delivered by prominent Islamist figures, began to publish a magazine named after the Society, and engaged in charity activities both in and outside Bahrain. The Society opened more Qur'an centres. As of 2010, it was operating more than twenty, employing around 150 teachers and accommodating up to a thousand pupils.[77] In addition to its Qur'an centres, the Society also expanded its influence to mosques, operating over fifty across Bahrain by 2012.[78]

As the popularity of secular ideologies and movements declined in Bahrain, the Society attracted new members from the Sunnis: not only figures from such business families as Jamil, al-Mir and Kuhaji, but also professionals such as teachers, public servants and university professors, joined the Society through the mid-1970s.[79] Reflecting its expanding activities and membership base, the Society opened several new branches in towns across Bahrain from 1983.[80]

---

75. For a comprehensive look into Yusuf al-Qaradawi's life and ideas, see Graf and Skovgaard-Petersen, *Global Mufti*.
76. See al-Qaradawi, 'Iftitah Mabna Jam'iyyat al-Islah bi al-Bahrain'.
77. '250 to vie for Quran honours.'
78. 'Banks back al-Islah in distributing their CSR allocations during Ramadan.'
79. The Administrative Council of al-Islah Society in 2011 illustrates this diversity. Isa bin Muhammad was still President; three other members of the Board of Directors were Abd al-Aziz Jalal al-Mir, Muhammad Abdullah Jamil and Muhammad Abd al-Wahid al-Kuhaji. Among the members of al-Islah who served on the committees, Hashim Muhammad al-Madani was a professor at the University of Bahrain, as was Raid Ibrahim al-Jawdar. Abd al-Aziz Muhammad al-Madfai was Director of a high school in Bahrain, Hasan Yusuf al-Hammadi was a senior director of government schools reviews in the Ministry of Education, and Hashim Yusuf Satar was a public servant in the Ministry of Interior. See *al-Islah Magazine*, No. 175, March 2011, p. 6.
80. In 2011 the Society had branches in Hadd, Muharraq, Manama, Madinat Isa, Rifa and Madinat Hamad.

Despite the visible activism and increasing influence of the Brotherhood in Bahrain, this had not troubled the regime. Relations between the two remained on good terms. This was in part because the Society's president was a member of the ruling family, Isa bin Muhammad Al Khalifa, who possibly kept the Society loyal to the regime. It was also critical that the regime continued to have the Shia problem throughout the 1990s and 2000s. In the mid-1990s, for example, Bahrain witnessed massive street protests led by the Shias, which took the country hostage on and off for almost five years. In such an environment the Brotherhood could have exposed the regime, which was not only Sunni but also supportive of the Brotherhood, to an existential threat if it had joined the Shia-dominated opposition. Not surprisingly, the Brotherhood did not join the opposition.[81]

The protests subsided when the ruler died of a heart attack in 1999. The new ruler, Hamad bin Isa, was relatively young, forty-nine, and, as hoped by many, promised reforms. To this end, the new ruler issued a general amnesty for political prisoners and exiles, and abolished the State Security Law and State Security Court. More importantly, he formed a forty-six-member committee to draft the National Action Charter, which was to become Bahrain's constitution after its approval.[82]

The charter was subjected to a referendum in 2001 and overwhelmingly approved by the Bahrainis, both Sunnis and Shias. A year later, the ruler signed the charter, making it the constitution. However, especially the Shia political groups soon objected. This was because the constitution envisioned a bicameral system. Only the lower house was to be elected through direct and free elections. The upper house, on the other hand, was to be appointed by the ruler and would have considerable legislative powers. More critically, the constitution stated that the parliament could not propose amendments to the monarchical and bicameral nature of the political system.[83]

The Brotherhood in Bahrain continued to be pro-regime in the new constitutional period. One of their own, the long-standing president of al-Islah

---

81. See Fakhro, 'The uprising in Bahrain: An assessment'.
82. Bahrain had a constitution enacted by the ruler in 1973. But the ruler abrogated it in 1975 and the country had been ruled under emergency laws.
83. See Wright, 'Fixing the Kingdom: Political evolution and socio-economic challenges in Bahrain.'

Society, Isa bin Muhammed Al Khalifa, was appointed by the new ruler to the committee that drafted the National Action Charter. The Brotherhood formed a political organisation, Islamic Platform or Jam'iyyat al-Minbar al-Watani al-Islami (the Society of National Islamic Platform) or al-Minbar, in March 2002 and participated in the first elections under the new constitution held in October 2002. The Shias' leading organisations boycotted the elections, criticising the constitution on the grounds that the upper house, appointed by the ruler, also had legislative powers.

The Brotherhood declared its allegiance to the 2002 constitution, an act that the Salafis refrained from on the grounds that the Qur'an was their only source of law.[84] The Brotherhood even became an advocate of the constitution. For example, it organised a seminar with Bahrain's National Democratic Institute on the constitution. It is telling that a major Shia political group, Jam'iyyat al-Wifaq al-Watani al-Islamiyya (the Concord National Islamic Society) or al-Wifaq, boycotted the seminar on the grounds that the constitution was illegitimate. In the seminar, two members of the Brotherhood made presentations: al-Minbar's president, Salah Ali Muhammad, and al-Islah's president and a board member of al-Minbar, Isa bin Muhammad Al Khalifa. The seminar's objective was to illustrate that the constitution gave the National Assembly 'ample legislative authority'.[85]

By declaring its allegiance to the constitution and even defending it, the Brotherhood in Bahrain lent legitimacy to the regime and its reform efforts. The support from al-Minbar was critical especially for the new ruler of Bahrain, Hamad bin Isa. However limited they might be, his reforms still 'created a climate of hope'. The Brotherhood in Bahrain helped to create that climate, which the new ruler desperately needed. As Wehrey noted, in such a climate 'groups that otherwise might have been inspired toward radicalism by the unfolding events in Iraq and the rise of Iran were effectively "nationalized" and developed vested stakes in the Bahraini political project'.[86]

The Brotherhood's support was also critical because at the time the new ruler was also seeking to appease the US in the latter's war on terrorism. Bahrain contributed a frigate to the US-led international military campaign against al-Qaeda and the Taliban regime in Afghanistan, even winning the praise of the Bush administration. In return for this small but symbolically significant contribution, the US president George W. Bush designated

---

84. Wehrey, *Sectarian Politics in the Gulf*, p. 62.
85. 'NDI tackles the 2002 Constitution.'
86. Wehrey, *Sectarian Politics in the Gulf*, p. 64.

Bahrain a major non-NATO ally. Bahrain also made a similar contribution to the US-led military campaign that toppled the Saddam regime in Iraq.[87]

Embroiling Bahrain in such highly controversial US-led campaigns against two Muslim countries, the ruler of Bahrain exposed himself to criticism at home, especially from the Islamists. But the Brotherhood in Bahrain kept its silence, even though it organised massive street protests against the US in Egypt, for example.

The only issue that the Brotherhood in Bahrain raised in the succeeding years that was embarrassing for the regime was the issue of Bahrainis held by the US in Guantanamo. A member of al-Minbar, Muhammad Khalid Ibrahim, was openly critical of the US to the extent that, according to a Wikileaks document, he refused to meet US officials and called for the release of Bahraini detainees in Guantanamo.[88] Yet this seems to have been Muhammad Khalid's personal choice, not a position taken by all al-Minbar members. The same Wikileaks document in fact described the chairman of al-Minbar, Salah Ali Muhammad, as 'moderate' and 'a prominent advocate for the rights of women and children'.

There were other issues to which the Brotherhood in Bahrain turned a blind eye. For example, Khalifa bin Salman Al Khalifa, who had been the prime target of criticism from the opposition in Bahrain, continued to occupy the position of prime minister. There was widespread corruption in Bahrain, and the bicameral system, with an appointed upper house, could effectively block any initiative started in the lower house. More scandalously, a report, known as the Bandar Report, exposed in 2006 that the regime was actively engineering ways to marginalise the Shias in parliament. The report implicated several figures sympathetic to or affiliated with al-Islah Society and al-Minbar.[89]

---

87. 'Bahrain', p. 232.
88. 'Survey of parliamentary blocs.'
89. According to the report, the leadership ring consisted of five figures working directly under the Minister of Cabinet for State Affairs, Ahmad Ateyatallah al Khalifa. Three of them were claimed to have either sympathy for or affiliation with al-Islah and al-Minbar. They were Dr Raid Muhammad Abdullah al-Shams, Muhammad Ali Muhammad al-Qaid and Jamal Yusuf Muhammad al-Asiri, who was a former editor of *al-Islah Magazine*. The report, prepared by Salah al-Bandar, an advisor to the Ministry of Cabinet for State Affairs, is available in both English and Arabic at http://www.bahrainrights.org/en/node/528.

The Brotherhood in Bahrain did not speak out on any of these controversial issues, even though it had every opportunity to embarrass the regime, al-Minbar having won in the 2002 election seven seats out of the forty in the parliament. Its rival Salafi group, Jam'iyyat al-Asalah al-Islamiyya (the Islamic Authenticity Society) or al-Asalah, won five seats. Despite the doctrinal differences, the two groups cooperated in the parliament, forming, in the absence of any other organised group, a powerful bloc. On at least two occasions al-Minbar and al-Asalah forced the government to be more careful about religious sensitivities in Bahrain. In 2004, for example, they prevented the shooting of a reality television show in Bahrain, accusing the programme makers of allowing young men and women to stay in the same house. The next year, the government banned alcohol in restaurants and five-star hotels in large part to appease the two Islamist groups.

Despite the protests and violence that erupted over the findings of the Bandar Report, the Shia political groups did not boycott the 2006 elections. The largest of them, al-Wifaq, won seventeen seats. Al-Minbar secured seven seats again and al-Asalah eight. With another eight seats won by independent Islamists, the parliament was divided into two sectarian halves. The ongoing street protests led by the Shias did not help, further polarising the parliament.

However, an opportunity emerged for both sides to work together in the new parliament. The government had failed to proceed with twenty-five laws passed by the previous parliament, which had been dominated by the Sunni political groups. This practically meant that the government had vetoed those laws. The Sunni Islamist deputies, one of whom was al-Minbar's Muhammad Khalid, accused the government of dismissing the parliament. But this opportunity was lost despite an initial attempt to form an informal committee to work on the vetoed laws.[90]

The Shias and Sunnis in the parliament were deeply divided on how far to go in challenging the regime. Later in the parliamentary term, al-Wifaq moved to call into question Ahmad bin Atiyatallah concerning his involvement in activities documented by the Bandar Report. This move was defeated in parliament by the Sunni groups. In reaction, the Sunni groups put forward their own motion, calling into question a Shia minister, Mansur bin Rajab,

---

90. 'Al-Wifaq courts Sunnis and government, but risks Shia impatience.'

on charges of corruption. Al-Wifaq made other attempts in the parliament and even sought to reach out to the Sunni groups. But all attempts failed.[91]

Despite al-Wifaq failing to bring any tangible change in the system throughout its second term, it still scored an electoral victory in the 2010 election: all of its eighteen candidates won but still failed to form a majority in the parliament. Previously serving as the regime's bulwark, both al-Minbar and al-Asalah significantly lost in the elections. Al-Minbar competed for eight seats but won only two of them. al-Asalah also contested eight seats but won only three. The independents, on the other hand, won seventeen seats.

Al-Wifaq was hopeful that it could achieve more in the new parliament. As an al-Wifaq deputy, Abd al-Jalil Khalil noted, the parliament had 'a cocktail of independents . . . so coming up with a united front for them is highly unlikely although possible'.[92] Yet the regime soon reacted, by shutting down al-Wifaq's newspaper, *al-Wasat*, and cracking down on other media outlets. Bahrain's prime minister even called for regional cooperation to fight what he called 'cyber terror'. But as Frederic Wefrey noted, by doing so the regime handed the Shia information sphere to 'a younger cadre of unlicensed, informal activists', who 'were savvier in the use of Facebook and Twitter, which connected them to activists in Tunisia, Egypt, and, to a lesser extent, Libya'.[93] In other words, the regime undermined the very group, al-Wifaq, that could have played a moderating role when massive protests erupted in Bahrain on 14 February 2011.

Like Bahrain, Qatar also maintained its prior friendly relations towards the Brotherhood. This was the case despite the fact that Qatar was more similar to the UAE than to Bahrain. Like the UAE, Qatar did not have a sizeable Shia opposition. Furthermore, like the UAE, Qatar also undertook educational reforms that might have generated an Islamist opposition. In the geopolitical context shaped by the global and regional religious resurgence, Qatar continued to employ Brothers in its state institutions and even provided new opportunities. Kamal Naji, for example, continued to be employed in the Ministry of Education as the Foreign Cultural Relations Advisor to the minister after he

---

91. See Wefrey, *Sectarian Politics in the Gulf*, pp. 67–8.
92. Cited in al-A'ali, 'Independents the biggest winners'.
93. Wehrey, *Sectarian Politics in the Gulf*, p. 75.

stepped down as the Director of Education in 1979. Kamal Naji later became the Director of the Center for Muslim Contribution to the Civilisation and remained in the post until his death in 1997. The Center was founded in 1983 by, and named after, Muhammad bin Hamad Al Thani, the brother of the then emir, Khalifa bin Hamad, and the Minister of Education.[94]

Yusuf al-Qaradawi, who founded the College of Shariah and Islamic Studies at Qatar University, served as the Dean until 1990. He continued to be affiliated with it as he went on to serve as the Director of the Center for Sirah [the life of the Prophet] and Sunnah [the Traditions of the Prophet] Research, which he founded in 1980. Yusuf al-Qaradawi also served on the founding Board of Trustees of the Center for Muslim Contribution to the Civilisation, which also included another prominent Brother, Izz al-Din Ibrahim from the UAE.[95]

The only setback for the Brotherhood in this period was that in 1986 the Presidency of Shariah Courts and Religious Affairs stopped the publication of the journal, *al-Ummah*. First published in 1980, it was put under the editorship of a Syrian Muslim Brother, Umar Ubaid Hasanah.[96] and gave a precious opportunity to the Brotherhood in Qatar to spread its message.[97]

It is not clear whether there was any pressure from the state to stop the publication. The announcement provided no reason, just stating that it was 'due to some circumstances'.[98] The most likely reason is that due to falling

---

94. The Centre still functions as the Muhammed bin Hamad Centre for Muslim Contribution to Civilisation in the Faculty of Islamic Studies at Hamad bin Khalifa University. See http://www.qfis.edu.qa/research-centres/mohammed-bin-hamad-center. For more information on the Centre, see the foreword in al-Suyuti, *The Perfect Guide to the Sciences of the Qur'an*.
95. Al-Suyuti, *The Perfect Guide to the Sciences of the Qur'an*, pp. ix–x.
96. Umar Ubaid was born in 1935 and studied law at the University of Damascus. He may have escaped Syria in 1980 in the midst of the growing conflict between Hafez al-Asad and the Muslim Brotherhood. Ashour, 'Tajrabat al-Ikhwan al-Muslimun fi Qatar', p. 192. Yusuf al-Qaradawi mentions Yusuf al-Muzaffar, whom he addresses as 'our son', as the chief editor, and Umar Ubaid Hasanah as a member of the editorial team, whom he addresses as 'our friend'. See al-Qaradawi, 'Majallat -Al-Ummah- wa Majallat -Al-Doha-'.
97. Among the prominent Brothers who contributed to the journal were Yusuf al-Qaradawi, Muhammad al-Ghazali, Muhammad Qutb, Hasan al-Huwaidi, Umar Ubaid Hasanah, Mana al-Qattan, Abd al-Salam Bassouni. See al-Kuwari, 'Hal Min 'Awdat al-Majallat al-Ummah?'.
98. Cited in al-Kuwari, 'Hal Min 'Awdat al-Majallat al-Ummah?'.

oil prices the state of Qatar had to introduce budget cuts. The journal may have been a victim of these.[99] Considering the domestic and regional context, there seems to be no compelling reason why the state of Qatar should have gone against the Brothers and stopped the journal at this time. It should be kept in mind that the editor of the journal, Umar Ubaid Hasanah, remained in Qatar, received citizenship in 1994 and found other employment, including membership of the Committee of Curriculum Development of Islamic Education in the Ministry of Education, the Supreme Council for Family Affairs and the Public Authority for Radio and Television, and teaching in the Faculty of Shari'a and Islamic Studies at Qatar University.[100]

As previously mentioned, Qatar's reform of its education system began in the mid-1990s and like that of the UAE also expanded education in English. To this end, the state established the Qatar Foundation for Education, Science and Community Development in 1995 as one of the first acts of the new ruler, Hamad bin Khalifa Al Thani. The Foundation set out to expand education in English at all levels, but especially at university level. To do this, the Qatar Foundation initiated a major educational project, which came to be known as the Education City. The Education City first founded the Qatar Academy in 1998, which offered education in English from primary to high school levels. In the same year, the Education City became home to the first US university, the Virginia Commonwealth University, which offered degrees in art and design. In 2001 the Education City opened the Academic Bridge Programme, to prepare high school graduates for higher education in English. Throughout the 2000s, the Education City brought more universities to Qatar and greatly expanded higher education opportunities.[101] All of these campuses offered their programmes in English and, more controversially from a religious/conservative perspective, were mixed-gender. Qatar's public university, Qatar University, also sought to expand education in English and began working with the RAND to reform its curriculum. Qatar University

99. I thank Jassim Sultan for this insight. Email exchange, 27 July 2014.
100. Umar Ubaid appears as the Head of the Sheikh Ali bin Abdullah Foundation of Knowledge Studies. See http://www.sheikhali-waqfia.org.qa/SF/Ar/Static/WaqfiaManager.aspx.
101. As part of the Education City, Virginia Commonwealth, Cornell, Texas A&M, Carnegie Mellon, Georgetown, Northwestern, HEC Paris and University College London have opened campuses in Qatar.

also introduced a mandatory foundation programme for all students and added majors taught in English.

Even though these steps had been just as controversial in Qatar as in the UAE, they had not inspired any notable opposition from the Brotherhood. Some leading Brotherhood figures in Qatar even sent their daughters to study in the US universities that had campuses in the Education City, implicitly granting religious legitimacy to these institutions.[102]

As a further gesture to the state, the Brotherhood even declared its own dissolution in Qatar in 1999. It is difficult to pinpoint the exact reason behind this radical decision. Even if there was pressure from the state, overt or covert, it is yet to be documented. The decision was most likely taken, Mustafa Ashour claimed, not because of an escalating conflict with the regime, but rather as 'the outcome of years of studies and reflection'.[103] A leading Brotherhood figure in Qatar, Jassim Sultan, who led the dissolution, confirmed that the state was already carrying out its religious duties and that there was basically no functional need for a Brotherhood organisation in Qatar.[104]

The Brotherhood's rather submissive attitude in Qatar makes sense if it is considered that around the same time it had been facing setbacks elsewhere in the Arab world, including Saudi Arabia and the UAE. Qatar was one of the very few states in the Arab world where the Brotherhood had maintained any sort of working relationship. The Brotherhood could not risk this relationship.

Furthermore, during the same process, the state continued to be quite generous to the Brotherhood. This was how Qatar differed from the UAE. The case of Yusuf al-Qaradawi is again illustrative. He was given a precious opportunity when the state established the Al Jazeera network in 1995. Al-Qaradawi became a regular guest on a weekly religious programme, *al-Shariah wa'l-Hayat* [*The Shariah and the Life*], in which he expressed his views and issued his religious opinions, fatwas, on a variety of matters, including those most of interest to Arabs.[105] Through this programme

---

102. I know two of them who studied at Georgetown University's campus.
103. Al-Turabi and al-Mubarak, 'Qatar's introspective Islamists'.
104. See the discussion in Ashour, 'Tajrabat al-Ikhwan al-Muslimin fi Qatar', p. 188. For a detailed discussion on the dissolution, see Freer, *Rentier Islamism*, pp. 88–91.
105. The matters on which al-Qaradawi expresses his opinions range from elections to women. On the latter issue, see Sakr, 'Women, development and Al Jazeera'.

al-Qaradawi reached out to millions of Arabs and became a religious celebrity in the Arab world.[106]

The state of Qatar also involved Yusuf al-Qaradawi in its Education City project. He was involved in the foundation of the Education City's Qatar Faculty of Islamic Studies, serving as the chair of the school's advisory committee. The committee also included another prominent Brother, Izz al-Din Ibrahim, from the UAE. In 2008 the school established a research centre and named it after al-Qaradawi: Markaz al-Qaradawi li'l Wasatiyya al-Islamiyya wa'l-Tajdid (Al-Qaradawi Center for Islamic Moderation and Renewal).[107]

Al Jazeera was also an employer of many Brotherhood figures from the other Arab countries. Visiting the network in 2001, Fuad Ajami, for example, observed that most reporters of were 'either pan-Arabists . . . or Islamists'.[108] The Brotherhood's dominance in the network probably increased after the appointment of Wadhah Khanfar as general manager in 2003. The Brotherhood's networkist character must have helped in gaining a disproportionate influence, if not a total dominance at the network.[109]

In addition to employment opportunities for the Brotherhood, Al Jazeera became a valuable platform for the movement's leading figures. As well as Yusuf al-Qaradawi, many others, from Rashid al-Ghannushi of Tunisia to Hasan al-Turabi of Sudan, appeared numerous times.[110]

In the same period, Qatar also became home to many Brotherhood figures and other Islamists from elsewhere in the Arab world. Al-Qaradawi's student from Libya, Ali al-Sallabi, lived in exile in Doha from 1999. Hamas' leader, Khaled Meshaal, also shuttled between Damascus and Doha throughout the

---

106. Shadid, 'Al-Jazeera star mixes tough talk with calls for tolerance'.
107. See the center's website at http://www.qfis.edu.qa/research-centres/alqaradawi-center
108. Ajami, 'What the Muslim world is watching'.
109. See Gillespie, 'The new face of Al Jazeera'.
110. Not just Brotherhood figures but all Islamists benefited from Al Jazeera as a platform. Even Turkey's ruling party, the Justice and Development Party, which hailed from Turkey's political Islam tradition, benefited from Al Jazeera's sympathetic coverage. In recognition of this, a pro-JDP columnist, Hakan Albayrak described the network as 'Turkey's official media apparatus'. Albayrak added: 'Al Jazeera and especially Wadhah Khanfar have greatly contributed to the shining of Turkey as a star.' See Albayrak, 'Vaddah Hanfer'e vefa'.

2000s. With employment opportunities in both education and media, Qatar turned into what Andrew Hammond called 'a mini Ikhwanistan'.[111]

This chapter has argued that in the new geopolitical context shaped by the Iranian revolution and the subsequent religio-political activism, the Muslim Brotherhood became more oppositional, first in Kuwait and the UAE and later in Saudi Arabia. It is important to reiterate that in no period over the course of modern state building have the Gulf states experienced any forced state secularisation. On the contrary, as discussed in Chapters 2 and 4, they have always been religious states, and Saudi Arabia more so than the others. The fact that the Muslim Brotherhood became oppositional in Kuwait, the UAE and Saudi Arabia, but not in Bahrain and Qatar, suggests that the level of state religiosity does not seem to have had any impact on its actions.

By the end of the 2000s, the Gulf states already had divergent attitudes towards the Muslim Brotherhood: Bahrain and Qatar still had friendly relations, while Kuwait, the UAE and Saudi Arabia had, to say the least, ambivalent relations with the movement. The Arab Spring would solidify these divergences by pushing the UAE and Saudi Arabia to an opposite extreme. More specifically, the UAE and Saudi Arabia became increasingly and more openly hostile towards the Muslim Brotherhood as the latter came to acquire a renewed geopolitical significance.

---

111. Hammond, 'Arab awakening: Qatar's controversial alliance with Arab Islamists'.

6

THE ARAB SPRING

The Arab Spring started on 17 December 2010, when Muhammad Bouazizi, a Tunisian street vendor, set himself on fire in protest against the local authorities' maltreatment and callousness. Bouazizi's self-immolation immediately sparked protests in his home town, Sidi Bouzid. Soon these spread to other towns in Tunisia and in less than a month had brought down Tunisia's long-ruling strongman, Zein al-Abidin bin Ali. Tunisia set the precedent, inspiring millions elsewhere in the Arab world to protest in their own countries.

The protests erupted in Egypt in late January and brought down another long-ruling Arab autocrat, Hosni Mubarak, in less than three weeks. Inspired and emboldened by the success of protesters in Tunisia and Egypt, hundreds of thousands poured onto the streets in Libya, Syria, Yemen and Bahrain in protest at their governments. In large part thanks to foreign intervention, the protests succeeded in toppling two further long-ruling autocrats, Ali Abdullah Salih in Yemen and Muammar Gaddafi in Libya. Foreign intervention was also decisive in both Bahrain and Syria. While it saved the regime in Bahrain, it deepened the regime crisis in Syria and plunged the country into a long civil war.

The Arab Spring fundamentally changed the geopolitical context in the Middle East. Leaving aside the possibility that Iran could further expand its sphere of influence in the Arab world, the Arab Spring paved the way for the formation of a new regional axis, an axis that reflected the rise of the Muslim

Brotherhood especially in Egypt, the Arab world's giant. In the first post-Arab Spring elections held in three rounds from November 2011 to January 2012, the movement's newly founded political party, Hizb al-Hurriyah wa'l-'Adalah (the Freedom and Justice Party, or FJP) scored critical electoral victories. The party won 47 per cent of the seats in the lower house and 38 per cent of the seats in the upper house. Even though the dissolution of the parliament by the Constitutional Court in June 2012 was a major blow, the movement scored another, even more critical electoral victory the same month, winning the presidential elections. A Brotherhood-affiliated figure and the leader of the FJP, Muhammad Morsi, was elected and sworn in as the president of Egypt.

Even before Morsi was elected, Turkey had expressed great enthusiasm in developing stronger relations with Egypt. Turkey's president, Abdullah Gül, was the first world leader to visit Egypt after Mubarak stepped down. Six months after this visit, Turkey's prime minister, Recep Tayyip Erdoğan, also visited Egypt and received a hero's welcome. Immediately thereafter, Turkey's Foreign Minister, Ahmet Davutoğlu, expressed Turkey's desire to form a new axis of power. 'This is what we want,' he said, adding, 'This will not be an axis against any other country –not Israel, not any other country, this will be an axis of democracy, real democracy.' It would be an axis 'of the two big nations in our region, from the north to the south, from the Black Sea down to the Nile Valley in Sudan'.[1]

After Muhammad Morsi became president, Turkey and Egypt made more tangible moves. When Morsi visited Turkey in September 2012 he received a wholehearted welcome, and in a highly symbolic gesture attended the ruling party's congress, where he also delivered a speech. 'The Egyptian and Turkish people', he said, 'have many common goals', such as 'to ensure that people and nations are the source of power' and 'to support the nations that are fighting for peace and want to get rid of their oppressive brutal dictators'.[2]

In November 2012, Erdoğan visited Egypt again, signing some twenty agreements, almost all of them seeking to expand cooperation between Turkey and Egypt in fields such as transportation, communication, agriculture,

1. Shadid, 'Turkey predicts alliance with Egypt as regional anchors'.
2. Muhammad Morsi's speech is available at https://www.youtube.com/watch?v=2Xx9I8mLhPM.

health services, tourism, urban development and culture.[3] More symbolically, Erdoğan gave a speech at Cairo University, bombastically stating, 'Today and tomorrow, we will continue to be in solidarity with Egypt, walk together with Egypt, and undertake all necessities our brotherhood requires.' Erdoğan also prophesied that 'Egypt and Turkey, two powerful states of the region, will be the assurance of peace, stability and tranquility of this geography.'[4]

In the following months, Turkey and Egypt continued to seek ways to strengthen their relations. For example, they signed a tourism partnership agreement in February 2013,[5] another one to expand cooperation in the media in April 2013[6] and finally, three separate agreements on rail, maritime and overland transportation in June 2013.[7]

What made the Turkey–Egypt rapprochement particularly important was that Turkey's ruling Justice and Development Party (JDP) shared an ideological affinity with the Muslim Brotherhood: both hailed from the broader political Islamic movement and had been building ties throughout the 2000s.[8] Thus, what appeared to be forming in the Middle East was an axis between Turkey and Egypt grounded in the same religious ideology. King Abdullah of Jordan remarked in April 2013, 'I see a Muslim Brotherhood crescent developing in Egypt and Turkey.'[9]

The formation of an axis between Turkey and Egypt in the Middle East could inspire and further embolden the Islamists in the Gulf, who had already been inspired by the Arab Spring. More troublingly, these two countries could in the near future support the Islamists in the Gulf.[10] This could be troubling for Saudi Arabia, the UAE and Kuwait, where the Brotherhood had a history of opposition. The transnational nature of the Brotherhood was well known – Saudi Arabia made a contribution through organisations such as the

---

3. 'Türkiye ile Mısır arasında 27 anlaşma imzalandı.'
4. 'Erdoğan Mısır'dan çok sert çıktı.'
5. Farouk, 'Egypt, Turkey sign tourism partnership agreement'.
6. El-Dabh, 'Egypt and Turkey sign media agreement'.
7. 'Turkey, Egypt sign transportation agreements.'
8. Merley, *Turkey, The Global Muslim Brotherhood and the Gaza Flotilla*.
9. Goldberg, 'The modern king in the Arab Spring'.
10. See my analysis, Başkan, *Turkey and Qatar in the Tangled Geopolitics of the Middle East*, ch. 6.

Muslim World League – and could no longer be ignored as it rose to power in Egypt and became an influential political player in Tunisia and Yemen. The stage was thus set for a repetition of the 1950s and 1960s, when an ideology of pan-Arab socialism inspired opposition at home and was in power in more populous regional states, such as Egypt, Iraq and Syria.

The so-called Muslim Brotherhood crescent had a short life, however, as the Egyptian military staged a coup against Muhammad Morsi and took over the government on 3 July 2013. Refusing to acknowledge the legitimacy of the coup, the Brotherhood in Egypt organised a series of protests and attracted a violent military reaction. The ensuing crackdown on the Brotherhood was unprecedented since the 1950s and 1960s.[11] Three Arab Gulf states, Saudi Arabia, the UAE and Kuwait, rushed to extend diplomatic and financial aid to Egypt. Saudi Arabia pledged $5 billion, the UAE $3 billion and Kuwait $4 billion. Their support proved critical to the success of the coup, coming at a time when the International Monetary Fund had postponed negotiations with Egypt for a loan. Saudi Arabia and the UAE took additional steps and declared the Muslim Brotherhood a terrorist organisation in March 2014 and November 2014 respectively. By not taking this measure, Kuwait proved that it had a much freer political environment and hence was more tolerant of oppositional activities than other the Gulf states. Bahrain and Qatar also did not declare the Muslim Brotherhood a terrorist organisation, but for their own reasons.

Troubled Monarchies: Saudi Arabia, the UAE and Kuwait

Saudi Arabia

The Arab Spring was troubling for all the Gulf states for a variety of reasons. Saudi Arabia's immediate concern was not geopolitical. It feared it might itself be a victim. After Hosni Mubarak stepped down in Egypt, online petitions began to circulate in Saudi Arabia calling for political reform. The online activists also began to call for demonstrations across the country and even set 11 March 2011 as the date to start them, naming it 'Day of Rage'. However, the regime pre-empted the protests and took measures to prevent them. On 23 February 2011 the regime announced economic measures worth

11. Dunne and Williamson, 'Egypt's unprecedented instability by the numbers'.

$36 billion to address problems such as inflation, housing, education costs and unemployment, in order to appease any potential protesters.[12]

The regime also mobilised its Wahhabi religious scholars in an effort to de-legitimise the protests. To this end, on 7 March 2011 the Committee of Senior Religious Scholars issued a fatwa, which was published and extensively discussed in newspapers, distributed throughout mosques and disseminated in online discussion forums. In the fatwa, the Committee first affirmed the Islamic credentials of the regime: 'Allah', affirmed the fatwa, 'bestowed upon this country unification in its leadership based on the light of the guidance of the book and the tradition.' According to the fatwa, Saudi Arabia 'has maintained its Islamic identity' and was blessed by God 'with the service to two noble shrines' for which it 'has won a special priority in the Islamic world'. The fatwa then called the citizens to strengthen their internal cohesion and mutual intimacy, and remain alert against any developments that could undermine them. More critically, the fatwa affirmed, it was 'illegal to issue statements and take signatures for the purposes of intimidation and inciting the strife'. This was 'contrary to what Allah Almighty commanded in His words'. The legal way, the fatwa assured, to improve welfare in the country was 'the mutual advice' which the religious scholars had been historically performing.[13]

In order to further de-legitimise the protest preparations, the regime also waged a massive media campaign suggesting that Iran was involved and hence the protests would be exclusively Shia. A similar de-legitimising discourse had already developed in Bahrain, portraying the protests there as being at the instigation of Iran, and the Saudi public was exposed to this literature. With these pre-emptive measures and the heavy presence of security forces on the streets, no large-scale protests erupted on 11 March across Saudi Arabia, though some did take place in the Shia-dominated eastern region, with Shias predominantly participating.[14]

In order to further cement the loyalty of the Sunnis and weaken the ongoing protests in the Shia regions, the regime announced another financial-aid

12. Murphy, 'Saudi Arabia's King Abdullah promises $36 billion in benefits'.
13. 'A fatwa from the Council of Senior Scholars in the Kingdom of Saudi Arabia warning against mass demonstrations.'
14. Al-Nafjan, 'Saudi Arabia's day of little rage'.

package almost a week after the failed Day of Rage. The regime increased the minimum wage and pledged to pay two months' extra salary for government workers, provide financial help to university students, pay a monthly stipend to the unemployed, build half a million housing units for low-income families, spend $4.3 billion on medical facilities and create 60,000 new jobs in the security forces.[15] Between the two packages, Saudi Arabia was pledging to spend a staggering $130 billion.

Saudi Arabia thus thwarted massive street protests from the Sunni majority within its borders. But the Arab Spring still inspired some leading religious figures of the Sahwa movement.[16] Salman al-Awdah was one of them. The piece he posted on his own website, islamtoday.net, is a good illustration of how he perceived the Arab Spring. In contrast to the Saudi regime and the Wahhabi religious scholars who had reservations and concerns, al-Awdah enthusiastically embraced the Arab Spring. He didn't make any specific comment on the developments in Tunisia almost until the end. Then on his TV programme, *Al-Hayat Kalimah (The Life is Word)*, aired on 31 January 2010, he hinted that he was following developments in Tunisia and even recommended being 'alert to the needs and aspirations of the people'.[17] Al-Awdah made his strongest statement about Tunisia on the day Zein al-Abidin bin Ali stepped down. On his TV programme aired on 14 February 2010, he said,

> I say to our rulers in the Arab countries ... feed your people before they eat you! Fight financial and administrative corruption. Perhaps the most important meal to provide to the people is the meal of freedom for it is not the bread only, which keeps the man alive.[18]

Al-Awdah believed in the transformative impact of the new means of communication on the beliefs and ideas of the youth. He claimed that the Arab people acquired new aspirations and hopes and now wanted to become like others. This was not unique to Tunisia. Therefore, what happened in Tunisia

---

15. 'Saudi king warns against unrest while boosting benefits.'
16. See al-Rasheed, 'Divine politics reconsidered'.
17. The programme's videos are available on Salman al-Awdah's website at http://hklive.islamtoday.net/archive.
18. Salman al-Awdah made almost the same statement in his Twitter account: https://twitter.com/salman_alodah/status/25903594960064512.

could also happen elsewhere, in Egypt, in Jordan, even in the Arab Gulf states. Before it was too late, al-Awdah warned, this problem had to be addressed.[19]

When protests erupted in Egypt, al-Awdah became even more enthusiastic, following the developments closely and issuing statements daily on his Twitter account. He even went to Egypt and visited Tahrir Square in Cairo with the prominent Muslim Brotherhood figure, Yusuf al-Qaradawi.[20] In his first reaction, on 26 January 2011, he emphasised the significance of freedom for the nations. 'The free people,' he remarked, were 'the people that deserve worthy of survival and of life [and that are] capable of overcoming difficulties'. 'Freedom,' he noted, was not some 'abstract decision', it was 'a program for life and development'.[21]

On 30 January, al-Awdah warned Arab and Islamic governments about the gravity of the situation and to 'engage in reform projects rather than turn against revolutions'. He further declared, 'demanding rights and end of oppression is not rebelling against the ruler and not against the sources of Shariah; enjoying what is good and forbidding what is evil is desirable and this is a part of rights.'[22] By stating this, al-Awdah was opposing the state-affiliated Wahhabi religious scholars that explicitly declared protests and demonstrations as forbidden in Islam.

Over the following days, al-Awdah continued to issue statements: he often expressed his admiration for the people of Egypt, again and again declaring his support for the people's demands and calling on the government to respect them, criticised the regime's attempts to crack down on the protests and called on all governments to implement fundamental reforms.[23]

19. The video is available at http://hklive.islamtoday.net/archive.
20. Salman al-Awdah acknowledged his visit in his programme, *The Life is Word*, on MBC on 28 February 2011. He must have gone to Egypt immediately after the massive protests erupted there. The episode is available at http://hklive.islamtoday.net/archive.
21. https://twitter.com/salman_alodah/status/30371832989229056
22. Salman al-Awdah's Twitter statements on 30 January 2011 are available at https://twitter.com/salman_alodah/status/31500523442016256 and https://twitter.com/salman_alodah/status/31701209970647040.
23. See, for example, https://twitter.com/salman_alodah/status/32105407291850752; https://twitter.com/salman_alodah/status/32105743750533120; https://twitter.com/salman_alodah/status/32895653717745665; https://twitter.com/salman_alodah/status/32911819148365824; https://twitter.com/salman_alodah/status/33146080602357760; https://twitter.com/salman_alodah/status/33498312221016064 and https://twitter.com/salman_alodah/status/33510008503279616.

His article posted on his own website, islamtoday.net, is a summary of how al-Awdah perceived the Arab Spring. 'These past few nights', he stated, 'I have been unable to sleep. Instead, I have been watching the news, captivated by the events that are unfolding in Egypt.' Feeling 'overjoyed' at times but 'saddened' at others, al-Awdah prophesied that 'something truly unprecedented in the Arab world' was unfolding. Why was this happening? This was a critical question to reflect on, especially for 'the rulers who think they are immune to change'.

Al-Awdah warned that no Arab leader should believe that he was special. As it had happened in Tunisia and Egypt, it could happen elsewhere, in 'Yemen, Morocco, Algeria, Jordan, or the Gulf states'. 'Before you hear the outcries . . . calling for the fall of the regime,' al-Awdah advised, 'please proclaim your commitment to substantial and radical reform.' What was needed in the Arab world was 'a new relationship between the ruler and the ruled, one that is not based on fear and coercion, but on recognition, partnership and respect'.[24]

Al-Awdah also expressed similar views on *The Life is Word* on MBC. In the episode aired on 28 January 2011, for example, he presented Tunisia as a model and emphasised the importance of new media, especially Facebook. He also noted that this was not a revolution for bread only. It was also about freedoms, especially political ones. The protests showed that 'the Arab governments are no longer able to accommodate the new generation'. They were, he argued, 'living in a state of senility or traditionalism, their personalities and programmes'.[25]

In the episode aired on 4 February 2011, al-Awdah again prophesied that other Arab countries were not immune to the protests: 'Causes may vary, but death is one . . . humans are humans; the needs of humans, their aspirations, their longings, their demands for rights . . . their feelings and humans are the same whichever country they are in.' Other Arab countries, al-Awdah advised, should study the causes of the revolutions to avoid the same problems: 'Correct the conditions, propagate justice, give people freedoms, give

---

24. Al-Awdah, 'Has Egypt's hour of reckoning come?' As I noted, this piece is a collection of statements al-Awdah made on his Twitter account from 26 January 2011 to 7 February 2011.
25. The episode is available at http://hklive.islamtoday.net/archive.

an order to priorities, dismiss officials when they do mistakes, appoint people accepting accountability and responsibility and even punish them when their mistakes are proven.'[26]

With these statements, Salman al-Awdah hit a nerve in Saudi Arabia. Not surprisingly, the 4 February episode turned out to be the last episode of *The Life is Word*. MBC, owned by a Saudi prince, Al-Waleed bin Talal al Saud, suspended al-Awdah's programme, a clear message that al-Awdah's enthusiasm for the Arab Spring was not welcomed by the regime.

Yet Salman al-Awdah continued to issue statements supporting and defending the revolution in Egypt. On 11 February, the day Egypt's long-ruling autocrat, Hosni Mubarak, stepped down, al-Awdah congratulated the Egyptians: 'congratulations from heart on the great success of the revolution of the Egyptian youth, tonight was born Egypt with a new spirit and the armless people defeated their executioners'.[27] Al-Awdah also defended the right of citizens to stage peaceful demonstrations: this right was part of the social contract between the ruler and the ruled in republican systems and was guaranteed by constitutions in all democracies.[28]

Salman al-Awdah was also enthusiastic about the protests in Syria, Yemen and Libya. He called for political reform, criticised regime violence and often praised the protesters, for example, declaring those killed by the regime as martyrs. He also visited Libya and met with the president of the transitional council, Ali al-Sallabi, a close associate of Yusuf al-Qaradawi. The two, al-Awdah reported, prayed together, thanking God for the success of the revolution in Libya. They also prayed for the revolutionaries in Syria and Yemen.[29]

While enthusiastic and outspoken about the protests and revolutions elsewhere in the Arab world, al-Awdah was more reserved about the protests in Bahrain and Saudi Arabia. Only following the regime's brutal crackdown on the protests in Bahrain did he react: 'belittling blood, whoever its source is,

26. The episode is available at http://hklive.islamtoday.net/archive.
27. https://twitter.com/salman_alodah/status/36117670759763968
28. https://twitter.com/salman_alodah/status/36776269551108096 and https://twitter.com/salman_alodah/status/36790588074504192
29. https://twitter.com/salman_alodah/status/68878138532302849 and https://twitter.com/salman_alodah/status/68879394080436224

is a crime'.[30] But he was less radical about the regime: he advised the regime and the protesters start a dialogue on necessary reforms.[31]

Al-Awdah was also reserved at home. He was among the signatories of a petition entitled 'Toward a State of Rights and Institutions' addressed to the king on 23 February 2011. The petition warned that the ongoing revolutions in other Arab countries proved that the rulers had to listen to their people, otherwise serious consequences would follow. Saudi Arabia, the petition declared, was in dire need of radical reforms. The petition proposed a number, the most significant of which was the establishment of a fully elected consultative council with legislative supervisory powers.[32]

Yet al-Awdah did not go too far. He did not, for example, give his blessing to the efforts to organise street protests in Saudi Arabia and remained silent on the suppression of the Shia-led protests in the eastern regions. However, though al-Awdah did not directly target Saudi Arabia, his comments could easily be interpreted as implicit criticisms of the regime. Not surprisingly, in late July 2011 Saudi Arabia banned Salman al-Awdah from travelling abroad, a ban that remained in place for several years.

Yet, al-Awdah continued to express his views, devoting his attention to Egypt, Syria and Yemen. He praised, for example, the putting on trial of Hosni Mubarak, the ex-President of Egypt: his trial would also be 'a trial of the Arab system and his fall will also be the fall of the Arab system'.[33] The trial was also going to make 'all leaders of the world look back to their own accounts'.[34]

Al-Awdah also expressed his satisfaction with the elections in Tunisia and Egypt. On 24 October 2011 he congratulated the Tunisians for successfully conducting elections and the Muslim Brotherhood-affiliated Harakat al-Nahda (the Renaissance Movement) or al-Nahda for receiving the largest share of the votes.[35] The next day, al-Awdah also called Rashid al-Ghannouchi, the founder and long-time leader of al-Nahda, and congratulated him on his victory.[36] The

30. https://twitter.com/salman_alodah/status/38684333204180992
31. https://twitter.com/salman_alodah/status/38684730673213440
32. The petition is available at http://ahewar.org/debat/show.art.asp?aid=247642.
33. https://twitter.com/salman_alodah/status/99117829495853057
34. https://twitter.com/salman_alodah/status/99519594179477504
35. https://twitter.com/salman_alodah/status/128541019015888897
36. https://twitter.com/salman_alodah/status/128597373411786752

whole process, al-Awdah declared on 11 November 2011, illustrated that the Islamists were not to be scared and proved them as reasonable partners.[37] Al-Awdah was also jubilant about the presidential elections in Egypt. When the first round was held, al-Awdah described it as 'a new beginning and a glorious historic day'.[38] Al-Awdah prayed to God 'to pick the best for Egypt, return it to the central stage and to the leadership of the Arab and especially the broader Islamic world'. Al-Awdah also prayed to God 'to inspire Muslim rulers . . . open their hearts and minds for the reform that will save their countries from sedition and strife'.[39]

Even though Al-Awdah had distanced himself from Muhammad Morsi, he was not jubilant about the military coup that overthrew Morsi in July 2013. His first reaction was to pray to God to 'save Egypt, unite their words [give them unity], reconcile their hearts, and prevent them from the vice of the evils, the bad intent of the wicked'.[40] More importantly, he legitimised peaceful opposition to the military coup by declaring, 'if the Egyptian people accept this new situation, they deserve it. But, opposing it peacefully is also their right.'[41] Al-Awdah thus put himself at odds with the regime in Saudi Arabia, which extended its financial and diplomatic support to Egypt immediately after the coup.

Al-Awdah became increasingly critical of the military as it became more violent towards the protesters. On 26 July 2013 he suggested that the army should return to barracks, claiming that its involvement in the 1952 revolution might have been the reason for Egypt's defeat in 1967 and its return to barracks for the victory in 1973.[42] On 27 July 2013 al-Awdah was particularly harsh: 'those who justify killing the opposition have no human values and have lost their sense of patriotism'. He added, 'we are against the killing of innocent people, regardless of who the killer or the victim is, and of their political affiliations'.[43]

37. https://twitter.com/salman_alodah/status/134943082511745024
38. https://twitter.com/salman_alodah/status/205287399327150081
39. https://twitter.com/salman_alodah/status/205421863025901568; https://twitter.com/salman_alodah/status/205422061064163329; https://twitter.com/salman_alodah/status/205422351842680832
40. https://twitter.com/salman_alodah/status/352549194415869953
41. https://twitter.com/salman_alodah/status/352791822432600066
42. https://twitter.com/salman_alodah/status/360775188914249729
43. https://twitter.com/salman_alodah/status/361069556720091136 and https://twitter.com/salman_alodah/status/361199865272877056

The UAE

The Arab Spring did not generate massive street protests in the UAE but it still unsettled the regime. In early March 2011, some 130 UAE citizens petitioned president Khalifa bin Zayed Al Nahyan demanding political reform. The petitioners demanded that the Federal National Council be elected by universal suffrage and have legislative and supervisory powers.[44] In April 2011, four non-governmental organisations, the Lawyers' Association, Teachers' Association, al-Shuhuh National Heritage Association and United Arab Emirates University Faculty Association, joined them and penned a letter voicing the same demands.[45]

The UAE's reaction was immediate. First, it arrested five outspoken dissidents: Ahmad Mansur, Fahad Salim Dalak, Ahmad Abd al-Khaleq, Naser bin Ghaith and Hassan Ali al-Khamis.[46] These came to be known as the UAE 5, being officially accused in July 2011 of publicly insulting the country's leadership, and were sentenced to jail (Mansur for three years and the others for two years) in November 2011. Second, the UAE dissolved the elected boards of two associations, the Lawyers' Association and Teachers' Association, and appointed its own officials to their boards. Third, the UAE mobilised its oil wealth. A day before the petition was submitted, the president ordered investment of $1.5 billion in water and electricity services in the northern Emirates.[47] Later the same month, the UAE increased pensions for military personnel and those employees retired from the Defence Ministry by 70 per cent. It also implemented limited political reform. In September 2011, it increased the size of the Electoral College that elects the Federal National Council from 6,689 to 129,274.

---

44. Established in 1971, this council had been an advisory body appointed by the rulers of the seven emirates until 2006. Since 2006, an electoral college of six thousand UAE citizens, appointed by the rulers, had elected half of the council members. The other half continued to be appointed by the rulers. The text of the petition and names of the signatories are available at http://www.ipetitions.com/petition/uaepetition71/.
45. The letter is dated 6 April 2011 and is available at http://www.uaeec.com/vb/archive/index.php/t-237248.html?s=c0031530a33ee9fd2940bfcb5cd62031.
46. In the same wave of arrests, Fahad Salim al-Shehhi, the head of al-Shuhuh National Heritage Association, was also arrested but released a week later. Among these names, only Ahmad Mansur was one of the 133 petitioners.
47. 'Dh5.7 bn allocated for new water and electricity projects in northern emirates.'

The UAE marked 40 years of independence on 5 December 2011. As the day approached, the president pardoned the five dissidents who had been sentenced to jail for insulting the country's leadership. They were not the only ones. The president also pardoned another 554 prisoners and settled their debts and fines.[48] Furthermore, the UAE also increased the salaries of all federal government employees, with judicial authorities, employees of the Ministry of Health and government teachers receiving as much as 100 per cent increases in their salaries. In another political-legal reform, the UAE announced that the UAE women married to non-citizens could apply for citizenship for their children. Finally, the state established a $2.7 billion fund to help citizens on low incomes pay off their personal loans.[49]

Using both the carrot and the stick, the UAE thus deflected the Arab Spring. President Khalifa bin Zayed was both proud and conciliatory on the fortieth anniversary.[50] However, the UAE was about to wage a campaign against the Muslim Brotherhood.

Just a few days after the anniversary celebrations, the UAE revoked the citizenship of six members of al-Islah Society: Muhammad Abd al-Razzaq al-Siddiqi, Ali Hussain al-Hammadi, Shahin Abdullah al-Husni, Hussain Munif al-Jabri, Hasan Munif al-Jabri and Ibrahim Hassan al-Marzuqi.[51] It turned out that the citizenship of another al-Islah member, Ahmad Ghaith al-Suwaidi, had already been revoked around seven months previously.[52]

Soon the UAE became vocal in its attitude towards the Brotherhood. In a speech delivered in Manama, Bahrain in early 2012, the Police Chief of

---

48. 'Sheikh Khalifa pardons 554 prisoners for National Day.'
49. 'President issues National Day resolutions.'
50. For Sheikh Khalifa's statement, see 'Shaikh Khalifa addresses the nation on National Day'.
51. Ali Husain al-Hammadi and Shahin Abdullah al-Husni appear among the signatories of the March 2011 petition.
52. According to an unnamed official, these six individuals 'perpetrated over the past years acts threatening the national security of the UAE through their connection with suspicious regional and international organizations and personalities'. See 'Citizenship of 6 naturalized Emiratis revoked by President', *Gulf News*, 22 December 2011. According to a statement from the Gulf Center for Human Rights, the seventh person, Ahmad Gaith al-Suwaidi, lost his citizenship seven months previously. See Gulf Center for Human Rights, 'UAE'.

Dubai, Dahi Khalfan al-Tamim, openly declared the Brotherhood as a serious threat to Gulf security. More specifically, al-Tamim claimed that the US was working to overthrow the Gulf regimes and grooming the Muslim Brotherhood in their place.[53]

Dahi Khalfan was not alone in the UAE state in his suspicions and criticisms of the Muslim Brotherhood. The Minister of Foreign Affairs, Sheikh Abdullah bin Zayed Al Nahyan, often joined Dahi Khalfan in waging a crusade against the movement. As early as February 2012, a prominent Emirati columnist, Sultan al-Qasimi, quoted Sheikh Abdullah asking for clarification from the Muslim Brotherhood in Egypt that it 'will not seek to export the revolution to the Gulf' and 'will not compromise on Gulf security'.[54]

Later in the year, Sheikh Abdullah became certain that the Muslim Brotherhood posed a serious threat to the Gulf states. He raised the issue in a joint news conference with the Minister of Foreign Affairs of Ukraine, held on 8 October 2012 in Abu Dhabi. Sheikh Abdullah was reported to have said, 'The Muslim Brotherhood's thinking does not recognise borders or sovereignty of nations. So it is not unusual that the international Brotherhood organisation works to make inroads upon sovereignty and laws of countries.'[55]

It was not just a rhetorical campaign against the Brotherhood. The UAE also started a wave of arrests in March 2012: Muhammad Al-Siddiqi was detained on 9 April, Muhammad al-Mansuri on 16 July and Muhammad al-Rukn on 17 July. Even Sultan bin Kayid al-Qassimi, a member of the ruling family of Ras al-Khaimah, was detained on 20 April.[56] The UAE also targeted Egyptians visiting the country, arresting more than ten on the charge of recruiting Egyptian expats in the UAE and collecting money for the Muslim Brotherhood in Egypt.[57] By late January 2013, the UAE had detained ninety-four citizens,

---

53. Dahi Khalfan's speech is available at http://www.thememriblog.org/blog_personal/en/41653.htm.
54. Al-Qassemi, 'Will Egypt's Muslim Brotherhood mend ties with Gulf States?'
55. 'Shaikh Abdullah slams Muslim Brotherhood.'
56. For the names of detainees, see http://www.echr.org.uk/?page_id=207. Al-Islah Society provides more detailed information about only forty-seven of the detainees on its website. See http://www.aleslaah.net/site/thred.php?id=25&page=1.
57. 'UAE busts cell "linked to Egypt Brotherhood".'

known as the UAE 94, and officially charged them with opposing the basic principles of governance and seizing political power in the UAE.[58]

This was quite unexpected, because al-Islah Society had been by and large politically inactive throughout 2011. Some leading figures had signed the petition submitted to the UAE president, including Muhammad al-Rukn, Muhammad al-Mansuri, Sultan bin Kayid al-Qassimi, Muhammad Abd al-Razzaq al-Siddiqi and Ahmad Saqr al-Suwaidi, but they constituted a minority of the signatories. Furthermore, Muhammad al-Rukn defended the UAE 5 as their lawyer and Muhammad al-Mansuri frequently spoke in the international media about the arrests. Yet the efforts of these few individuals could easily be interpreted as their own personal initiatives, not as organisational undertakings of al-Islah Society, and the UAE might not have implicated the whole movement.

More interestingly, unlike their colleagues elsewhere in the Gulf, the Brotherhood figures in the UAE had remained more or less silent about the Arab Spring. Muhammad al-Rukn's statements on his Twitter account had been hardly political. In fact, he joined Twitter in May 2011. Muhammad Abd al-Razzaq al-Siddiqi did not issue any statement on Twitter until December 2011. When he began, he gave a personal account of what was happening in the UAE.

Al-Siddiqi began to post his statements on Twitter a few weeks after his citizenship was revoked.[59] In his first post, he said, 'we have been patient in our country for twenty years', suffering from 'great crimes committed by corrupt people within the security apparatus'. There was an evil plan these corrupt figures were executing 'to control every aspect of the state'. To this end, they were installing their like, 'corrupt elements', in all state institutions from the security apparatus to the ministries. These corrupt elements had also been working 'to isolate the rulers from the people' and even 'managed to strip rulers of their roles . . . in shaping policies of the country'.[60]

---

58. See the full statement, 'Statement by Attorney General on the organization which seeks to oppose basic principles of the UAE system of governance and to seize power'.
59. For a brief biography of Muhammed Abdul Razzaq al-Siddiq, see Gümüşlüoğlu, 'Sıddık'ın hayatının izinde'.
60. https://twitter.com/malsiddiq/status/152186261359181826; https://twitter.com/malsiddiq/status/152186704999096320; https://twitter.com/malsiddiq/status/152187053071802368; https://twitter.com/malsiddiq/status/152190899760283648; https://twitter.com/malsiddiq/status/152191147106762752

These corrupt figures had also targeted al-Islah Society, the Muslim Brotherhood's branch in the UAE, for twenty years, and other charitable, social and educational organisations. Al-Siddiqi claimed that these corrupt figures had also sought to destroy his own foundation, Dar al-Khayrat, a charitable foundation 'whose patriotism has been observed both domestically and internationally'.[61]

Muhammad al-Siddiqi also called upon the rulers and those working in the security services to 'cleanse their councils and offices of these corrupt people'. He called on those working in the apparatus to 'either switch to other departments or to leave this job in the name of religion'. He added, 'let us live in peace and sleep with no bitterness or hatred'.[62] It was al-Islah Society,[63] al-Siddiqi claimed, that 'brought up the youth in goodness in schools, universities and associations' and that 'founded charitable organizations'. 'The advocates of corruption', on the other hand, al-Siddiqi claimed, wanted 'to clear out the country for Shakira and her likes'.[64]

The UAE's hosting of music concerts was also the work of the same corrupt figures. On 31 December 2011, al-Siddiqi shared a picture of a newspaper article, which had a photograph of the world-famous singer Shakira during her concert in Abu Dhabi, and said, 'Look at these shameless concerts, held on the soil of our pure nation through consultation and implementation of corrupt consultants.' Al-Siddiqi added, 'Fear God Almighty. Our beloved nation is in the noble Arabian peninsula, kilometres away from Mecca al-Mukarramah and Medina al-Musharrafah.'[65]

Al-Siddiqi also criticised the UAE's policies towards the Arab Spring countries, as a result of which, he claimed, the UAE had been losing its

61. https://twitter.com/malsiddiq/status/152187395717083136; https://twitter.com/malsiddiq/status/152472852560494592; https://twitter.com/malsiddiq/status/152473493907320833; https://twitter.com/malsiddiq/status/152473940609081344
62. https://twitter.com/malsiddiq/status/152191744140787712; https://twitter.com/malsiddiq/status/152487922556342272; https://twitter.com/malsiddiq/status/152494079882698752
63. Muhammed al-Siddiq attributes this to, if literally translated, 'advocates of the Reform', by which he most likely meant the members of Al-Islah Society.
64. https://twitter.com/malsiddiq/status/153185871330410496; https://twitter.com/malsiddiq/status/153190766397755392
65. https://twitter.com/malsiddiq/status/153164617399545856; https://twitter.com/malsiddiq/status/153172803963731969

excellent relations established during Sheikh Zayed's reign. The UAE was sacrificing its relations with Arab and non-Arab countries, such as Egypt, Turkey, Morocco, Tunisia, Yemen and Syria. Was this because, al-Siddiqi asked, these countries elected the Muslim Brotherhood? Even the US was working to secure its interests and communicating with the Brotherhood. Why should the UAE, al-Siddiqi asked, not do the same and pursue its own interests? At the very least, al-Siddiqi suggested, 'let us wait and see what happens . . . why do we sacrifice the future of our relations?' He again blamed the corrupt advisers, who had the delusion that 'this is an American-Zionist-Iranian plan and that the Muslim Brotherhood will fail within months'. The UAE, al-Siddiqi claimed, was building its foreign relations on an illusion[66] and pursuing, due to the corrupt advisers' hatred of the Muslim Brotherhood, foolish foreign policies.[67]

Qatar, on the other hand, in al-Siddiqi's view, 'correctly understood the new situation. Therefore it now occupies the hearts of the Arab peoples.'[68] In contrast, the UAE had 'lost the legacy of love' its founder, Sheikh Zayed, 'built in the hearts of Arab people' and had 'replaced it with hatred'.[69] The UAE had to revise its foreign policy and 'think about the Muslim Brotherhood objectively'.[70]

Al-Siddiqi also made his sympathy for the Muslim Brotherhood clear. The Brotherhood's understanding of Islam was moderate and based on love. It was because of this understanding that people loved the Brotherhood and the Brotherhood spread around the world. However, al-Siddiqi also emphasised that al-Islah Society was independent and did not follow 'any external

---

66. https://twitter.com/malsiddiq/status/156800324944920578; https://twitter.com/malsiddiq/status/156802004516208640; https://twitter.com/malsiddiq/status/156802973090070528; https://twitter.com/malsiddiq/status/156804056541700096; https://twitter.com/malsiddiq/status/156807373216956416; https://twitter.com/malsiddiq/status/156808167425183746; https://twitter.com/malsiddiq/status/156808941685325825.
67. https://twitter.com/malsiddiq/status/162621979856351232; https://twitter.com/malsiddiq/status/162624248710574080; https://twitter.com/malsiddiq/status/162625097604141056
68. https://twitter.com/malsiddiq/status/156813584398159873
69. https://twitter.com/malsiddiq/status/156814657175298048
70. https://twitter.com/malsiddiq/status/157579366870695936

organization'.⁷¹ Al-Siddiqi also clarified his personal relationship with the Brotherhood: there was 'nothing wrong with learning from their thought and educational program'.⁷²

In February 2012, al-Siddiqi spoke of Syria. The regime in Syria was like 'the people of "Ad"', mentioned in the Qur'an, who 'unjustly sought dominance on earth saying, "Who is more powerful than us?"'⁷³ 'Let us arise!' al-Siddiqi called. 'Let us help our Syrian brethren with all we have. Prayer, money, assistance, advice.'⁷⁴ Al-Siddiqi was not highly critical of the UAE's stance on Syria. He even thanked the government for 'dismissing the ambassador [of Syria] and sending aid'. But the UAE could do more: it could 'provide full political, financial, media and military support to Syria' and even prepare 'an army to get rid of the tyrant'.⁷⁵

Yet al-Siddiqi also observed a general disinterest in UAE society about Syria.⁷⁶ Friday sermons, for example, did not touch on the issue.⁷⁷ Al-Siddiqi again accused the corrupt elements in the security apparatus: 'the criminals of the security apparatus want to kill our mosques, sermons and religion'.⁷⁸ The security apparatus was simply handing the sermon text to the prayer leaders and forbidding them to 'say anything outside' the text.⁷⁹ In the UAE,

71. https://twitter.com/malsiddiq/status/157895681573523456; https://twitter.com/malsiddiq/status/157897304102289408; https://twitter.com/malsiddiq/status/157897855955251200; https://twitter.com/malsiddiq/status/157898378401955841; https://twitter.com/malsiddiq/status/157900236176625665
72. https://twitter.com/malsiddiq/status/172790731130417152
73. https://twitter.com/malsiddiq/status/166614972649050113
74. https://twitter.com/malsiddiq/status/166975239350263809
75. https://twitter.com/malsiddiq/status/166614972649050113; https://twitter.com/malsiddiq/status/166983087648014336; https://twitter.com/malsiddiq/status/167334540463964161; https://twitter.com/malsiddiq/status/167339851086168064; https://twitter.com/malsiddiq/status/167349567690510336
76. https://twitter.com/malsiddiq/status/168068742591430657; https://twitter.com/malsiddiq/status/168069584748937216; https://twitter.com/malsiddiq/status/168075289379864577
77. https://twitter.com/malsiddiq/status/168062137200156672. On 20 February 2012, al-Siddiq said, in sermons in the UAE, 'it is absolutely forbidden to pray for Syria or Palestine': https://twitter.com/malsiddiq/status/171683206934966273.
78. https://twitter.com/malsiddiq/status/168077577095872512
79. https://twitter.com/malsiddiq/status/171683982134624256

al-Siddiqi declared, 'mosques are not for God, but for the corrupt security apparatus'.[80] The UAE was transforming into, al-Siddiqi pithily observed, a police state that was 'fighting against Islam and preachers'.[81] He also made a call: 'We must stand against the security apparatus before they ruin our religion and our world with their immorality and corruption.'[82]

As a religious scholar, al-Siddiqi brought up religious arguments against the UAE. But he also expressed his views, albeit rarely, on the ideal political system. For example, he claimed that 'governance based on consultation' was 'the right way of governance', a way the Prophet of Islam and his successors, the four caliphs, also adopted. That way of governance could take place only when 'people feel they are exercising their right to manage their own affairs'. People, wherever they are, al-Siddiqi declared, had 'the right to choose who represents them in the three branches of the government'.[83]

In late February 2012, there were reports of the UAE deporting dozens of Syrians. Al-Siddiqi apologised to those who were deported, according to him, for 'no good reason'. He extended his apology to all 'nations of revolutions' who were offended by the UAE's 'security apparatus', and also apologised to Qatar-based Yusuf al-Qaradawi, who raised the issue of deportation in his weekly programme on Al Jazeera.[84] Al-Siddiqi later shared the video of al-Qaradawi's remarks and once again apologised to al-Qaradawi for 'what the ignorant ones said about him'.[85]

Al-Siddiqi was also vocal in his criticism of the arrests of some leading members of al-Islah Society. When Salih al-Zufeiry was arrested, he said, 'my heart aches for the imprisonment of a blessed Sheikh like Salih al-Zufeiry'. When Ahmad Ghaith al-Suwaidi was arrested, Al-Siddiq said it was 'a crime

---

80. https://twitter.com/malsiddiq/status/171684544431394817
81. https://twitter.com/malsiddiq/status/158960747240624128
82. https://twitter.com/malsiddiq/status/168079965655543808
83. https://twitter.com/malsiddiq/status/168787632514539520; https://twitter.com/malsiddiq/status/168788556964298753; 2 April 2012: https://twitter.com/malsiddiq/status/186908284224155648
84. https://twitter.com/malsiddiq/status/174214017701773312; https://twitter.com/malsiddiq/status/174217198989090816; https://twitter.com/malsiddiq/status/174218179940327424
85. https://twitter.com/malsiddiq/status/176644958516822016; https://twitter.com/malsiddiq/status/176727033680887808

against the nation. He is known for this loyalty and righteousness.'[86] This was, al-Siddiqi declared, 'a year of oppression in the UAE'.[87] If Sheikh Zayed were alive, al-Siddiqi rhetorically asked, 'Would these violations of human dignity have taken place?'

On the same day he asked this question, Muhammad Abd al-Razzaq al-Siddiqi was arrested and, along with some ninety other UAE citizens, charged with forming an organisation that aimed to overthrow the government. On 2 July 2013 the Federal Supreme Court sentenced al-Siddiqi to ten years' imprisonment.

Kuwait

Unlike Saudi Arabia and the UAE, Kuwait had a more vibrant civil society, freer media and active parliamentary life. When the Arab Spring erupted, Kuwait was already in the midst of domestic political agitation.[88] The Arab Spring changed the regional environment within which political activism was taking place in Kuwait. For example, there had already been a campaign waged on the Internet at least since November 2010, which demanded the prime minister, Nasser bin Muhammad Al Sabah, step down. The slogan of the campaign resembled that of the protesters who rose against the regimes elsewhere in the Arab world during the Arab Spring: 'the people demand the downfall of Nasser'. The campaign led to a demonstration, joined by members of the parliament and activists, on 8 December 2010, which was dispersed forcefully by the regime. The prime minister barely survived a motion of no confidence but even so was able to stave off the mounting pressure.

Yet with the developments in Tunisia and Egypt, youth groups became emboldened again, asking for the resignation of the Interior Minister, a member of the ruling Al Sabah family, and calling for protests against the regime on 8 February 2011. The minister resigned on the 7th and the protests were postponed to 8 March. With 2011 being the fiftieth and twentieth

---

86. https://twitter.com/malsiddiq/status/180399317532672000 and 4 April 2012: https://twitter.com/malsiddiq/status/187623777214005252
87. https://twitter.com/malsiddiq/status/176180600070340608
88. For the following account, I benefited from Dazi-Heni, 'The Arab Spring impact on Kuwaiti "Exceptionalism"'; Tétreault, 'Looking for revolution in Kuwait'; Ghabra, 'Kuwait'.

anniversaries of Kuwait's independence from Britain and Iraq respectively, the regime announced a financial aid package worth $5.3 billion, including a one-off payment of $3,500 and fourteen months' free food baskets to every Kuwaiti family.

The Kuwaitis seemed to have been bought off. Only a few hundred stateless people, known as the bidoun, staged demonstrations and demanded Kuwaiti citizenship. Soon after, however, in early March 2011, some youth groups began another campaign that called for the resignation of the prime minister and greater political reforms. Despite their weekly meetings outside parliament, Kuwait did not witness street protests for several months to come. In September 2011 oil workers went on strike and forced the government to increase their salaries. While this move by the government stopped strikes in the oil industry, it set off strikes in other public sectors.

Further complicating the situation, Kuwait was about to go through what Shafiq Al-Ghabra called its own Watergate Scandal. In Autumn 2011 a public investigation found that several members of the parliament had received suspicious money transfers totalling millions of dollars. The prime minister was accused of bribing them. The allegations energised the opposition again, which began to organise protests against the prime minister. In mid-November 2011, the protests intensified and ended with parliament being stormed. Outside the parliament, tens of thousands of Kuwaitis protested.

The protesters achieved their objective. The prime minister resigned on 28 November. In a way, this was Kuwait's moment in the Arab Spring. More than a week later, the ruler of Kuwait dissolved the parliament 'due to the deteriorating conditions that led to difficulties in achieving progress and threatened the country's higher interests'. Kuwait was going to overcome the crisis by going 'back to the people to choose their representatives'.[89] Unfortunately, however, Kuwait could not. The new elections held in early February 2013 created an even more oppositional parliament, with thirty-five of the fifty seats going to opposition figures. A new series of protests and demonstrations would hit Kuwait again in October 2012.

Like their colleagues elsewhere in the Gulf, Brotherhood figures in Kuwait also embraced and enthusiastically supported the Arab Spring. Even Tariq

---

89. 'Emir of Kuwait dissolves parliament', *BBC News*, 6 December 2011.

al-Suwaidan, a figure devoted to preaching, did not hide his enthusiasm. When Zein al-Abidin bin Ali stepped down, al-Suwaidan was jubilant: 'To my brothers in green Tunisia,' he said, 'you have revolted against despotism (tughyan) today and succeeded.' He also gave advice to the Tunisians: 'do not ever accept despotism (tughyan) again'.[90]

Three days later, al-Suwaidan named political despotism (istibdad) as the most important obstacle the Islamic nation [ummah] faced in front of a reawakening. Next came financial and administrative corruption in al-Suwaidan's list of obstacles, followed by the nature of religious scholars' relations with the rulers, foreign intervention and Zionist occupation.[91]

In particular, the problem of political despotism (tughyan or istibdad) would repeatedly appear in al-Suwaidan's statements. When the protests erupted in Egypt, for example, he addressed the Egyptians: 'to our brothers and sisters in Egypt and the others in oppressed Arab countries, the change has started. So do not accept anything other than a radical change of despotism (tughyan).'[92]

A few days later, al-Suwaidan penned a piece for Qatar's *al-Watan* daily newspaper and cited several factors that led to the revolution, such as corruption, despotism, difficult life conditions, youth unemployment, lack of freedoms and human dignity. In the same piece, he declared those killed by the regime during the protests as 'martyrs', for their blood was spilled 'for the country and freedom'. Al-Suwaidan repeated his advice to the protesters not to accept anything less than a total overhaul of the regime. 'Not just individuals,' he asserted, 'the whole regime had to go . . . You are free. Do not accept humiliation. You started your revolution with dignity and complete it with dignity.' He added, 'May God give you victory over all tyrants.'[93]

When Hosni Mubarak stepped down, al-Suwaidan was joyful: 'We thank God . . . for the liberation of Egypt and the end of this despotic regime.' He added, 'We ask God to make this a start for the liberation of the rest of our people from despotism.'[94] As protests erupted elsewhere in the Arab

90. https://twitter.com/TareqAlSuwaidan/status/26296231290478592
91. https://twitter.com/TareqAlSuwaidan/status/27230525328457728
92. https://www.facebook.com/Dr.TareqAlSuwaidan/posts/197752730235022
93. Al-Suwaidan, 'Thawrat al-Sha'b al-Masri'.
94. https://www.facebook.com/Dr.TareqAlSuwaidan/posts/100878449993048

world, al-Suwaidan once again declared his happiness: 'Thank God. I lived to witness these revolutions that rocked the thrones of tyrants in the Arab world,' and added, 'I did not die in the era of tyranny.'[95] Earlier, al-Suwaidan declared those killed during the protests in Egypt 'martyrs'. Later he would declare all 'those who were killed in the Arab protests' as 'the masters of martyrs'[96] and 'the most noble of martyrs'.[97]

Al-Suwaidan also stated his views on Syria, Libya and Yemen. He was especially attentive to the developments in Libya. He called the rebels there 'our brothers' and asked religious scholars 'to raise their voices for the victory'. If they did not, he warned, the next generations would curse the current rulers and men of religion who remained silent.[98] Al-Suwaidan also wrote a highly emotional commentary on Libya for Qatar's *al-Watan* daily, in which he harshly criticised the regime in Libya for corruption, mismanagement of the country's wealth, brutality and despotism. He ended his commentary with a call to the rebels: 'I do not make my call to this regime because it is moronic . . . arrogant . . . criminal. But I speak in the name of our people that our hearts, our tongues and our times are with you until you become liberated from the tyranny of this regime.'[99] When Muammar Gaddafi was arrested, al-Suwaidan was unequivocal: 'I congratulate the Islamic nation [ummah], especially Libya,' he said, 'for the overthrow of the tyrant.' He added, 'I pray that all tyrants face a similar fate.'[100]

Al-Suwaidan was equally concerned about Syria. In late May 2011, he said, 'the Syrian people are heroic and will not give up even if thousands of martyrs fell'.[101] He called on everyone to stand with the protesters and support human rights in Syria: 'Those who hesitate . . . should re-think the values they adhere to.'[102] Al-Suwaidan was highly sceptical of the regime. He did not

---

95. https://twitter.com/TareqAlSuwaidan/status/39748705183744001
96. As he had earlier, al-Suwaidan added, 'God willing (insha Allah)' to this declaration: https://twitter.com/TareqAlSuwaidan/status/71542857885958144.
97. https://twitter.com/TareqAlSuwaidan/status/102847446325006336
98. https://www.facebook.com/Dr.TareqAlSuwaidan/posts/10150094591441677
99. Al-Suwaidan, 'Al-Thawrat al-Libiyya wa Junoun al-Hukm'.
100. https://twitter.com/TareqAlSuwaidan/status/127035806375354368
101. https://twitter.com/TareqAlSuwaidan/status/75219207675060224
102. https://twitter.com/TareqAlSuwaidan/status/101988058500579329

believe that Bashar al-Assad would undertake any reform, even if he declared so.[103] Al-Suwaidan also turned his anger against Russia, which stood with the Assad regime. 'It is time for Arabs', he declared, 'to act collectively against Russia.' Then Russia 'would be forced to choose between the people and the tyrants'.[104] Al-Suwaidan also signed the religious edict (fatwa) prepared by Yusuf al-Qaradawi and supported by more than a hundred religious scholars. The edict declared it obligatory 'to break away from the Bashar regime' and 'to support the Syrian revolution and the Free Army'.[105] He added, 'Whoever supports the Syrian regime is a traitor and whoever funds it is an enemy, including Russia, China, Iran and Hezbollah.'[106]

Al-Suwaidan also supported the protesters turning to violence against the Syrian regime. This was because 'protests were met with violence' in Syria: 'The people have the right to defend themselves with every possible weapon.'[107] He also responded to those 'who say that the Syrian revolution has to stay non-violent': 'Look at what the regime did in the last 12 months.'[108] Not surprisingly, al-Suwaidan supported Saudi Arabia and Qatar 'for calling for arming the Syrian fighters of religion (mujaheden)'.[109]

While he was enthusiastic about the protests in Egypt and elsewhere, al-Suwaidan was more tolerant towards the regime in Bahrain. However, he did not seek to de-legitimise the protests either. In a statement addressed to the protesters to clarify his position, he declared his firm belief in 'people's right in freedom, in human rights, and in people's full political participation', adding irrespective of 'their religion and sect'. Al-Suwaidan also stated his refusal of any foreign involvement in Bahrain's affairs, be that Iran or any other state. More significantly, in the same statement he also noted Bahrain's

---

103. https://twitter.com/TareqAlSuwaidan/status/104087199955435520 and 10 September 2011: https://twitter.com/TareqAlSuwaidan/status/112592754906894337
104. https://twitter.com/TareqAlSuwaidan/status/162988799431950338. See also https://twitter.com/TareqAlSuwaidan/status/162992501605679104
105. https://twitter.com/TareqAlSuwaidan/status/168069925389336577
106. https://twitter.com/TareqAlSuwaidan/status/168445961641803776
107. https://twitter.com/TareqAlSuwaidan/status/170488348421533696
108. https://twitter.com/TareqAlSuwaidan/status/174241861425299458
109. https://twitter.com/TareqAlSuwaidan/status/174165417357619200. See also https://twitter.com/TareqAlSuwaidan/status/210091626293493761

different approach to the protests and attributed this to Bahrain's crown prince. Al-Suwaidan described the crown prince's prevention of the Special Forces' intervention in the protests and his call for comprehensive dialogue as 'rational and gentle'. Al-Suwaidan ended his statement with a prayer, 'I ask God to give Bahrain security, stability, renaissance, revival, love and harmony',[110] a prayer against neither the regime nor the protesters.[111]

Al-Suwaidan visited Egypt in June 2011 and saw there was an 'atmosphere of freedom'. 'I hope', he declared, this atmosphere 'continues and Egypt remains the leader of the development of our nation [ummah]'.[112] Because of this freedom, Egypt was also 'the leader of creativity'.[113] Egypt was leading a change, a change that would not be restricted 'to Egypt and Arabs, but to Muslims and the world'. This was 'a turning point in history'.[114]

In the relatively open political environment in Kuwait, Tareq al-Suwaidan could speak out more freely. In September 2011 he even joined other Kuwaitis and protested in front of the parliament 'to demand radical change and the overthrow of corrupt figures'. In Kuwait, he claimed, an atmosphere of freedom came with the demand for the overthrow of Kuwait's prime minister.[115] Even though the protests lasted longer than expected, al-Suwaidan still expressed hope: 'I am not pessimistic,' he said. 'I can confidently say that the current government is the most ineffective government Kuwait has ever had.' He called on the government to 'leave now'.[116] Three weeks later, he repeated his call: 'Leave now before things get worse', and joined the protesters again in order to 'reject corruption'. He added, 'I consider abstaining from participation to be weakness and carelessness.' Al-Suwaidan was also appreciative of the relatively freer environment in Kuwait. 'Thank God for

---

110. https://www.facebook.com/notes/10150097720291677/
111. Two weeks later, al-Suwaidan issued another statement on Bahrain and reiterated similar views: https://www.facebook.com/notes/10150110099821677/
112. https://twitter.com/TareqAlSuwaidan/status/76706412297846784
113. https://twitter.com/TareqAlSuwaidan/status/76951533308223488
114. https://twitter.com/TareqAlSuwaidan/status/79152538288533505
115. https://twitter.com/TareqAlSuwaidan/status/116551545880977409; https://twitter.com/TareqAlSuwaidan/status/116577006132531200; https://twitter.com/TareqAlSuwaidan/status/116578597904465921; https://twitter.com/TareqAlSuwaidan/status/126781183852949504
116. https://twitter.com/TareqAlSuwaidan/status/132414320356229120

blessing with freedom,' he said, and added, 'If I were tweeting in another country, I would have been arrested or assassinated.'[117]

Tareq al-Suwaidan also showed great interest in Egypt's elections. When the Muslim Brotherhood-affiliated Freedom and Justice Party won the first round of parliamentary elections, for example, he claimed that Zionists were growing 'worried' and rhetorically asked, 'What is the opinion of those who accuse them [Islamists] of treason?'[118] When the presidential elections approached, he declared, 'I salute Egyptians for their perseverance and their insistence to make their revolution succeed,' and added, 'I pray that Egypt elects the strong and honest to lead it.' Reiterating Egypt's importance, al-Suwaidan stated, 'For the Islamic nation [ummah] will not experience a renaissance without Egypt.'[119]

When it turned out that the Muslim Brotherhood-backed Muhammad Morsi would face Ahmad Shafik in the second round of the presidential election, al-Suwaidan declared his support for the former: 'it is better in any democracy not to have one party controlling all institutions'. But in the case of Egypt, where the previous regime had a candidate, 'then electing Morsi is better'.[120] This was because 'the revolution will not be complete if all major pillars of the Mubarak regime, who crippled Egypt for decades, are not removed'.[121] With a Shafik win, the old regime would be back in power.[122]

When Morsi finally won, al-Suwaidan thanked God who, paraphrasing a verse (3:26) from the Qur'an, 'grants his dominion to whom he wishes and takes his dominion away from whom he wishes, who exalts whom he wishes and abases whom he wishes'. Al-Suwaidan then hoped that Morsi's presidency was a blessing for the Islamic nation [ummah].[123] He also congratulated Egypt and Egyptians on Morsi's victory. But he also warned, 'the

---

117. https://twitter.com/TareqAlSuwaidan/status/140090224561766400; https://twitter.com/TareqAlSuwaidan/status/140903163606745088; https://twitter.com/TareqAlSuwaidan/status/140737914865856512
118. https://twitter.com/TareqAlSuwaidan/status/143399432271036416
119. https://twitter.com/TareqAlSuwaidan/status/198139166519857153
120. https://twitter.com/TareqAlSuwaidan/status/206261648976117761
121. https://twitter.com/TareqAlSuwaidan/status/206424064024248320
122. https://twitter.com/TareqAlSuwaidan/status/208777935539273728
123. https://twitter.com/TareqAlSuwaidan/status/216903248102178818

battle for development, freedom and justice has begun'. The first battle was 'to regain the powers of the people and the parliament'.[124]

After the military issued an ultimatum to Muhammad Morsi, al-Suwaidan clearly stated, 'I respect people's will, but reject the military rule.'[125] After the coup was executed and Morsi was overthrown, al-Suwaidan repeatedly expressed his objections to military rule and its intervention in politics. 'The coup in Egypt, the censorship of media, the campaign of arrests,' al-Suwaidan said, 'are dangerous' and must come to an end 'as soon as possible'.[126] Egypt was in crisis and there was no way out 'except restoring Morsi to presidency' and 'all sides agree on a shared plan'.[127] Mubarak had no legitimacy because he 'rigged the elections'. But Morsi had legitimacy because he 'came through free elections'.[128] 'Military coups' were ugly. And, al-Suwaidan declared, 'We will all stand against any coup, even if it is against Baradei, Moussa and Sabahi.'[129]

Al-Suwaidan was furious when pro-Morsi supporters met with violence. 'How many deaths', he rhetorically asked, 'do Sisi supporters need before they wake up to the brutality of the military rule?'[130] He was furious when protesters were killed. 'The shedding of innocent blood in Egypt' was forbidden in religion [haraam], and 'whoever supports or condones it' was 'a partner in crime'.[131]

Al-Suwaidan criticised everyone who supported the military coup in Egypt. The Salafis, the liberals, the Tamarod (Rebellion) movement and the US received their share of his criticisms. Of the liberals, for example, he said, 'Arab liberals justify dictatorship against their opponents, thus have betrayed

---

124. https://twitter.com/TareqAlSuwaidan/status/216900851841761280 and https://twitter.com/TareqAlSuwaidan/status/216907200730374144
125. https://twitter.com/TareqAlSuwaidan/status/352041053643214848
126. https://twitter.com/TareqAlSuwaidan/status/352713833875374080. See also 6 July 2013: https://twitter.com/TareqAlSuwaidan/status/353417091564568577; https://twitter.com/TareqAlSuwaidan/status/353463222872981505; 8 July 2013: https://twitter.com/TareqAlSuwaidan/status/354165084257402880
127. https://twitter.com/TareqAlSuwaidan/status/354159062277046273
128. https://twitter.com/TareqAlSuwaidan/status/355574943389458433
129. https://twitter.com/TareqAlSuwaidan/status/355608970922172416 and https://twitter.com/TareqAlSuwaidan/status/355577080014045184
130. https://twitter.com/TareqAlSuwaidan/status/361014435185299456
131. https://twitter.com/TareqAlSuwaidan/status/361213547641974784

the foundation of liberalism.' Now, he suggested, the liberals 'should look for another disguise to hide behind'.[132] As for the US, al-Suwaidan stated in English, 'The USA claims to support democracy in the world', and 'respects the will of the people then fails miserably when it supports the coup' in Egypt.[133]

Al-Suwaidan was also critical of countries, including Saudi Arabia, the UAE and Kuwait, which extended financial aid to Egypt's new government. In mid-August 2013, he was harsh: 'May God punish those who support the coup with money or helped in the bloodshed.'[134] He was openly against Kuwait's support for the coup. On the same day, he invited 'all anti-coup people' in Kuwait 'to gather in front of the Egyptian consulate' so that 'the Kuwait government would see the amount of popular opposition to the brutal coup'.[135] Two days later, he declared, 'We apologise to the great Egyptian people for Kuwait's support of the coup and for the killing of the innocent. We leave them to God to judge.'[136] A day later, al-Suwaidan was fired from the al-Resalah channel owned by the Saudi Prince, Al-Waleed bin Talal al Saud, for his staunch opposition to the military coup.

Undeterred by the dismissal, al-Suwaidan declared that the coup destroyed all the achievements of the Arab Spring: an elected president was overthrown, hundreds of people killed, thousands injured, media censored, military rule restored and Mubarak set free.[137] His overall assessment was: 'All Arab Spring nations moved forward.' But Egypt was an exception. 'It moved backward.'[138]

The case of Tareq al-Suwaidan illustrates that Muslim Brotherhood figures in Kuwait were emboldened and inspired by the Arab Spring. Although the regime had already been facing an oppositional Brotherhood, the rise of the so-called Muslim Brotherhood Crescent could further complicate the situation for Kuwait as a Brotherhood-dominated Egypt allied with Turkey could disproportionately change the regional context in favour of the opposition.

132. https://twitter.com/TareqAlSuwaidan/status/363906572319481856
133. https://twitter.com/TareqAlSuwaidan/status/363428443473461248
134. https://twitter.com/TareqAlSuwaidan/status/367598994048180224
135. https://twitter.com/TareqAlSuwaidan/status/367622947990933504
136. https://twitter.com/TareqAlSuwaidan/status/368467643562729472
137. https://twitter.com/TareqAlSuwaidan/status/370258514490695680
138. https://twitter.com/TareqAlSuwaidan/status/371642567269810176

Special Cases: Bahrain and Qatar

Bahrain

Bahrain was also troubled by the Arab Spring but did not take the extreme step of declaring the Muslim Brotherhood a terrorist organisation. This was because, unlike Saudi Arabia, the UAE and Kuwait, Bahrain still had cordial relations with the Brotherhood. With its dwindling oil revenues and deeply divided society, Bahrain was the most vulnerable of the Gulf states to the Arab Spring.[139] It had already witnessed massive protests and the Shia majority had been growing restless throughout the 2000s. In late January 2011 there were indications on social media of preparations to stage massive protests. In early February there were calls to start the protests on 14 February. Massive protests did indeed erupt on that day, with protesters demanding political, economic and social reforms. The state responded with a combination of soft and hard measures: on the one hand it sought to appease the protesters by holding talks with their leaders and promising reforms. Fortunately, the protesters were by and large Shias, whose leaders could be identified. On the other hand the regime resorted to violence, killing a protester on the first day.

As the days passed, the protests did not subside but instead grew in intensity. Bahrain experienced a cycle of protests and state violence, which fed off each other. In late February the protesters began to demand the fall of the regime rather than reforms. As the regime proved incapable of stopping the protests, other Gulf States rushed to help. On 10 March Saudi Arabia, Kuwait, Qatar and the UAE announced that they would provide $10 billion in aid to Bahrain. Four days later, the Gulf Cooperation Council's joint military force, the Jazeera Shield Forces, entered Bahrain to protect vital sites on the island, relieving Bahrain's own security forces of this task. The following day the regime declared a state of emergency, enabling the security forces to take more forceful measures against the protesters. A massive crackdown in the ensuing month effectively ended the protests, leaving a crippled economy and a more deeply divided society.

---

139. The most detailed narrative of the developments in Bahrain can be found in a report prepared by a commission led by a respected international lawyer and academic, Mahmoud Cherif Bassiouni. The commission was established by the King of Bahrain, Hamad bin Isa Al Khalifa, in early July 2011. The report is available at http://www.bici.org.bh/BICIreportEN.pdf.

In Bahrain, the regime found in the Muslim Brotherhood a loyal ally against the protesters. Al-Islah Society, led by a member of the ruling family, Sheikh Isa bin Muhammad Al Khalifa, had by and large remained silent on the developments in the Arab world. This was understandable, as an enthusiastic embrace of the protests elsewhere in the Arab world would be a difficult and hypocritical attitude to hold if similar protests were to erupt in Bahrain.

Yet the Society did not keep silent when the protests indeed erupted in Bahrain. Its first statement appeared in February 2011 issue of the Society's journal, with the cover page depicting Bahrain's flag. In the statement, the Society declared it had been following the events 'with great sorrow and sadness' and prayed to God not to drag the country 'into further escalation' towards which, the Society believed, 'some hidden hands are trying to push' it. Praising the king for the measures taken, the Society also offered 'condolences to the families of the victims' and prayed to God 'to give them patience and solace'. The Society emphasised that the current regime, with its institution and the rule of Al Khalifa family, was legitimate and any demand for reform had to be voiced 'through constitutional means'. The call for the overthrow of the regime was, the Society believed, 'totally unacceptable'. The Society warned that 'escalation in sectarian conflict' would bring 'no outcome' and would also prevent the country's fight with 'corruption' and efforts to improve 'living conditions'. The Society also asserted that the events in Bahrain had no similarity with what had happened in Tunisia and Egypt, where 'all classes and members of the nation and active political forces have rallied'. In contrast, 'a small group of a purely sectarian nature' was seeking 'to replicate it in Bahrain'. The Society ended its statement praying to God 'to protect the Kingdom of Bahrain from sedition and bless all its people with the blessings of security and stability'.[140]

When the protests were quelled, the Society issued another statement on 5 April. In it the Society expressed its satisfaction with 'the gradual return of security and stability in the country'. After thanking God, the Society praised the king and the security forces for their efforts in bringing about this outcome. The Society also extended its thanks to the rulers of 'the Gulf

---

140. Jam'iyyat al-Islah, 'Bayan min Jam'iyyat al-Islah bi Sha'n al-Ahdath al-Akhirah fi Bilad wa Tada'ayatiha'.

Cooperation Council' for their support of Bahrain and for sending the Jazeera Shield Forces.

The Society commended its own members for their participation in popular committees formed 'to contribute to maintaining security, strengthening cooperation and solidarity among the members of the society, combating the smear campaigns that targeted Bahrain's reputation at home and abroad'. The Society also thanked its members 'who made personal contact with and communicated with different Islamist personalities and Islamic movements in Gulf countries and the Arab and Muslim world' to present 'the truth of the schemes that are targeting the Kingdom of Bahrain'.

The Society believed that the tragic events in Bahrain 'revealed a dangerous plan that targeted the stability and security of the country'. More critically, the Society claimed, the Iranian regime had blatantly intervened, in order to open up 'a large crack in the national unity shared by the people of Bahrain'. The Society also called on 'the authorities to hold accountable those who are found guilty of taking part in this malicious scheme, and those who tried to paralyze life in this country, mounted attacks against security forces, citizens and residents'.[141]

The Society was then silent for a number of months. It only became outspoken about the situation in Syria one year after the protests there started. On 4 February 2012 the Society prayed for Syria: 'O God, be with our brothers in Syria. O God, be helpful to them . . . O God, be supportive of them . . . O God, protect them.'[142] Two days later, the Society called on prayer leaders in Bahrain to pray for Syria and Bahrain. The Society also organised a variety of events and programmes[143] and took part in the establishment of a national committee to help the Syrians. The Society believed that the revolution in Syria was undermining Iran. It shared with its followers two quotes, stating this belief. In one, Dr Al-Harbash said the revolution in Syria had awakened the Islamic nation [ummah] and was destroying 'the Iranian–Safavid project' that endangered the Gulf.[144] In another quote, Abd al-Halim Murad claimed 'the Safavid–Zionist–Crusader triangle' was at work in Syria because what

141. http://www.twitlonger.com/show/9maf27
142. https://twitter.com/eslahbh/status/165856718058815488
143. https://twitter.com/eslahbh/status/177397015217577984
144. The tweet does not specify the name of Dr Harbash, but he must be Jaman al-Harbash, a prominent figure from the Kuwaiti Muslim Brotherhood: https://twitter.com/eslahbh/status/178536706771922947.

was happening there was 'the decisive battle'.¹⁴⁵ It is important to note that such a stance on Syria did not put the Society at odds with Bahrain or, for that matter, Saudi Arabia.

In late May 2012, members of al-Islah Society and al-Minbar visited Qatar-based Yusuf al-Qaradawi. Al-Qaradawi described the events in Bahrain as 'sectarian' and claimed that they targeted Bahrain's stability and security.¹⁴⁶ A month later, both the Society and al-Minbar issued a statement congratulating Muhammad Morsi, the Muslim Brotherhood and the FJP for winning the Egyptian presidential elections. The statement also prayed to God 'to bestow upon Egypt security, stability and prosperity, so it would fulfill its role of supporting the Arab and Muslim causes'. The statement also asked Egypt to support the Palestinians against 'the regional plans and projects'.¹⁴⁷

More critically, after Morsi was sworn in as president, a delegation from Society and al-Minbar visited Egypt and met with Muhammad Badi, the supreme guide of the Muslim Brotherhood. The headline of the article reporting the visit quoted Badi as saying, 'the stability of Bahrain and all other Gulf states means stability of Egypt – I refused to meet the Iranian ambassador several times until his country shifts its position on Gulf states and Syria'. The piece further quoted Badi as saying, 'the leadership and people and dynamic powers in Bahrain are capable of solving their problems independently, without the slightest amount of foreign intervention'. Badi further confirmed that the fate of 'the Egyptian and Bahraini peoples . . . is one, and we will not allow any harm to befall the Bahraini people, and their kingdom, which is dear to our hearts, and we will not allow any interventions in their internal affairs, or any bargaining'.¹⁴⁸

In mid-April 2013, al-Islah Society organised a public lecture by Dr Sultan al-Amin, the Secretary General of the Supreme Council of Islamic Affairs in Egypt, who was highly sympathetic to Muhammad Morsi. He said, for example, 'I see a religious worshipper in Dr Morsi.' Al-Amin also

---

145. Abd al-Halim Murat was a member of the Bahraini parliament from al-Asalah: https://twitter.com/eslahbh/status/178540081366310913.
146. https://twitter.com/eslahbh/status/206026237179736066
147. https://twitter.com/eslahbh/status/217325753023471617; https://twitter.com/eslahbh/status/217326400342982657; https://twitter.com/eslahbh/status/217327966907154432; https://twitter.com/eslahbh/status/217328628965449729
148. https://twitter.com/eslahbh/status/222782694885572608

reminded his listeners that for Morsi, 'the security of Egypt begins in the entire Gulf' and that the Egyptian people were 'conscious of the Iranian plan in Egypt'.[149]

In the following months, the Society was again silent and kept its silence even about the military coup in Egypt. Having adopted a pro-regime attitude during the protests, the Muslim Brotherhood proved itself a loyal ally of the regime in Bahrain. Therefore, while the UAE and Saudi Arabia declared the movement a terrorist organisation, Bahrain did not.

Qatar

Among all the Gulf States, Qatar was the country least affected by the Arab Spring. It witnessed almost no public discontent or unrest. No groups were formed to stage demonstrations against the regime or to submit petitions. The only development that can be associated with the Arab Spring was that a former professor at Qatar University, Ali al-Kuwari, started meetings by invitation only in mid-March 2011 and continued to hold them almost every month until February 2012. A total of seventy-three Qatari citizens[150] attended all twelve meetings but failed to turn these into a mass pressure group.

The only tangible outcome of the meetings was a book written by Ali al-Kuwari published in Beirut, Lebanon in October 2012. Even the title of the book is illustrative of how little Qatar was affected by the Arab Spring: *al-Sha'b Yurid al-Islah fi Qatar . . . Aidan* (in Arabic) or *The People Want Reform . . . in Qatar, Too*. Because the book was critical of the political, economic, social and cultural systems, if not directly of Qatar's rulers, it was banned in Qatar. Yet neither Ali al-Kuwari nor any person who attended the meetings has since been arrested. The only similar instance occurred in November 2011 when the regime arrested a poet, Muhammad al-Dhib al-Ajami, for writing a poem allegedly insulting the ruler of Qatar and inciting a rebellion.

---

149. https://twitter.com/eslahbh/status/323404657441517568; https://twitter.com/eslahbh/status/323496370562531329; https://twitter.com/eslahbh/status/323511461840314368; https://twitter.com/eslahbh/status/323512194698457088
150. The names are available at http://dr-alkuwari.net/sites/akak/files/names-until-moday_17.pdf.

Like other the Gulf states, Qatar mobilised its financial largesse, increasing basic salaries, social allowances to military personnel of officer rank by 120 per cent, military personnel of other ranks by 50 per cent and civilian state employees by 60 per cent. Qatar also raised the pensions of the same groups by the same percentages.[151] Yet this move came in September 2011, months after the Arab Spring had already shown signs that it would not spread to the Gulf countries. As such, the staggering salary increases were not the regime's attempt to pacify a society in turmoil but as the regime's reward for society's passivity in a time of unrest elsewhere in the Arab world.

More critically, unlike other Gulf states, Qatar did not seem to be alarmed by the rise of the Muslim Brotherhood. This was despite Brotherhood figures in Qatar wholeheartedly welcoming the Arab Spring. This can be seen in statements by Yusuf al-Qaradawi, the Brotherhood's most iconic figure in the Gulf.[152] When Zein al-Abidine Bin Ali stepped down on 14 January 2011, al-Qaradawi praised the Tunisians and described them as setting an 'example for the Arab peoples and the other suppressed people and crushed masses of the entire world'.[153] Just four days after the protests broke out in Egypt, Yusuf al-Qaradawi explicitly called on the Egyptians to oust Hosni Mubarak. Speaking on Al Jazeera, he said Mubarak's 'regime must learn a lesson from the happenings in Tunisia. I advise Mubarak to leave Egypt. Having been in the saddle for 30 years is enough'.[154] Two days later, on 31 January, Qaradawi declared those killed by the police to be 'martyrs' and renewed his call on Mubarak to leave power to the people.[155] One week after Mubarak stepped down on 11 February, al-Qaradawi was in Tahrir Square in Cairo and delivered a sermon to the millions gathered there. He praised the youth and the people of Egypt, encouraging them to protect the revolution and work hard to solve Egypt's problems, and called on Egypt's armed

---

151. Toumi, 'Public sector in Qatar to get 60 per cent pay rise'.
152. For a lengthier discussion, see Warren, 'The "Ulama" and the Arab Uprisings 2011–2013'.
153. See 'Al-Qaradawi yawzah mawkufihi min al-Bu'azizi'.
154. 'Mubarak must go, says Qaradawi.'
155. 'Protestors killed in Egypt are martyrs, says Qaradawi.'

forces to respect the revolution. In his concluding remarks, al-Qaradawi addressed the other Arab leaders:

> Don't be arrogant! Don't delude yourselves! Don't stop History! Nobody will be able to fight the divine decrees, nor to delay the day when it rises. This world has changed and the world has evolved. The Arab world has changed from the inside. So, do not stand against the peoples (sha'b). Try to come to an understanding with them! Don't deceive them! Don't try to get them with empty words! It is not possible that peoples (sha'b) remain silent. Dialogue with them in a real dialogue, not to patch things up, but with constructive actions, constructive actions that put things in their places, respect the minds of people (nâs) and respect the minds of the peoples (sha'b)!¹⁵⁶

In Yemen and Libya too, al-Qaradawi took a strong pro-revolutionary stand. Soon after the protests started in Libya, on 21 February 2011 al-Qaradawi, for example, issued a religious declaration, a fatwa, on the life of the Libyan leader, Muammar Gaddafi. He said on a programme aired on Al Jazeera, 'I give this fatwa: officers and soldiers, those who can, kill Muammar al-Gaddafi . . . thus save the people and the ummah from the evil of this mad person.'[157]

Meanwhile, al-Qaradawi had also been active in declaring his unequivocal support for the Syrian revolution almost from the beginning. Soon after the protests erupted in Syria, al-Qaradawi said in his Friday sermon on 25 March 2011, 'Winds of change are not far from Syria.' He added, 'Nothing comes for free in the world. The blood of martyrs in Dar'a [the town where the first protests broke out in Syria] killed by bullets will be a torch leading you to victory and all should back and support civilians of Dar'a in the revolution.'[158] In August 2011, al-Qaradawi gave his endorsement to a fatwa issued by religious scholars from Kuwait. The fatwa, among other things, called on all Arab

---

156. Translated by Dr Yahya Michot of Hartford Seminary. The text of the full translation of the sermon is available at http://www.beliefnet.com/columnists/cityofbrass/2011/03/the-khutbah-sermon-of-yusuf-al.html#.
157. Al-Qaradawi issued this fatwa on a programme on Al Jazeera, which can be found at http://www.youtube.com/watch?v=bEe8GouMrtY.
158. 'Qaradawi backs Syrian revolution.'

and Muslim countries to assist financially the Syrian people and cut all their ties with the Syrian regime. This fatwa fell short of calling for direct military aid for the Syrian people, but that call also came. In February 2012, around the same time the Gulf States began to make calls for military action against the regime in Syria, al-Qaradawi joined some hundred religious scholars and issued a fatwa calling on other Muslim states to help the Free Syrian Army.[159]

Yet al-Qaradawi showed little interest in the protests in Bahrain. He refused the request of a prominent Shia scholar from Najaf, Iraq, to support the protests. Worse, he dismissed them as sectarian. In his Friday sermon delivered on 18 March 2011, two days after Saudi Arabia-led Gulf forces had intervened in Bahrain, al-Qaradawi said, 'Truly the Bahrain revolution, it is not a revolution, rather it's a sectarian uprising . . . It's Shia against Sunni, I am not against the Shia, I'm against fanaticism . . . they aren't peaceful, they're using weapons'.[160]

Al-Qaradawi also observed the post-Mubarak developments in Egypt. He closely followed both the parliamentary and presidential elections and issued regular statements, even in his Friday sermons. In mid-October 2011 he was certain that the future was bright. The nineteenth century "was the century of capitalism and the 20th century was the century of communism'. Al-Qaradawi declared the twenty-first century would be 'the century of Islam'.[161] As the first round of parliamentary elections approached, he unequivocally declared his support for the Muslim Brotherhood. He dismissed the accusation that the Brotherhood had an excessive desire 'to seize power' and even argued that the movement unnecessarily 'shied away from it'.[162] He even added, 'the interest of our country now lies in the rise of the Muslim Brotherhood to power'. This was 'their role and duty'.[163] When the Brotherhood scored a victory in the parliamentary elections, al-Qaradawi confidently declared, 'I am not surprised at all by the performance of the Muslim Brotherhood in the Egyptian elections.'[164]

---

159. 'Fatwa on Syria by 107 scholars.'
160. Cited in Warren, 'The "Ulama" and the Arab Uprisings 2011–2013', p. 17.
161. https://twitter.com/alqaradawy/status/126281478890983425
162. https://twitter.com/alqaradawy/status/140449927338795008
163. https://twitter.com/alqaradawy/status/140843997504614400
164. Yusuf al-Qaradawi was surprised by the electoral success of the Salafis in the elections: https://twitter.com/alqaradawy/status/171172911271510016

After the parliamentary elections, al-Qaradawi turned his attention to the presidential elections and supported the candidacy of Abdul Moneim Abul Futouh, who was also a member of, but not officially nominated by, the Muslim Brotherhood. He was, according to al-Qaradawi, the 'most suitable compared to the rest of the candidates'.[165] Al-Qaradawi was concerned that the Brotherhood would not 'nominate an Islamist presidential candidate' and publicly asked the movement not to 'let down the one who represents them', who was 'Abul Futouh'.[166]

Yet when the Brotherhood nominated Muhammad Morsi, Yusuf al-Qaradawi did not express any discontent, at least publicly. In the second round of presidential elections, al-Qaradawi even declared, 'Making Shafik [Morsi's rival] fail in the elections is a religious, Shar'i, and moral duty.'[167] During the election process, al-Qaradawi not only declared his 'trust' in the Muslim Brotherhood, but also advised the movement 'to engage all the competent noble people' and listen to and reassure 'the Copts', who had some concerns.[168]

When Morsi was elected as Egypt's president, the al-Qaradawi-led al-Ittihad al-'Alemi al-'Ulama' al-Muslimin (International Union of Muslim Religious Scholars) issued a statement congratulating him and also met with him.[169] Al-Qaradawi also supported Morsi especially after he began to take some controversial steps. In late November, for example, al-Qaradawi declared that Morsi's decisions 'met the demands of the people', adding that he also supported 'these decisions'.[170] Furthermore, al-Qaradawi noted, Morsi had 'the right to take these measures', as God had placed that responsibility 'upon his shoulder'.[171] Al-Qaradawi also added that neither Morsi

---

165. https://twitter.com/alqaradawy/status/163300875689930752
166. https://twitter.com/alqaradawy/status/168710607967764480
167. https://twitter.com/alqaradawy/status/208568096569556992
168. https://twitter.com/alqaradawy/status/209994757383012352 and https://twitter.com/alqaradawy/status/210322824886358016
169. https://twitter.com/alqaradawy/status/217628375605456898 and https://twitter.com/alqaradawy/status/221346122717868034
170. Al-Qaradawi particularly noted that he supported the sacking of the Prosecutor General: https://twitter.com/alqaradawy/status/272006870829527040; https://twitter.com/alqaradawy/status/272006959186710529.
171. https://twitter.com/alqaradawy/status/272780152805670912

nor his party had any interest in taking these decisions, but Egypt had. Morsi's decisions were, al-Qaradawi declared, 'in the national interest'.[172]

Al-Qaradawi also declared his support for the new Egyptian constitution. 'This constitution project,' he said, 'Egypt has never seen one like it before.'[173] Al-Qaradawi called on all Egyptians to cast their vote in the referendum on the new constitution and announced that he would vote 'yes'. The constitution, even though it had some objectionable components, was 'overall a great constitution'.[174]

Immediately after the coup, al-Qaradawi issued a fatwa: the Shariah, the fatwa claimed, made it incumbent upon Muslims to fully obey 'the chosen ruler, to implement his commands, and accept his directives in all matters of life, as long as two conditions are met'. Discussing these conditions, the fatwa claimed that they were not met in order for Muslims to disobey Morsi. It was necessary, therefore, that Morsi 'remain the president and no one can claim any right to depose him'. Al-Qaradawi ended his fatwa with a call to

> all of the Egyptian people . . . to stand together united on one platform to protect the fruits of the revolution . . . freedom, democracy, and liberation from every dictatorship. We must not abandon them for any despotic ruler, whether he is military or civil, for this is what happened to some nations that ended up losing their freedom and did not regain it until years later.[175]

In the succeeding months, al-Qaradawi continued to make similar statements, sparing no one in Egypt in his criticism. Individuals from Abdel Fattah el-Sisi to Ali Gomaa, the Sheikh of al-Azhar, repeatedly received their share of al-Qaradawi's criticism.[176] He eventually even criticised the UAE and Saudi Arabia. In January 2014, for example, he criticised the UAE for its support of the Egyptian government and claimed that the UAE 'has always been opposed

---

172. https://twitter.com/alqaradawy/status/272780152805670912 and https://twitter.com/alqaradawy/status/272780828499648512
173. https://twitter.com/alqaradawy/status/274872313521004544
174. https://twitter.com/alqaradawy/status/278458600916144128 and https://twitter.com/alqaradawy/status/278458828889145344
175. Al-Qaradawi, 'Fatwa of Shaikh Yusuf Qaradawi on the military coup in Egypt'.
176. Schenker, 'Qaradawi's war for Egypt'.

to Islamic rule', a remark the UAE considered an 'insult'.[177] In the same month, al-Qaradawi gave an interview to Reuters and said that the Saudis were supporting those 'who are far from God and Islam' and who 'kill innocent Egyptians'. He also called on the Saudis 'to stand with the Egyptian people against the murderers and executioners, to stand with the right against wrong, to stand with the slain against the killer, to stand with the oppressed against the oppressors'.[178]

For Qatar, however, Yusuf al-Qaradawi's enthusiasm for the Arab Spring was not troubling. This was in large part because al-Qaradawi's stand on the Arab Spring ran parallel to Qatar's own. Unlike other Gulf states, Qatar seemed untroubled by the Arab Spring.[179] It even welcomed the rise of the Muslim Brotherhood. This was most likely because Qatar had been friendly towards the Brotherhood[180] and, more importantly, had nurtured strong ties with the transnational Brotherhood movement.[181] Qatar was so confident of its relations with the Brotherhood that the prime minister and Minister of Foreign Affairs, Hamad bin Jassim Al Thani, prophesied after the first round of parliamentary elections in Egypt that Islamists would assume political power in the Arab world and said, 'We shouldn't fear them, let's co-operate with them', adding that moderate Islamists could even be useful 'in fighting against the extremists'.[182]

Qatar also became the prime financial backer of Egypt during Muhammad Morsi's presidency. Qatar's ruler, Hamad bin Khalifa, was the first and only

---

177. 'UAE, Saudi Arabia and Bahrain recall their ambassadors from Qatar.'
178. Bakr, 'Influential cleric urges Saudis to stop backing Egypt's dominant military'.
179. For Qatar's foreign policy during the Arab Spring, see Ulrichsen, *Qatar and the Arab Spring*.
180. David Roberts argues that because the Brotherhood's society base in Qatar was weak and therefore could not pose a serious internal threat, Qatar was able to pursue an active foreign policy during the Arab Spring and hope to benefit from the rise of the Muslim Brotherhood. See Roberts, 'Qatar and the Muslim Brotherhood'. Yet I should add that the Brotherhood's penetration into UAE society was not that deep either. The opposition the Brotherhood waged in the UAE did not involve any grassroots societal mobilisation, but rather generated an oppositional discourse that challenged the legitimacy of the state. See al-Zoby and Başkan, 'Discourse of oppositionality in the Arab Spring'.
181. See Chesnot and Malbrunot, *Qatar Papers*.
182. Khalaf and Saleh, 'West "should not fear Islamist movements"'.

Gulf leader who visited Egypt during Morsi's presidency. During this visit, Qatar announced it was going to provide $2 billion in financial aid to Egypt. Just a week after this visit, Qatar's prime minister, Hamad bin Jassim, visited Egypt. In November 2012 Hamad bin Khalifa was back in Cairo, holding talks with Egypt's Muhammad Morsi and Turkey's Recep Tayyip Erdoğan concerning the ongoing crisis in Gaza. Qatar continued to support Egypt under the Morsi administration and had extended a total of $8 billion in financial aid by the time he was overthrown, the largest donor to Egypt in this period.

When the military overthrew Morsi, Qatar was less enthusiastic than other Gulf states. But its new ruler, Tamim bin Hamad Al Thani, still congratulated the interim president, Adli Mansour, and declared that Qatar would continue to support Egypt. Yet Egypt refused Qatar's offer and in September 2013 returned the $2 billion that Qatar had deposited in Egypt's Central Bank during Morsi's presidency.[183]

Qatar, however, became critical of the military's crackdown on the Muslim Brotherhood and, more importantly, became a safe haven for many Brotherhood figures escaping Egypt. When Egypt declared the Muslim Brotherhood a terrorist organisation in late December 2013, Qatar condemned the declaration. A statement from the Ministry of Foreign Affairs said, 'the decision to designate popular political movements as terrorist organisations, and labeling peaceful demonstrations as terrorism, did not succeed in stopping the peaceful protests'.[184]

Qatar's relations with Egypt inevitably deteriorated. Egypt even accused Qatar of supporting the Brotherhood. The deterioration in relations culminated in March 2014 in Egypt's formal withdrawal of its ambassador to Qatar, who had been absent since early February. In a statement, the Egyptian government said, 'It is for Qatar to clearly determine its position, whether it will stand on the side of Arab solidarity, unified ranks and protection of national security . . . or on the other side, and bear the consequences and responsibility for that.'[185]

Qatar's embrace of the Arab Spring and tolerance towards the Muslim Brotherhood eventually led to another major crisis. In March 2014, Saudi

---

183. See 'Egypt's Central Bank returns $2 billion Qatari deposit'.
184. 'UPDATE 2 – Egypt summons Qatari envoy after criticisms of crackdown.'
185. 'Egypt recalls envoy from Qatar following Gulf decision.'

Arabia, the UAE and Bahrain joined Egypt and withdrew their ambassadors from Doha. The three states accused Qatar of intervening in their internal affairs by supporting an organisation that was considered a threat to 'the security and stability of GCC countries'.[186] There is no doubt that the organisation referred to in the statement was the Muslim Brotherhood.

In November of the same year, the three Gulf states returned their ambassadors to Doha, but not because the crisis was resolved. The crisis was merely shelved and erupted again in June 2017. This time the crisis was deeper and much more severe: the three Gulf States not only withdrew their ambassadors, but also expelled Qatar's ambassadors and imposed a blockade. This crisis had lasted for almost three and half years and was resolved in early 2021.[187]

---

186. Cited in Abdullah, 'Motives and consequences of ambassador withdrawals from Doha'.
187. For a detailed account, see Ulrichsen, *Qatar and the Gulf Crisis* (London: Hurst Publishers, 2020). Gümüşlüoğlu, *Körfez'den Notlar*, also contains a number of insightful articles on the subject.

CONCLUSION

I authorise and give up my Right of Governing my selfe, to this man, or to this Assembly of men, on this condition, that thou give the Right to him, and Authorise all his Actions in like manner . . . This is the Generation of that great Leviathan, or rather (to speak more reverently) of that Mortall God, to which we owe under the Immortall God, our peace and defence . . . And he that carryeth this Person, is called Soveraigne, and said to have Soveraigne Power.[1]

The mortal God analogy Thomas Hobbes employs in reference to the modern state is not coincidental. The concept of sovereignty, which is the defining feature of the modern state, is also the defining feature of God in theology, be it Islamic or Christian. Furthermore, one might interpret the verse in Islam's Holy Book, the Qur'an, 'He to whom belongs the domination of the Heavens and the earth, no son has He begotten, nor has He a partner in his sovereignty', to argue that in Islam God does not share that feature with any other being.[2]

As the absolute sovereign, the modern state also claims supreme legislative authority within its territory, an authority exclusively attributed in

---

1. Cited in Elshtain, 'Sovereign God, sovereign state, sovereign self', pp. 1363–4.
2. Qur'an 25:2. Caveat: This is one possible interpretation of the said verse. Muslims might interpret it quite differently.

religions like Islam to God only. One might interpret the following verses in the Qur'an to suggest that Islam strongly orders to rule by Allah's revelation and attributes the three worst qualities to 'those who do not judge in accordance with Allah's revelation': 'kafirun (unbelievers)', 'zalimun (transgressors)' and 'fasiqun (disobedient sinners)'.[3]

There is thus an intimate link between the theology of God and the political theory of the modern state. Some scholars have observed this link.[4] Carl Schmitt, for example, claimed, 'All significant concepts of the modern theory of the state are secularized theological concepts . . . transferred from theology to the theory of the state, whereby, for example, the omnipotent God became the omnipotent lawgiver.'[5] It might sound outrageous to some people with religious sensibilities, but the modern state ambitiously seeks to put itself in place of God. This is what the secularisation of the state is. In this sense, all modern states, including the Gulf states, are secular states, no matter what kind of relationship they have built with religion and religious actors.[6]

There are serious practical implications of modern sovereign state building. That is, the modern sovereign state expands its activities into fields where religious actors have historically functioned, such as derivation from the sources of religious rulings, norms and values for their followers, and adjudication and mediation among disputants in accordance with religious rulings, norms and values derived from the sources of religion, education and even welfare services.

To be more specific, over the course of its development the modern state either totally takes over or at the very least strictly regulates those public functions/services that religion's representatives had historically undertaken. Most importantly, the modern state takes over and monopolises the power to make laws, or unmake or amend them if necessary. Equally critically, the modern state monopolises the power to interpret and, through its own bodies, apply laws. The modern state also propagates its own norms and values

3. Qur'an, 5:44, 45 and 47. Caveat: This is one possible interpretation of the said verses. Muslims might interpret them quite differently.
4. A classic in this genre is Kantorowicz, *The King's Two Bodies*.
5. Schmitt, *Political Theology*, p. 36.
6. I develop this idea in Başkan, *From Religious Empires to Secular States*. For a more beautiful discussion, see Elshtain, *Sovereignty*.

and seeks to ingrain them in its citizens through its education system. To this end, the modern state either monopolises or strictly regulates education, both secular and religious. If it so wishes, the modern state may even monopolise or at the very least regulate and supervise purely religious services.

Over the course of this total overhaul, state–religion relations inescapably change. The Gulf states are no exception to this. This book lays out the broad contours of the changes in state–religion relations as the Gulf states have become modern states. In the particular context of the Gulf, religious actors had historically operated in two major fields: justice and education. They shared the former field with others such as the ruling families, merchants and tribal leaders, yet autonomously, at least in theory, derived their rulings from sources of religion and applied them in their courts. In the field of education, however, they had a total monopoly. Needless to say, religious actors also served as prayer leaders and preachers in mosques.

As the Gulf states became modern states, four of them, Bahrain, Kuwait, Qatar and the UAE, eventually developed variants of the Ottoman model of state–religion relations. They have created new courts that expanded at the expense, and eventually restricted the jurisdiction, of religious courts. They have also supplied religious courts with codified laws to apply to matters within their jurisdictions, the exception being Bahrain's still uncodified family law for Shias. They have created new schools that teach modern sciences more heavily than religion. In the meantime, they have also become the dominant provider of religious education through religious schools. Finally, they have also come to regulate and supervise the religious field and engage in some sort of religious calling, or Da'wah, to spread the message of Islam.

Saudi Arabia differs from the other four Gulf states in fundamental ways. First of all, Saudi Arabia has kept religious courts as the backbone of its legal system and has not yet provided any codified laws. Therefore, religious judges are left with considerable autonomy in the derivation of rulings from the sources of Islam. Second, Saudi Arabia has also created new schools, but these teach religion more heavily than the schools of the other Gulf states. Moreover, Saudi Arabia has also become the dominant provider of religious education, but differently from other the Gulf states, through running more religious schools and universities. Like other the Gulf states, Saudi Arabia also regulates and supervises the religious field and engages in religious calling.

Bahrain, Kuwait, Qatar and the UAE depart from the Ottoman model in one critical respect: they do not have an office like the Office of the Sheikh al – Islam, which issues religious sanction for state policies if necessary. In this regard, Saudi Arabia is similar to the Ottoman model as it also has a body of religious scholars, which issues religious sanction, fatwa, for state policies if necessary.

The modern state inescapably confronts religious actors. What sort of capital, symbolic or otherwise, religious actors can mobilise for or against the modern state inevitably shapes state–religion relations in any country. This is the claim illustrated in this book. More specifically, the book shows that by the time it began to build modern state institutions, Saudi Arabia had a native class of religious scholars with a strong intra-group solidarity and moral authority. None of the other Gulf states had such a religious group. Kuwait had a number of native religious scholars but they did not constitute an organised group with internal solidarity and some sort of homogeneity in theology, jurisprudence or social background. Bahrain, Qatar and the UAE also had religious scholars but they were few in number and mostly foreigners. Only in Saudi Arabia, therefore, could religious scholars effectively protect their class interests. Hence, Saudi Arabia developed a model of state–religion relations in which religious scholars have kept their overall influence in the expanding state institutions and the political system.

In addition to the presence or absence of religious actors sharing certain features, The book has also paid attention to the geopolitical context within which modern state building takes place and the domestic opposition that gets inspiration from that context. However, this factor does not determine the model per se, but rather affects the discourse of the modern state.

The book has also traced the Gulf states' attitudes towards the Muslim Brotherhood. In the 1950s and 1960s, all Gulf states were quite friendly towards the movement because they faced similar challenges. With the discovery of oil, the Gulf states were able to embark on their own modern state building and expanded their institutions in a relatively short period of time. However, they had no prior experience and needed professionals, importing them from other Arab countries such as Egypt, Syria, Iraq and Palestine. This reliance on foreign professionals had a downside because they could be ideologically inclined towards pan-Arab socialism. This would not be a problem if in the same period the Gulf states had not been geopolitically and ideologically challenged by pan-Arab-socialist regimes that came to power in other Arab countries. Furthermore, in this early stage of oil-financed state building the Gulf states had not yet fully instituted their welfare systems and were facing domestic opposition that adopted a pan-Arab socialist political discourse. In this domestic and regional context, the Muslim Brotherhood proved an acquiescent and loyal ally for the Gulf states.

This honeymoon period lasted until the 1970s. By then the conditions that led the Gulf states to adopt friendly attitudes towards the Muslim Brotherhood had begun to disappear: the Egyptian-led geopolitical challenge receded and the secular domestic opposition in the Gulf weakened. Then a series of domestic and regional developments began to shake friendly state–Muslim Brotherhood relations in the Gulf: the 1979 Iranian revolution, the decline in oil prices, Iraq's invasion of Kuwait, the rise of al-Qaeda and the 9/11 attacks.

Starting in the 1980s, the Gulf states diverged in their attitudes towards the Brotherhood: while Bahrain and Qatar have maintained friendly relations, Kuwait, the UAE and Saudi Arabia developed ambivalent attitudes towards the movement. Over the next three decades idiosyncratic factors, such as the presence of a relatively free political system in Kuwait, a native class of religious scholars in Saudi Arabia and the Shia as the majority of the population in Bahrain left their own country-specific imprints on evolving state–Brotherhood relations. With the onset of the Arab Spring, during which the Muslim Brotherhood came to acquire an unprecedented geopolitical significance, Saudi Arabia and the UAE became more openly hostile towards the movement. Because it has a relatively free political system, Kuwait was more flexible and therefore less hostile towards the movement.

The two historical processes this book has traced seem at first sight to be unrelated. Indeed, Saudi Arabia and the UAE have different models of state–religion relations, but eventually adopted similar attitudes towards the Muslim Brotherhood. Qatar and the UAE have similar models of state–religion relations, but eventually adopted opposing attitudes towards the Brotherhood. Hence, there does not seem to be a correlation between state–religion relations and state–Muslim Brotherhood relations.

Yet the two issues are linked at another level. We have to recognise that as a mass religious movement the Muslim Brotherhood has always faced a predicament in the Gulf. To put it bluntly, it cannot offer much to its members. The state in the Gulf is rentier, providing almost all public services free of charge. The state is also the largest employer of its citizens and the prime source of wealth in the Gulf. Elsewhere in the Muslim world, the Brotherhood and other religious groups could expand their membership base, and as a result become influential political and social actors, by running parallel welfare systems to those of the state. In the Gulf, the rentier state has suffocated the very space the Brotherhood could flourish in.

The Brotherhood's most critical social function in the Gulf could be to act like a social network, the members of which promote one another in the public and private sectors. The Brotherhood has also faced a formidable rival in this field too. Tribe has continued to be functional in the Gulf, providing its members with the kind of social safety net the Brotherhood and other religious groups provide elsewhere in the Muslim world.

The Gulf was not fertile ground for the Muslim Brotherhood to sink deep roots and flourish. Not surprisingly, therefore, the movement's social base has remained very narrow. In other words, the Brotherhood has never become a grassroots mass movement in the Gulf. Even in the UAE, where the state seems to perceive a serious and real Brotherhood threat, the movement possibly does not have even a thousand sympathisers.[7]

Because it cannot mobilise thousands onto the streets, the only opposition the Brotherhood can pose in the Gulf is by questioning the religious and moral foundations of the state.[8] Yet the Gulf states do not take even this limited opposition lightly. This is because they have their own predicament when facing the Brotherhood. That is, when they confront the Brotherhood they have to maintain their historical image, which is highly respectful of religion, religious figures and religious institutions. At the very least, the Gulf states declare Islam as their religion, recognise the Islamic law as a source of

---

7. According to a Wikileaks cable, Muhammad bin Zayed, Abu Dhabi's Crown Prince, estimates that 'there are up to 700 Muslim Brotherhood sympathizers in the UAE'. See 'UAE minimizing influence of Islamic extremists'.
8. See al-Zoby and Başkan, 'Discourse of oppositionality in the Arab Spring'.

law and derive from the religious law certain rulings to be applied in penal and personal cases. To boost their image, the Gulf states also make major financial contributions to mosques and other religious activities and services.[9] This predicament is serious for the Gulf states that rule over relatively conservative and religious societies. It is worth recalling that this is in large part of their own doing because as part of their investment in religion they have also built a school system with a curriculum that incorporates religion at all levels.

This relationship between the state and religion in the Gulf also complicates the Brotherhood's predicament. It seriously limits the scope for criticism of the state on religious grounds. An alternative for the Brotherhood has been to expand that scope to matters that are not strictly religious, such as corruption and foreign policy. And this is more in line with what Hasan al-Banna preached decades ago: 'Islam is a comprehensive system which deals with all spheres of life. It is a state and a homeland . . . It is morality and power . . . It is a culture and a law . . . It is material and wealth . . . It is Jihad and a call . . . And finally, it is true belief and worship.'[10] By expanding that scope, however, the Brotherhood hits sensitive nerves and inescapably raises the ire of the Gulf states. The Brotherhood's fortunes in the Gulf might ebb and flow in the coming decades, but with its totalistic view of Islam, the movement will constantly test the upper limits of the Gulf states' religious credentials.

The challenge is, how far can the modern state go to improve these credentials? Of the Gulf states, Saudi Arabia has gone the furthest. Yet it has still faced religious opposition, more than Qatar and the UAE have ever faced. For Saudi Arabia, adding a more religious flavour to state policies has proven to be ineffective in preventing the emergence of religious opposition. And this must be the irony of state–religion relations in the Gulf. No matter how far a state goes to improve its religious credentials, it still might not be enough.

---

9. Fox, *A World Survey of Religion and the State*.
10. Al-Banna, *Six Tracts of Hasan Al-Banna*, p. 5.

BIBLIOGRAPHY

Online Sources

The Religion and State Project: http://www.thearda.com/ras/
Al Mubarak family website: http://www.mubarak.org
Saudi Arabia's laws: https://www.boe.gov.sa
Bahrain's laws: https://www.bahrain.bh
Kuwait's laws: https://www.e.gov.kw/sites/kgoenglish/Pages/HomePage.aspx
Qatar's laws: http://www.legal.gov.qa/Default.aspx?language=en
UAE's laws: http://www.elaws.gov.ae/EnLegislations.aspx
UNESCO Educational Reports: http://www.ibe.unesco.org/en/ibedocs/national-reports
Qatar Digital Library: https://www.qdl.qa/en
World Bank, *World Development Indicators*: https://databank.worldbank.org/source/world-development-indicators
Michael Herb, Kuwait Political Database: http://www2.gsu.edu/~polmfh/database/database.htm
Al-Islah Society's Twitter posts: http://twitter.com/eslahbh
Muhammad al-Siddiqi's Twitter posts: http://twitter.com/malsiddiq
Salman al-Awdah's website: http://hklive.islamtoday.net/archive
Salman al-Awdah's Twitter posts: http://twitter.com/salman_alodah
Tareq al-Suwaidan's Twitter posts: http://twitter.com/TareqAlSuwaidan
Tareq al-Suwaidan's Facebook posts: http://www.facebook.com/Dr.TareqAlSuwaidan
Yusuf al-Qaradawi's Twitter posts: http://twitter.com/alqaradawy

Sources in Turkish

'Erdoğan Mısır'dan çok sert çıktı', *CNNTürk*, 17 November 2012.
'Türkiye ile Mısır arasında 27 anlaşma imzalandı', *Yeni Şafak*, 17 November 2012.
Albayrak, Hakan, 'Vaddah Hanfer'e vefa', *Yeni Şafak*, 24 September 2011.
Albayrak, Sadık, *Son Devir Osmanlı Uleması*, v. 1–5 (Istanbul: Istanbul Buyuksehir Belediyesi, 1996).
Gümüşlüoğlu, Feyza, 'Sıddık'ın hayatının izinde: BAE-Islah ilişkilerine genel bir bakış', *Star Gazetesi*, 7 May 2016: https://www.star.com.tr/acik-gorus/siddikin-hayatinin-izinde-baeislah-iliskilerine-genel-bir-bakis-haber-1109567/
Gümüşlüoğlu, Feyza and Zekeriya Kurşun, 'Katar Krizi, Birleşik Arap Emirlikleri İhvan'ı ve Kilit Bir İsim', ORDAF Görüş, 4 July 2017: https://ordaf.org/katar-krizi-birlesik-arap-emirlikleri-ihvani-ve-kilit-bir-isim-hasan-ahmed-el-dikki/
Gümüşlüoğlu, Feyza, *Körfez'den Notlar* (İstanbul: Mana Yayınları, 2019).
Hamidullah, Muhammad, *İslam'da Devlet İdaresi*, translated by Hamid Aktaş (İstanbul: Beyan Yayınları, 2007).
Kurşun, Zekeriya, *Necid ve Ahsa'da Osmanlı Hakimiyeti: Vehhabi Hareketi ve Suud Devleti'nin Ortaya Çıkışı* (Ankara: Türk Tarih Kurumu, 1998).
Kurşun, Zekeriya, *Basra Körfezi'nde Osmanlı-İngiliz Çekişmesi: Katar'da Osmanlılar, 1871–1916* (Ankara: Türk Tarih Kurumu, 2004).
Yargı, Mehmet Ali, *Suudi Arabistan'ın Yargı Sistemi*, 2nd edn (İstanbul: Marmara Üniversitesi İlahiyat Fakültesi Yayınları, 2014).

Sources in Arabic

"Abd al-'Azim al-Dib .. Al-'Alim al-Muhaqqiq', *IkhwanWiki.Com*, no date: https://www.ikhwanwiki.com/index.php?title=عبد_العظيم_الديب
'Al-'Alim al-Jalil: 'Abdullah bin Suleiman bin 'Abd al-Rahman al-Dosari', *alduwasser.net*, no date: http://www.alduwasser.net/vb/showthread.php?t=3928
Al-Kharafi, Abd al-Muhsin J., 'Yusuf Jassim Muhammad al-Hajji: Al-Mutafanni bi Samat', *Al-Qabas*, 21 May 2016: https://alqabas.com/en/article/42035-youssef-jassim-muhammad-alhajji-the-dedicated-silence-12#
'Al-Mustashar 'Abdullah al-'Aqil', *Ikhwanwiki.com*, no date: https://www.ikhwanwiki.com/index.php?title=العقيل_عبد_الله
'Al-Qaradawi yawzah mawkufihi min al-Bu'azizi', *AlJazeera*, 19 January 2011: http://mubasher.aljazeera.net/news/القرضاوي-يوضح-موقفه-من-البوعزيزي
'Al-Sheikh Hasan 'Abd al-Zahir … Nujoum al-Da'wa La Taghib', *Ikhwanwiki.com*, no date: https://www.ikhwanwiki.com/index.php?title=الشيخ_عبد_حسن_الظاهر.._نجوم_الدعوة_لا_تغيب

'Al-Sheikh Fathi al-Khawli ... Rumouz al-'Ata", *Ikhwanwiki.com*, no date: https://www.ikhwanwiki.com/index.php?title=فتحي_الخولي

'Liqa' Hawl Sirat al-Sheikh wa Masiratahu', *binbaz.org*, no date: https://binbaz.org.sa/old/457

'Muhammad Mahmoud al-Sawwaf ... Ra'ed al-Harakat al-Islamiyya fi'l 'Iraq', *Ikhwanwiki.com*, no date: https://www.ikhwanwiki.com/index.php?title=الصواف_محمود_محمد

'Tarikh al-Ihwan al-Muslimun fi'l Bahrain', *Ikhwanwiki.com*, no date: https://www.ikhwanwiki.com/index.php?title=البحرين

Al-Antably, Ashraf Aid and Abduh Mustafa Desouki, 'Al-Sheikh 'Izz al-Din Ibrahim', *Ikhwanwiki.com*, no date: https://www.ikhwanwiki.com/index.php?title=إبراهيم_الدين_عز

Al-Aqil, Abdullah, 'Al-Akh al-Da'iyya 'Abd al-Rahman 'Ali al-Jawdar (Abu Ahmad)', *Ikhwanwiki.com*, no date: https://www.ikhwanwiki.com/index.php?title=(أحمد_أبو)_الجودر_علي_الرحمن_عبد_الداعية_الأخ

Al-Aqil, Abdullah, 'Mubarak Rashid al-Khatir al-Mu'arikh al-Adib ... wa'l Sha'ir al-Da'iayya', *Ikhwanwiki.Com*, no date: https://www.ikhwanwiki.com/index.php?title=مبارك_راشد_المؤرخ_الخاطر_الأديب.._والشاعر_الداعية

Al-Aqil, Abdullah, 'Ta'rif bi Rabitat al-'Alem al-Islami', *Ikhwanwiki.com*, no date/: https://www.ikhwanwiki.com/index.php?title=تعريف_بـ"رابطة_العالم_الإسلامي

Al-Bakri, Tariq, 'Al-Sheikh Ahmad Baze' al-Yasin', *Tarikh al-Kuwait*, March 2010: http://www.kuwait-history.net/vb/showthread.php?t=9655

Al-Bassam, Abdullah A., *'Ulama' Najd Khilal Thamaaniyat Qurun*, v.1–6 (Riyadh: Dar al-Asimah, 1998).

Al-Hamad, Said, "Isa bin Muhammed min al-Islah ila'l-Islah', *al-Ayam*, 24 March 2012: https://www.alayam.com/Article/courts-article/79497/Index.html

Al-Jaser, Najat Abd al-Qadir, *Al-Sheikh Yusuf bin 'Isa al-Qina'i*, 2nd edn (Kuwait: no publisher, 2007).

Al-Kuwari, Rabia Sabah, 'Hal Min 'Awdat al-Majallat al-Ummah?', *Islamweb*, 22 January 2009: http://articles.islamweb.net/media/index.php?page=article&lang=A&id=147735 (last accessed on 23 July 2014; unfortunately no longer functional).

Al-Nuqaidan, Mansour, 'Al-Ikhwan al-Muslimun fi'l Imarat al-Tamaddad wa'l Inhisar', in *Al-Ikhwan al-Muslimun wa'l Salafiyyun fi'l Khalij*, 2nd edn (Dubai: Al Mesbar Studies and Research Center, 2011).

Al-Qaradawi, Yusuf, '"Bi Rouz al-Ma'had al-Dini', *al-qaradawi.net*, 8 April 2016: https://www.al-qaradawi.net/node/4514

Al-Qaradawi, Yusuf, *Ibn al-Qaryah wa'l-Kuttab: Malamih Sirah wa Masirah*, v.2 (Cairo: Dar al Shuruq, 2002).

Al-Qaradawi, Yusuf, 'D. Hasan al Ma'ayarji .. Rajul al-'Ilm wa'l-tarbiyya wa'l-Qur'an fi dhammat Allah', *al-qaradawi.net*, 11 February 2008: https://www.al-qaradawi.net/node/3358

Al-Qaradawi, Yusuf, 'Al-'Awdat ila Qatar ba'da'l I'tiqal', *al-qaradawi.net*, 23 August, 2016: https://al-qaradawi.net/node/4509

Al-Qaradawi, Yusuf, 'Majallat -Al-Ummah- wa Majallat -Al-Doha-', *al-qaradawi.net*, 21 March 2018: https://www.al-qaradawi.net/content/132-مجلة-«الأمة»-و مجلة-«الدوحة»

Al-Qaradawi, Yusuf, 'Iftitah Mabna Jam'iyyat al-Islah bi'l-Bahrain 10 May 1983', *al-qaradawi.net*, 16 May 2018: https://www.al-qaradawi.net/content/144-افتتاح-مبنى-جمعية-الإصلاح-بالبحرين-10-مايو-1983م

Al-Rumi, Adnan S., *'Ulama' al Kuwait wa A'lamuha Khilal Thalathat Qurun* (Kuwait: Maktaba al-Manar al-Islamiyya, 1999).

Al-Shahabi, Ghassan, 'Al-Ikhwan al-Muslimun fi'l Bahrain Tahwilat al-'Uqud al-Sab'a', in *Al-Ikhwan al-Muslimun fi'l Khalij* (Dubai: Al Mesbar Studies and Research Center, 2012).

Al-Shaikh, Hisham Abd al-Wahhab, 'Li Mihat min Hayat al-Ustadh Qasim Yusuf al-Sheikh (3)', *al-Islah*, No. 168, July 2010.

Al-Sha'ir, Ebtasam, 'D. Said Salman Masirat 'Atirah fi khidmat al-'ilm wa'l-majtama'', *Al-Bayan*, 22 September 2009: https://www.albayan.ae/our-homes/2009-09-22-1.473321

Al-Suwaidan, Tareq, 'Thawrat al-Sha'b al-Masr', *Al-Watan*, 4 February 2011: https://ikhwanwayonline.wordpress.com/2011/02/04/السويدان-محمد-طارق-المصر-الشعب-ثور/

Al-Suwaidan, Tareq, 'Al-Thawrat al-Libiyya wa Junoun al-Hukm', *Al-Watan*, 20 February 2011: http://hamilalmisk2.blogspot.com/2011/07/blog-post.html

Al-Utaibi, Abdullah Bijad, 'Al-Ikhwan al-Muslimun wa'l Sa'udiyya al-Hijrah wa'l 'Alaqat', in *Al-Ikhwan al-Muslimun wa'l Salafiyyun fi'l Khalij*, 2nd edn (Dubai: Al Mesbar Studies and Research Center, 2011).

Ashour, Mustafa, 'Tajrabat al-Ikhwan al-Muslimun fi Qatar', in *Al-Ikhwan al-Muslimun wa'l Salafiyyun fi'l Khalij*, 2nd edn (Dubai: Al Mesbar Studies and Research Center, 2011).

Dubai Courts, 'Nabdhat Tarikhiyya: Qissat al-Qada' fi Dubai', no date: https://www.dc.gov.ae/PublicServices/CMSPage.aspx?PageName=CourtHistory

Husain, Abd al-Ghaffar, 'Al-Ikhwan al-Muslimun fi'l Imaraat', *Al-Khaleej*, 1 August 2012: http://www.alkhaleej.ae/studiesandopinions/page/f386335f-a354-4fc7-a6c2-dd476e573d3c

Jam'iyyat al-Islah, 'Bayan min Jam'iyyat al-Islah bi Sha'n al-Ahdath al-Akhirah fi Bilad wa Tada'ayatiha', *Majallat al-Islah*, No. 174 (February 2011).

Jinahi, Mahmoud Hasan, "Abd al-Rahman al-Jawdar ... 'Ala Darab al-Da'wa', *Ikhwanwiki.com*, no date: https://www.ikhwanwiki.com/index.php?title= الدعوة_درب_علی_..الجودر_الرحمن_عبد

Mousa, Muhammad and Abduh Moustafa Desouki, 'Tarikh al-Ikhwan al-Muslimun fi'l Kuwait', *Ikhwanwiki.com*, no date: https://www.ikhwanwiki.com/index. php?title=الكويت

Mukhtar, Omar T., *'Allamah Qatar al-Sheikh 'Abdullah Bin Ibrahim al-Ansari* (Doha: Markaz Shebab Barzan, 2006).

Sources in English

'250 to vie for Quran honours', *Gulf Daily News*, 19 December 2010.

'A fatwa from the Council of Senior Scholars in the Kingdom of Saudi Arabia warning against mass demonstrations', *IslamopediaOnline*, 10 March 2011.

'Al-Wifaq courts Sunnis and Government, but risks Shia impatience', *Wikileaks*, 22 March 2007: https://wikileaks.org/plusd/cables/07MANAMA263_a.html

'Ambassador's dinner with "Enlightened Conservative" religious figures', *Wikileaks*, 6 July 2009: https://wikileaks.org/plusd/cables/09RIYADH887_a.html

'Bahrain', in *The Middle East and North Africa 2004*, Taylor & Francis Group, 2004.

'Banks back al-Islah in distributing their CSR allocations during Ramadan', *Bahrain News Agency*, 11 August 2012.

'Citizenship of 6 naturalized Emiratis revoked by president', *Gulf News*, 22 December 2011.

'Dh5.7 bn allocated for new water and electricity projects in northern emirates', *Emirates 24/7 News*, 2 March 2011.

'Egypt's Central Bank returns $2 billion Qatari deposit', *Al Monitor*, 24 September 2013.

'Emir of Kuwait dissolves parliament', *BBC News*, 6 December 2011.

'Egypt recalls envoy from Qatar following Gulf decision', *Al-Akhbar English*, 7 March 2014.

'Fatwa of Shaikh Yusuf Qaradawi on the military coup in Egypt', translated by Muneeb Baig, *Albalagh*, 9 July 2013: http://www.albalagh.net/current_affairs/0104.shtml

'Fatwa on Syria by 107 scholars', *islam21c.com*, 21 February 2012.

'File 35/7 agitation for constitutional reforms in Bahrain', British Library: India Office Records and Private Papers, IOR/R/15/2/851: http://www.qdl.qa/en/archive/81055/vdc_100000000241.0x000122

'HADAS political bureau resigns', *Ikhwanweb*, 2 June 2009.

'Kuwaiti react to Sadat visit, Gok silent, but Kuwaitis love it Confidential," *Wikileaks*, 21 November 1977: https://wikileaks.org/plusd/cables/1977KUWAIT06565_c.html

'May 27 – June 5, 2007 Visit by US Commission on International Religious Freedom to Saudi Arabia', *Wikileaks*, 26 August 2007: https://wikileaks.org/plusd/cables/07RIYADH1787_a.html

'Ministry of Education dismissed eighty three Emirati teachers', *Wikileaks*, 22 December 2008: https://wikileaks.org/plusd/cables/08ABUDHABI1440_a.html

'Mubarak must go, says Qaradawi', *The Peninsula*, 29 January 2011.

'Naif says Muslim Brotherhood cause of most Arab problems', *Arab News*, 28 November 2002: https://www.arabnews.com/node/226291

'NDI tackles the 2002 Constitution', *Wikileaks*, 4 January 2004: https://wikileaks.org/plusd/cables/04MANAMA7_a.html

'President issues National Day resolutions', *Gulf News*, 30 November 2011.

'Protestors killed in Egypt are martyrs, says Qaradawi', *The Peninsula*, 31 January 2011.

'Qaradawi backs Syrian revolution', *The Peninsula*, 26 March 2011.

'Saudi king warns against unrest while boosting benefits', *BBC News*, 18 March 2011.

'Scholar who left cultural mark on the emirates', *The National*, 6 February 2010.

'Shaikh Abdullah slams Muslim Brotherhood', *Gulf News*, 8 October 2012.

'Shaikh Khalifa pardons 554 prisoners for National Day', *The National*, 27 November 2011.

'Shaikh Khalifa addresses the nation on National Day', *Khaleej Times*, 1 December 2011.

'Statement by Attorney General on the organization which seeks to oppose basic principles of the UAE system of governance and to seize power', *WAM Emirates News Agency*, 27 January 2013.

'Survey of Parliamentary Blocs', *Wikileaks*, 25 October 2004: https://wikileaks.org/plusd/cables/04MANAMA1619_a.html

'Terrorist finance: Designation of five Saudis', *Wikileaks*, 11 September 2007: https://wikileaks.org/plusd/cables/07RIYADH1894_a.html

'Terrorist finance: Post vetting of proposed terrorist finance targets', *Wikileaks*, 27 March 2003: https://wikileaks.org/plusd/cables/03KUWAIT1221_a.html

'The Brotherhood in Bahrain', *Asharq al-Awsat*, 22 June 2013: https://eng-archive.aawsat.com/theaawsat/features/the-brotherhood-in-bahrain

'The man behind UAE's first newspaper', *Gulf News*, 17 May 2002.

'Turkey, Egypt sign transportation agreements', *Anadolu News Agency*, 11 June 2013.
'UAE activist attempts to open independent human rights NGO', *Wikileaks*, 17 May 2004: https://wikileaks.org/plusd/cables/04ABUDHABI1589_a.html
'UAE busts cell "linked to Egypt Brotherhood"', *Al Jazeera*, 1 January 2013.
'UAE minimizing influence of Islamist extremists', *Wikileaks*, 10 November 2004: https://wikileaks.org/plusd/cables/04ABUDHABI4061_a.html
'UAE: Revocation of citizenship of seven human rights defenders and deprivation of basic human rights', *Gulf Center for Human Rights*, 16 January 2012.
'UPDATE 2 - Egypt summons Qatari envoy after criticisms of crackdown', *Reuters*, 4 January 2014.
'UAE, Saudi Arabia and Bahrain recall their ambassadors from Qatar', *Gulf News*, 5 March 2014.
'UAE lists Muslim Brotherhood as terrorist group', *Reuters*, 15 November 2014.
Abd Allah, Mohammed Morsy, *The United Arab Emirates: A Modern History*, 3rd edn (Abu Dhabi: Makarem G Trading and Real Estate, 2007).
Abd-Allah, Umar F., *The Islamic Struggle in Syria* (Berkeley: Mizan Press, 1983).
Abdelnasse, Walid M., 'Islamic organizations in Egypt and the Iranian revolution of 1979: The experience of the first few years', *Arab Studies Quarterly* 19, 2 (1997): 25–39.
Abdel Nasser, Gamal, *Egypt's Liberation: Philosophy of the Revolution* (Washington, DC: Public Affairs Press, 1955).
Abdel Nasser, Gamal, *Address by President Gamal Abdel Nasser at the International Labourers' Day Festivities May 1st, 1964* (Cairo: Information Department, 1964).
Abdullah, Jamal, 'Motives and consequences of ambassador withdrawals from Doha', *Al Jazeera Center for Studies*, 10 April 2014: https://studies.aljazeera.net/en/reports/2014/04/201441061248251708.html
Abu-Amr, Ziad, *Islamic Fundamentalism in the West Bank and Gaza: Muslim Brotherhood and Islamic Jihad* (Bloomington: Indiana University Press, 1994).
Abu-Rabi', Ibrahim M., *Intellectual Origins of Islamic Resurgence in the Modern Arab World* (Albany: State University of New York Press, 1996).
Abu Hakima, Ahmad, *History of Eastern Arabia: The Rise and Development of Bahrain and Kuwait* (Beirut: Khayats, 1965).
Acemoğlu, Daron, Simon Johnson and James Robinson, 'The colonial origins of comparative development: An empirical investigation', *American Economic Review* 91, 5 (2001): 1369–1401.
Adams, Charles, *Islam and Modernism in Egypt* (London: Oxford University Press, 1933).

Ajami, Fouad, 'What the Muslim world is watching', *The New York Times*, 18 November 2001.
Ajbaili, Mustapha, 'Saudi: Muslim Brotherhood a terrorist group', *Al Arabiya English*, 7 March 2014.
Altorki, Soraya and Donald P. Cole, *Arabian Oasis City: The Transformation of 'Unayzah* (Austin: University of Texas Press, 1989).
Al-A'ali, Mohammed, 'Independents the biggest winners', *Gulf Digital News*, 1 November 2010.
Al-Abed, Ibrahim, Paula Vine and Abdullah al Jabali (eds), *Chronicle of Progress, 25 Years of Development in the United Arab Emirates* (London: Trident Press, 1996).
Al-Anani, Khalil, *Inside the Muslim Brotherhood: Religion, Identity, and Politics* (New York: Oxford University Press, 2016).
Al-Assiri, Abdul-Reda and Kamal al-Monoufi, 'Kuwait's political elite: The cabinet', *The Middle East Journal* 42, 1 (1988): 48–58.
Al-Awadi, Hesham, *In Pursuit of Legitimacy: The Muslim Brothers and Mubarak 1982–2000* (London: Tauris Academic Studies, 2004).
Al-Awdah, Salman, 'Has Egypt's hour of reckoning come?', *IslamToday*, 7 February 2011.
Al-Azimi, Basim, 'The Muslim Brotherhood: Genesis and development', in Falah A. Jaber, *Ayatollahs, Sufis and Ideologues: State, Religion and Social Movements in Iraq* (London: Saqi Books, 2002).
Al-Azmeh, Aziz, *Secularism in the Arab World: Contexts, Ideas and Consequences*, translated by David Bond (Edinburgh: Edinburgh University Press, 2020).
Al-Banna, Hasan, *Five Tracts of Hasan Al-Banna (1906–1949)*, translated by Charles Wendell (Berkeley: University of California Press, 1975).
Al-Banna, Hasan, *Memoirs of Hasan al-Banna Shaheed*, translated by N. M. Shaikh (Karachi: International Islamic Publishers, 1981).
Al-Banna, Hasan, *Six Tracts of Hasan Al-Banna: A Selection from the Majmua'at Rasa'il al Imam al Shahid Hasan al Banna (1906–1949)* (Kuwait: International Islamic Federation of Student Organizations, 2006).
Al Fahim, Mohammed, *From Rags to Riches: A Story of Abu Dhabi* (London: London Center of Arab Studies, 1995).
Al-Ghadyan, Ahmed A., 'The judiciary in Saudi Arabia', *Arab Law Quarterly* 13, 3 (1998): 235–51.
Al-Ghazali, Zainab, *Return of the Pharaoh: Memoir in Nasir's Prison*, translated by Mokrane Guezzou (Leicester: The Islamic Foundation, 2006).

Al-Hedaithy, Mesaid Ibrahim, *Modernization and Islam in Saudi Arabia: A Sociological Study of 'Public Morality Committees'* (PhD Thesis, Durham University, 1989).

Al-Jarbou, Ayoub M., 'The role of traditionalists and modernists on the development of the Saudi legal system', *Arab Studies Quarterly* 21, 3 (2007): 191–229.

Al Juhany, Uwaidah M., *Najd Before the Salafi Reform Movement* (Reading: Ithaca Press, 2002).

Al-Kobaisi, Abdullah Juma, *The Development of Education in Qatar, 1950–1977: With an Analysis of Some Educational Problems* (PhD Thesis, Durham University, 1979).

Al-Kuwari, Ali Khalifa, *Oil revenue of the Arabian Gulf Emirates: Patterns of Allocation and Impact on Economic Development* (PhD Thesis, Durham University, 1974).

Al-Mdaires, Falah A., 'The Arab Ba'th Socialist Party and the Gulf Society', *Digest of Middle East Studies* 9, 2 (2000): 1–17.

Al-Mdaires, Falah A., *Islamic Extremism in Kuwait: From the Muslim Brotherhood to Al-Qaeda and other Islamic Political Groups* (London: Routledge, 2010).

Al-Muhairi, Butti S. B. A., 'Islamisation and modernization within the UAE Penal Law: Shari'a in the pre-modern period', *Arab Law Quarterly* 10, 4 (1995): 287–309.

Al-Muhairi, Butti S. B. A., 'The development of the UAE legal system and unification with the judicial system', *Arab Law Quarterly* 11, 2 (1996): 116–60.

Al-Muhairi, Butti S. B. A., 'The Islamisation of laws in the UAE: The case of the Penal Code', *Arab Law Quarterly* 11, 4 (1996): 350–71.

Al-Misnad, Sheikha Abdullah, *The Development of Modern Education in Bahrain, Kuwait and Qatar with Special Reference to the Education of Women and their Position in Modern Society* (PhD Thesis, Durham University, 1984).

Al-Mughni, Haya, *Women in Kuwait: The Politics of Gender* (London: Saqi Books, 2001).

Al-Mughni, Haya, 'The rise of Islamic feminism in Kuwait', *Review des Mondes Musulmans et de la Mediterranee*, 128 (2010): 167–82.

Al-Nafjan, Eman, 'Saudi Arabia's day of little rage', *The Guardian*, 12 March 2011.

Al-Qassemi, Sultan, 'Will Egypt's Muslim Brotherhood mend ties with Gulf states?', *Egypt Independent*, 7 February 2012.

Al-Rasheed, Madawi, *Politics in an Arabian Oasis: The Rashidis of Saudi Arabia* (London: I. B. Tauris, 1991).

Al-Rasheed, Madawi, *Contesting the Saudi State: Islamic Voices from a New Generation* (Cambridge: Cambridge University Press, 2007).

Al-Rasheed, Madawi, *A History of Saudi Arabia* (Cambridge: Cambridge University Press, 2010).

Al-Rasheed, 'Madawi, divine politics reconsidered: Saudi Islamists on peaceful revolution', LSE Middle East Center Paper Series No. 7 (London: London School of Economics, 2015).

Al-Rashoud, Talal, *Modern Education and Arab Nationalism in Kuwait, 1911–1961* (PhD Thesis, University of London, 2016).

Al-Suyuti, Imam Jalal-al Din 'Abd al-Rahman, *The Perfect Guide to the Sciences of the Qur'an*, translated by Hamid Algar, Michael Schub and Ayman Abdel Haleem (Reading: Garnet Publishing Ltd, 2011).

Al-Turabi, Amr and Tarek al-Mubarak, 'Qatar's introspective Islamists', *Asharq al-Awsat*, 18 June 2013.

Al-Uthaymin, Abd Allah S., *Muhammad ibn Abd al-Wahhab: The Man and His Works* (London: I. B. Tauris, 2009).

Al-Zoby, Mazhar and Birol Başkan, 'Discourse of oppositionality in the Arab Spring: The case of the Muslim Brotherhood in the United Arab Emirates', *International Sociology* 30, 4 (2015): 401–17.

Al-Zumai, Ali Fahed, *The Intellectual and Historical Development of the Islamic Movement in Kuwait* (PhD Thesis, University of Exeter, 1988).

Ali, Ahmed, Brian Pridham and Khaled Hroub (eds), *My Early Life: Sultan bin Muhammad al Qasimi*, translated by Domenyk Eades (London: Bloomsbury, 2011).

Anderson, J. N. D., 'Modern trends in Islam: Legal reform and modernisation in the Middle East', *International and Comparative Law Quarterly* 20, 1 (1971): 1–21.

Anderson, Perry, *Lineages of the Absolutist State* (London: N.L.B., 1974).

Ansary, Abdullah F., 'Combatting extremism: A brief overview of Saudi Arabia's approach', *Middle East Policy Council* 15, 2 (2008): 111–42.

Ansary, Abdullah F., 'Update: A brief overview of the Saudi Arabian legal system', *New York University School of Law* (August, 2015): http://www.nyulawglobal.org/globalex/Saudi_Arabia1.html

Anscombe, Frederick, 'The Ottoman role in the Gulf', in Lawrence G. Potter (ed.), *The Persian Gulf in History* (New York: Palgrave Macmillan, 2009).

Arjomand, Said Amir, *The Shadow of God and the Hidden Imam* (Chicago: University of Chicago Press, 1984).

Asad, Talal, *Formations of the Secular: Christianity, Islam, Modernity* (Stanford: Stanford University Press, 2003).

Awadh, Sami, *Islamic Political Groups in Kuwait: Roots and Influences* (PhD Thesis, University of Portsmouth, 1999).

Ayoob, Mohammed, *The Many Faces of Political Islam: Religion and Politics in the Muslim World* (Ann Arbor: University of Michigan Press, 2008).

Ayubi, Nazih N., *Political Islam: Religion and Politics in the Arab World* (London: Routledge, 1991).

Bahgat, Gawdat, 'Saudi Arabia and the War on Terrorism', *Arab Studies Quarterly* 26, 1 (2004): 51–63.

Baker, Raymond, *Islam without Fear: Egypt and the New Islamists* (Cambridge, MA: Harvard University Press, 2003).

Bakr, Amena, 'Influential cleric urges Saudis to stop back Egypt's dominant military', *Reuters*, 28 January 2014.

Ballantyne, W. M., 'The constitutions of the Gulf states: A comparative study," *Arab Law Quarterly* 1, 2 (1986): 158–76.

Banani, Amin, *The Modernization of Iran, 1921–41* (Stanford: Stanford University Press, 1961).

Baron, Beth, *The Orphan Scandal: Christian Missionaries and the Rise of the Muslim Brotherhood* (Stanford: Stanford University Press, 2014).

Başkan, Birol, *From Religious Empires to Secular States: State Secularization in Turkey, Iran, and Russia* (New York: Routledge, 2014).

Başkan, Birol, *Turkey and Qatar in the Tangled Geopolitics of the Middle East* (New York: Palgrave Macmillan, 2016).

Başkan, Birol, 'Book review: Rentier Islamism: The influence of the Muslim Brotherhood in Gulf monarchies', *Perspectives on Politics* 17, 1 (2017): 281–2.

Bayat, Asef, *Making Islam Democratic: Social Movements and the Post-Islamist Turn* (Stanford: Stanford University Press, 2007).

Belgrave, Charles, *Personal Column* (London: Hutchinson, 1960).

Berkes, Niyazi, *The Development of Secularism in Turkey* (Montreal: McGill University Press, 1964).

Birks, J. S. and C.A. Sinclair, *International Migration and Development in the Arab Region* (Geneva: International Labour Organization, 1980).

Brown, Carl, *Religion and State: The Muslim Approach to Politics* (New York: Columbia University Press, 2000).

Brown, Nathan, *Rule of Law in the Arab World: Courts in Egypt and the Gulf* (New York: Cambridge University Press, 1997).

Brown, Nathan, *When Victory is not an Option: Islamist Movements in Arab Politics* (Ithaca: Cornell University Press, 2012).

Brown, Nathan and Amr Hamzawy, *Between Religion and Politics* (Washington, DC: Carnegie Endowment for International Peace, 2010).

Brynjar, Lia, *The Society of the Muslim Brothers in Egypt: The Rise of an Islamic Mass Movement, 1928–1942* (Reading: Ithaca Press, 1998).

Burgat, François, *Face to Face with Political Islam* (New York: I. B. Tauris, 2003).

Calvert, John, *Sayyid Qutb and the Origins of Radical Islamism* (London: C. Hurst & Co., 2010).

Camus, Albert, *The Myth of Sisyphus and Other Essays*, translated by Justin O'Brien (New York: Vintage Books, 1983).

Carter, Robert, 'The history and prehistory of pearling in the Persian Gulf', *Journal of the Economic and Social History of the Orient* 48, 2 (2005): 139–209.

Casanova, Jose, *Public Religions in the Modern World* (Chicago: University of Chicago Press, 1994).

Chesnot, Christian and Georges Malbrunot, *Qatar Papers: Comment l'émirat finance l'islam de France and d'Europe* (Neuilly-sur-Seine Cedex: Michel Lafon, 2019) [In French].

Cole, Donald P., *Nomads of the Nomads: The Al Murrah Bedouin of the Empty Quarter* (Chicago: Aldine Publishing, 1975).

Cole, Juan R., 'Rival empires of trade and Imami Shi'ism in Eastern Arabia, 1300–1800', *International Journal of Middle East Studies* 19, 2 (1987): 177–204.

Commins, David, 'Traditional anti-Wahhabi Hanbalism in nineteenth-century Arabia', in Yitzchak Weisman (ed.), *Ottoman Reform and Islamic Regeneration: Studies in Honor of Butrus Abu-Maneh* (London: I. B. Tauris, 2005).

Commins, David, *The Wahhabi Mission and Saudi Arabia* (London: I. B. Tauris, 2009).

Commins, David, *The Gulf States: A Modern History* (New York: I. B. Tauris, 2012).

Cook, Michael, *Commanding Right and Forbidding Wrong in Islamic Thought* (New York: Cambridge University Press, 2004).

Crecelius, Daniel, 'The course of secularization in modern Egypt', in John Esposito (ed.), *Islam and Development: Religion and Socio-Political Change* (Syracuse: Syracuse University Press, 1980).

Crystal, Jill, *Oil and Politics in the Gulf: Rulers and Merchants in Kuwait and Qatar* (Cambridge: Cambridge University Press, 1990).

Davidson, Christopher, *Dubai: The Vulnerability of Success* (London: Hurst Publishers, 2009).

Davidson, Christopher, *Abu Dhabi: Oil and Beyond* (London: Hurst Publishers, 2009).

Dazi-Heni, Fatiha, 'The Arab Spring impact on Kuwaiti "exceptionalism"', *Arabian Humanities* [En ligne], 4, 2015; https://journals.openedition.org/cy/2868#text

DeLong-Bas, Natana J., *Wahhabi Islam: From Revival and Reform to Global Jihad* (New York: Oxford University Press, 2004).

Dessouki, Ali E. Hillal (ed.), *Islamic Resurgence in the Arab World* (New York: Praeger, 1982).

Dunne, Michele and Scott Williamson, 'Egypt's unprecedented instability by the numbers', Carnegie Endowment for International Peace Article, 24 March 2014: https://carnegieendowment.org/2014/03/24/egypt-s-unprecedented-instability-by-numbers-pub-55078

El-Affendi, Abdelwahab, *Turabi's Revolution: Islam and Power in Sudan* (London: Grey Seal, 1991).

El-Awaisi, Abd Al-Fattah Muhammad, *The Muslim Brothers and the Palestine Question 1928–1947* (London: I. B. Tauris, 1998).

El-Dabh, Basil, 'Egypt and Turkey sign media agreement', *Daily News Egypt*, 21 April 2013.

Elshtain, Jean Bethke, *Sovereignty: God, State, and Self* (New York: Basic Books, 2008).

Elshtain, Jean Bethke, 'Sovereign God, sovereign state, sovereign self', *Notre Dame Law Review* 66, 5 (April, 2014): 1355–78.

Enayat, Hamid, *Modern Islamic Political Thought: The Response of the Shi'i and Sunni Muslims to the Twentieth Century* (London: The Macmillan Press, 1982).

Esposito, John L. (ed.), *Voices of Resurgent Islam* (New York: Oxford University Press, 1983).

Esposito, John L., *Islam and Politics* (Syracuse: Syracuse University Press, 1984).

Esposito, John L., *The Islamic Threat: Myth or Reality?* (New York: Oxford University Press, 1995).

Esposito, John L. and John Voll, *Islam and Democracy* (New York: Oxford University Press, 1996).

Esposito, John L. and John O. Voll, *Makers of Contemporary Islam* (Oxford: Oxford University Press, 2001).

Esposito, John L. and François Burgat (eds), *Modernizing Islam: Religion in the Public Sphere in the Middle East and Europe* (New Brunswick, NJ: Rutgers University Press, 2004).

Euben, Roxanne, *Enemy in the Mirror: Islamic Fundamentalism and the Limits of Modern Rationalism* (Princeton: Princeton University Press, 1999).

Fakhro, Munira A., 'The uprising in Bahrain: An assessment', in Gary. S. Sick and Lawrence G. Potter (eds.), *The Persian Gulf at the Millennium: Essays in Politics, Economy, Security, and Religion* (New York: St Martin's Press, 1997).

Fandy, Mamoun, *Saudi Arabia and the Politics of Dissent* (New York: Palgrave, 1999).

Farha, Mark, *Lebanon: The Rise and Fall of a Secular State under Siege* (Cambridge: Cambridge University Press, 2019).

Farha, Mark, 'Arab secularism's assisted suicide', *The Century Foundation Report*, 25 April 2019: https://tcf.org/content/report/arab-secularisms-assisted-suicide/?agreed=1

Farouk, Dalia, 'Egypt, Turkey sign tourism partnership agreement', *Al Ahram English*, 13 February 2013.

Findlow, Sally, 'International networking in the United Arab Emirates higher-education system: global–local tensions', *Compare: A Journal of Comparative and International Education* 35, 3 (2005): 285–302.

Findlow, Sally, 'Higher education and linguistic dualism in the Arab Gulf', *British Journal of Sociology of Education* 27, 1 (2006): 19–36.

Fox, Jonathan, *A World Survey of Religion and the State* (New York: Cambridge University Press, 2008).

Freer, Courtney, *Rentier Islamism: The Influence of the Muslim Brotherhood in Gulf Monarchies* (Oxford: Oxford University Press, 2018).

Fyfe, A. Ann, *Wealth and Power: Political and Economic Change in the United Arab Emirates* (PhD Thesis, Durham University, 1989).

Gause III, F. Gregory, *The International Relations of the Persian Gulf* (Cambridge: Cambridge University Press, 2010).

Ghabra, Shafiq, 'Balancing state and society: The Islamic movement in Kuwait', *Middle East Policy* 5, 2 (1997): 58–72.

Ghabra, Shafeeq, 'Kuwait: At the crossroads of change or political stagnation', *Middle East Institute Policy Paper*, May 2014: https://www.mei.edu/publications/kuwait-crossroads-change-or-political-stagnation

Ghazal, Amal N., 'Power, Arabism and Islam in the writings of Muhib al-Din al-Khatib', *Past Imperfect* 6 (1997): 133–50.

Gibb, H. A. R., *Modern Trends in Islam* (Chicago: University of Chicago Press, 1947).

Gillespie, Kristen, 'The new face of Al Jazeera', *The Nation*, 26 November 2007.

Goldberg, Jeffrey, 'The modern king in the Arab Spring', *The Atlantic*, April 2013.

Graf, Bettina and Jakob Skovgaard-Petersen, *Global Mufti: The Phenomenon of Yusuf Al-Qaradawi* (London: Hurst Publishers, 2009).

Grimm, Dieter, *Sovereignty* (New York: Columbia University Press, 2015).

Habib, John, *Ibn Sa'ud's Warriors of Islam: The Ikhwan of Najd and their Role in the Creation of the Saudi Kingdom* (St Petersburg, FL: Hailer Publishing, 2005).

Hamid, Shadi and William McCants, *Rethinking Political Islam* (New York: Oxford University Press, 2018).

Haddad, Yvonne Y., John L. Esposito and John O. Voll (eds), *The Contemporary Islamic Revival: A Critical Survey and Bibliography* (New York: Greenwood Press, 1991).

Hallaq, Wael B., *An Introduction to Islamic law* (New York: Cambridge University Press, 2009).

Hallaq, Wael B., *The Impossible State: Islam, Politics, and Modernity's Moral Predicament* (New York: Columbia University Press, 2013).

Halverson, Jeffry R., *Theology and Creed in Sunni Islam: The Muslim Brotherhood, Ash'arism, and Political Sunnism* (New York: Palgrave Macmillan, 2010).

Hamed, Hamed A., *Islamic Religion in Qatar during the Twentieth Century: Personnel and Institutions* (PhD Thesis, University of Manchester, 1993).

Hamid, Shadi, *Temptations of Power: Islamists and Illiberal Democracy in a New Middle East* (New York: Oxford University Press, 2014).

Hammond, Andrew, 'Arab awakening: Qatar's controversial alliance with Arab Islamists', *openDemocracy*, 25 April 2013.

Hamzawy, Amr, 'Interview with Dr Badr al Nashi, President of the Islamic Constitutional Movement', *Carnegie Endowment*, August 2008: http://carnegieendowment.org/sada/?fa=20913

Hamzeh, A. Nizar, 'Qatar: The duality of the legal system', *Middle Eastern Studies* 30, 1 (1994): 79–90.

Hauslohner, Abigail, 'Egypt's Muslim Brotherhood finds havens abroad', *Washington Post*, 6 November 2013.

Haykel, Bernard, 'Jihadis and the Shia', in Assaf Moghadam and Brian Fishman (eds), *Self-Inflicted Wounds: Debates and Divisions within Al-Qa'ida and its Periphery* (West Point: Combatting Terrorism Center, 2010).

Heard-Bey, Frauke, *From Trucial States to United Arab Emirates* (Dubai: Motivate Publishing Ltd, 2005).

Hefner, Robert W., *The New Cambridge History of Islam*, vol. 6 (Cambridge: Cambridge University Press, 2010).

Hegghammer, Thomas, *Jihad in Saudi Arabia: Violence and Pan-Islamism since 1979* (New York: Cambridge University Press, 2010).

Herb, Michael, *All in the Family: Absolutism, Revolution and Democracy in the Middle Eastern Monarchies* (Albany: State University of New York Press, 1999).

Herb, Michael, *The Wages of Oil: Parliaments and Economic Development in Kuwait and the UAE* (Ithaca: Cornell University Press, 2014).
Hinnebusch, Raymond, *Syria: Revolution from Above* (New York: Routledge, 2001).
Hobbes, Thomas, *Leviathan* (London: Penguin, 1985).
Hourani, Albert, *Arabic Thought in the Liberal Age* (London: Oxford University Press, 1962).
Hroub, Khaled, *Hamas: Political Thought and Practice* (Washington, DC: Palestine Studies, 2000).
Huntington, Samuel, 'Will more countries become democratic?', *Political Science Quarterly* 99, 2 (1984): 193–218.
Irwin, Robert, 'Is this the man who inspired Bin Laden?', *The Guardian*, 31 October 2001.
Ismail, Salwa, *Rethinking Islamist Politics: Culture, the State and, Islamism* (London: I. B. Tauris, 2003).
Jamal, Amaney A., *Of Empires and Citizens: Pro-American Democracy or No Democracy at All?* (Princeton: Princeton University Press, 2012).
Johnson, Ian, *A Mosque in Munich: Nazis, the CIA, and the Rise of the Muslim Brotherhood in the West* (New York: Mariner Books, 2011).
Joyce, Miriam, *Bahrain from the Twentieth Century to the Arab Spring* (New York: Palgrave Macmillan, 2012).
Juergensmeyer, Mark, *The New Cold War? Religious Nationalism confronts the Secular State* (London: University of California Press, 1993).
Kantorowicz, Ernst, *The King's Two Bodies: A Study in Medieval Political Theology* (Princeton: Princeton University Press, 1957).
Kechichian, Joseph A., *Legal and Political Reforms in Saudi Arabia* (New York: Routledge, 2012).
Keddie, Nikki R., *An Islamic Response to Imperialism: Political and Religious Writings of Sayyid Jamal ad-Din "al-Afghani"* (Berkeley: University of California Press, 1968).
Keddie, Nicki, *Sayyid Jamal ad-Din "al-Afghani": A Political Biography* (Berkeley: University of California Press, 1972).
Kedourie, Elie, *Afghani and Abduh: An Essay on Religious Unbelief and Political Activism in Modern Islam* (London: Frank Cass, 1966).
Kepel, Gilles, *Muslim Extremism in Egypt: The Prophet and the Pharaoh* (Berkeley: University of California Press, 1985).

Kepel, Gilles, *The Revenge of God: The Resurgence of Islam, Christianity, and Judaism in the Modern World*, translated by Alan Braley (University Park: Pennsylvania State University Press, 1994).

Kepel, Gilles, *Jihad: The Trial of Political Islam*, translated by Anthony F. Roberts (Cambridge, MA: Harvard University Press, 2003).

Kerr, Malcolm, *Islamic Reform: The Political and Legal Theories of Muhammad Abduh and Rashid Rida* (Berkeley: University of California Press, 1966).

Khalaf, Roula and Heba Saleh, 'West "should not fear Islamist movements"', *Financial Times*, 30 November 2011.

Khatab, Sayed, *The Political Thought of Sayyid Qutb: The Theory of Jahiliyya* (London: Routledge, 2006).

Khedr, Ahmed Aly, 'Update: Overview of the Kuwait legal system', *New York University School of Law* (June, 2016): http://www.nyulawglobal.org/globalex/Kuwait1.html

Khuri, Fuad I., *Tribe and State in Bahrain: The Transition of Social and Political Authority in an Arab State* (Chicago: University of Chicago Press, 1981).

Krämer, Gudrun, *Hasan al-Banna* (London: OneWorld Publications, 2010).

Lacroix, Stéphane, *Awakening Islam: The Politics of Religious Dissent in Contemporary Saudi Arabia* (Cambridge, MA: Harvard University Press, 2011).

Lange, Matthew, 'British colonial legacies and political development', *World Development* 32, 6 (2004): 905–22.

Lapidus, Ira M., *A History of Islamic Societies*, 3rd edn (New York: Cambridge University Press, 2014).

Lawrence, Bruce B., *Shattering the Myth: Islam beyond Violence* (Princeton: Princeton University Press, 1998).

Lay, Daniel, *Radical Islam and the Revival of Medieval Theology* (Cambridge: Cambridge University Press, 2012).

Lefevre, Raphael, *Ashes of Hama: The Muslim Brotherhood in Syria* (Oxford: Oxford University Press, 2013).

Liebesny, Herbert J., 'Administration and legal development in Arabia: The Persian Gulf principalities', *Middle East Journal* 10, 1 (1956): 33–42.

Lombardi, Clark B., 'Constitutional provisions making Sharia "A" or "The" chief source of legislation: Where did they come from? What do they mean? Do they matter?', *The American University International Law Review* 28, 3 (2013): 733–74.

Long, David E., 'The Board of Grievances in Saudi Arabia', *Middle East Journal* 27, 1 (1973): 71–5.

Louër, Laurence, *Transnational Shia Politics: Religious and Political Networks in the Gulf* (New York: Columbia University Press, 2010).

Mahmoud, Saba, *Politics of Piety: The Islamic Revival and the Feminist Subject* (Princeton: Princeton University Press, 2005).

Mandaville, Peter, *Global Political Islam* (London: Routledge, 2007).

Mandaville, Peter, *Islam and Politics*, 2nd edn (London: Routledge, 2007).

Mann, Michael, 'The autonomous power of the state: its origins, mechanisms and results', *European Journal of Sociology* 25, 2 (1984): 185–213.

Marschall, Christin, *Iran's Persian Gulf Policy: From Khomeini to Khatami* (London: RoutledgeCurzon, 2003).

Marty, Martin E. and R. Scott Appleby (eds), *Accounting for Fundamentalisms* (Chicago: University of Chicago Press, 1994).

Matthee, Rudi, 'The Egyptian opposition on the Iranian revolution', in Juan R. I. Cole and Nikki R. Keddie (eds), *Shi'ism and Social Protest* (New Haven: Yale University Press, 1986).

Matthews, Roderic D. and Matta Akrawi, *Education in Arab Countries of the Near East: Egypt, Iraq, Palestine, Transjordan, Syria, Lebanon* (Washington, DC: American Council on Education, 1949).

Mayer, Ann Elizabeth, *Islam and Human Rights: Tradition and Politics* (Boulder: Westview Press, 1995).

Merley, Steven G., *Turkey, the Global Muslim Brotherhood and the Gaza Flotilla* (Jerusalem: Jerusalem Center for Public Affairs, 2011).

Micaud, Charles, Leon C. Brown and Clement H. Moore, *Tunisia; The Politics of Modernization* (New York: Frederick A. Praeger, 1964).

Milton-Edwards, Beverley, *Islamic Fundamentalism since 1945* (London: Routledge, 2005).

Mishal, Shaul and Avraham Sela, *The Palestinian Hamas* (New York: Columbia University Press, 2000).

Mitchell, Richard P., *The Society of the Muslim Brothers* (London: Oxford University Press, 1969).

Moubayed, Sami, *Steel and Silk: Men and Women who Shaped Syria 1900–2000* (Seattle: Cune Press, 2006).

Mouline, Nabil, *The Clerics of Islam: Religious Authority and Political Power in Saudi Arabia*, translated by Ethan S. Rundell (New Haven: Yale University Press, 2014).

Mousalli, Ahmad S., *Radical Islamic Fundamentalism: The Ideology and Political Discourse of Sayyid Qutb* (Beirut: American University of Beirut Press, 1992).

Murphy, Caryle, 'Saudi Arabia's King Abdullah promises $36 billion in benefits', *The Christian Science Monitor*, 23 February 2011.

Nasr, Seyyed Vali Reza, *Islamic Leviathan: Islam and the Making of State Power* (New York: Oxford University Press, 2001).

Onley, James, 'Britain and the Gulf shaikhdoms, 1820–1971: The politics of protection', Occasional Paper No. 4 (Doha: Center for International and Regional Studies, Georgetown University School of Foreign Service in Qatar, 2009).

Osman, Tarek, *Islamism: A History of Political Islam from the Fall of the Ottoman Empire to the Rise of ISIS* (New Haven: Yale University Press, 2017).

Ottaway, David, 'The king and us: US–Saudi relations in the wake of 9/11', *Foreign Affairs* 88, 3 (2009): 121–31.

Otto, Jan Michiel, *Sharia Incorporated: A Comparative Overview of the Legal Systems of Twelve Muslim Countries in Past and Present* (Leiden: Leiden University Press, 2010).

Pargeter, Alison, *The Muslim Brotherhood: The Burden of Tradition* (London: Saqi Books, 2010).

Peters, Rudolph, *Crime and Punishment in Islamic law: Theory and Practice from the Sixteenth to the Twenty-First Century* (Cambridge: Cambridge University Press, 2009).

Peterson, J. E., 'Saudi–American relations after 11 September 2001', *Asian Affairs* 33, 1 (2002): 102–14.

Peterson, J. E., 'Britain and the Gulf: At the periphery of empire', in Lawrence G. Potter (ed.), *The Persian Gulf in History* (New York: Palgrave Macmillan, 2009).

Phelps-Harris, Christina, *Nationalism and Revolution in Egypt: the Role of the Muslim Brotherhood* (The Hague: Mouton & Co., 1964).

Pierret, Thomas, *Religion and State in Syria: Sunni Ulama from Coup to Revolution* (New York: Cambridge University Press, 2013).

Pierson, Christopher, *The Modern State*, 2nd edn (London: Routledge, 1996).

Poggi, Gianfranco, *The Development of the Modern State* (Stanford: Stanford University Press, 1978).

Przeworski, Adam and Henry Teune, *The Logic of Comparative Social Inquiry* (Malabar: Krieger Publishing Company, 1970).

Qubain, Fahim I., 'Social classes and tensions in Bahrain', *Middle East Journal* 9, 3 (1955): 269–80.

Rabi, Uzi, 'Oil, politics and tribal rulers in eastern Arabia: The reign of Shakhbut (1928–1966)', *British Journal of Middle Eastern Studies* 33, 1 (2006): 37–50.

Radhi, Hassan Ali, *Judiciary and Arbitration in Bahrain: A Historical and Analytical Study* (Leiden: Brill, 2003).

Rahman, Habibur, *The Emergence of Qatar: The Turbulent Years, 1627–1916* (London: Kegan Paul International, 2005).
Rahnema, Ali (ed.), *Pioneers of Islamic Revival* (London: Zed Books Ltd, 1994).
Renan, Ernest, *Islam and Science*, 2nd edn, translated by Sally P. Ragep, 2011: https://www.mcgill.ca/islamicstudies/files/islamicstudies/renan_islamism_cversion.pdf
Retz, George S., *The Birth of the Islamic Reform Movement in Saudi Arabia* (London: Arabian Publishing, 2004).
Ricks, Thomas E., 'Briefing depicted Saudis as enemies: Ultimatum urged to Pentagon board', *The Washington Post*, 6 August 2002.
Rizvi, *Sayyid Muhammad, Muhibb ad-Din Al Khatib: A Portrait of a Salafi Arabist (1881–1969)*, (PhD Thesis, Simon Fraser University, 1991).
Roberts, David, 'Qatar and the Muslim Brotherhood: Pragmatism or preference', *Middle East Policy* 21, 3 (2014): 84–94.
Roberts, David, 'Qatar and the Brotherhood', *Survival: Global Politics and Strategy* 56, 4 (2014): 23–32.
Rohe, Mathias, *Themes in Islamic Studies: Islamic Law in Past and Present* (Leiden: Brill, 2014).
Rosenthal, Erwin I. J., *Islam in the Modern National State* (Cambridge: Cambridge University Press, 1965).
Ross, Michael, 'Does oil hinder democracy?', *World Politics* 53, 3 (2001): 325–61.
Roy, Olivier, *The Failure of Political Islam*, translated by Carol Volk (Cambridge: Cambridge University Press, 1994).
Rubin, Barry (ed.), *Revolutionaries and Reformers: Contemporary Islamist Movements in the Middle East* (Albany: SUNY Press, 2003).
Rubin, Barry (ed.), *The Muslim Brotherhood: The Organization and Policies of a Global Movement* (New York: Palgrave Macmillan, 2010).
Ruedy, John, *Islamism and Secularism in North Africa* (New York: Palgrave Macmillan, 1996).
Rumaihi, Muhammad G., *Bahrain: Social and Political Change since the First World War* (PhD Thesis, Durham University, 1973).
Sakr, Naomi, 'Women, development and al Jazeera: A balance sheet', in Mohamed Zayani (ed.), *The Al Jazeera Phenomenon: Critical Perspectives on New Arab Media* (London: Pluto Press, 2005).
Schenker, David, 'Qaradawi's war for Egypt', *Asharq al-Awsat*, 23 November 2013.
Schmitt, Carl, *Political Theology: Four Chapters on the Concept of Sovereignty*, translated by George Schwab (Cambridge, MA: The MIT Press, 1985).

Schwedler, Jillian, *Faith in Moderation: Islamist Parties in Jordan and Yemen* (New York: Cambridge: Cambridge University Press, 2006).

Sfeir, George N., 'An Islamic conseil d'etat: Saudi Arabia's Board of Grievance', *Arab Law Quarterly* 4, 2 (1989): 128–37.

Shadid, Anthony, 'Al-Jazeera star mixes tough talk with calls for tolerance', *The Washington Post*, 14 February 2003.

Shadid, Anthony, 'Turkey predicts alliance with Egypt as regional anchors', *International New York Times*, 18 September 2011.

Shehata, Samer S. (ed.), *Islamist Politics in the Middle East: Movements and Change* (New York: Routledge, 2012).

Shukri, Ahmad Ibrahim, *Education, Man Power Needs and Socio-Economic Development in Saudi Arabia* (PhD Thesis, University of London, 1972).

Sinclair, C. A., *Education in Kuwait, Bahrain and Qatar: An Economic Assessment* (PhD Thesis, Durham University, 1977).

Sivan, Emmanuel, 'Sunni radicalism in the Middle East and the Iranian revolution', *International Journal of Middle East Studies* 21, 1 (1989): 1–30.

Smith, Donald E., *Religion and Political Development* (Boston: Little, Brown Company, 1970).

Steinberg, Guido, *Religion and Staat in Saudi-Arabien- Die Wahhabitischen Gelehrten 1902–1953* (Würzburg: Ergon Verlag, 2002) [In German].

Steinberg, Guido, 'The Wahhabi Ulama and the Saudi State: 1745 to the present', in Paul Parts and Gerd Nonneman (eds), *Saudi Arabia in the Balance: Political Economy, Society, Foreign Affairs* (London: Hurst Publishers, 2005).

Tadros, Mariz, *The Muslim Brotherhood in Contemporary Egypt: Democracy Redefined or Confined?* (London: Routledge, 2012).

Tamimi, Azzam and John L. Esposito (eds), *Islam and Secularism in the Middle East* (London: C. Hurst & Co., 2002).

Teitelbaum, Joshua, *Holier Than Thou: Saudi Arabia's Islamic Opposition* (Washington, DC: The Washington Institute for Near East Policy, 2000).

Tétreault, Mary Ann and Haya Al-Mughni, 'Gender, citizenship, and nationalism in Kuwait', *British Journal of Middle Eastern Studies* 22, 1–2 (1995): 64–80.

Tétreault, Mary Ann, *Stories of Democracy* (New York: Columbia University Press, 2000).

Tétreault, Mary Ann and Robert A. Denemark (eds), *Gods, Guns & Globalization* (London: Lynne Rienner Publishers, 2004).

Tétreault, Mary Ann, 'Looking for revolution in Kuwait', *MERIP Report Online*, 1 November 2012: https://merip.org/2012/11/looking-for-revolution-in-kuwait/

Tibi, Bassam, *The Challenge of Fundamentalism: Political Islam and the New World Disorder* (Berkeley: University of California Press, 1998).
Tibi, Bassam, *Islamism and Islam* (New Haven: Yale University Press, 2012).
Tilly, Charles, *Coercion, Capital, and European States, AD 990–1992* (Cambridge, MA: Blackwell Publishing, 1990).
Tolstoy, Leo, *Anna Karenina*, translated by Marian Schwartz (New Haven: Yale University Press, 2014).
Toumi, Habib, 'Public sector in Qatar to get 60 per cent pay rise', *Gulf News*, 7 September 2011.
Trial, George T. and R. Bayly Winder, 'Modern education in Saudi Arabia', *History of Education Journal* 1, 3 (1950): 121–33.
Ulrichsen, Kristian C., *Qatar and the Arab Spring* (London: Hurst Publishers, 2014).
Ulrichsen, Kristian C., *Qatar and the Gulf Crisis* (London: Hurst Publishers, 2020).
United Nations, *Human Development Report 2016* (New York: The UN Development Programme, 2016).
United Nations Educational, Scientific and Cultural Organization (UNESCO), *International Yearbook of Education*, vol. 19 (Geneva: UNESCO, 1957).
Vassiliev, Alexei, *The History of Saudi Arabia* (London: Saqi Books, 2013).
Vogel, Frank E., *Islamic Law and Legal System: Studies of Saudi Arabia* (Leiden: Brill, 2000).
Voll, John Obert, *Islam: Continuity and Change in the Modern World* (Boulder: Westview, 1982).
Wahba, Hafiz, 'Wahhabism in Arabia', *IslamicReview* 17, 8 (1929): 279–89.
Warren, David H., 'The "Ulama" and the Arab Uprisings 2011–2013: Considering Yusuf al-Qaradawi, the Global Mufti, between the Muslim Brotherhood, the Islamic Legal Tradition, and Qatari Foreign Policy', *New Middle Eastern Studies*, 4 (2014): 2–32.
Wehrey, Frederic, *Sectarian Politics in the Gulf* (New York: Columbia University Press, 2014).
Wickham, Carrie R., *Mobilizing Islam: Religion, Activism and Political Change in Egypt* (New York: Columbia University Press, 2002).
Wiktorowicz, Quintan, *The Management of Islamic Activism: Salafis, the Muslim Brotherhood, and State Power in Jordan* (Albany: State University of New York Press, 2001).
Wilkinson, John C., *Ibadism: Origins and Early Development in Oman* (New York: Oxford University Press, 2010).

Wright, Steven, 'Fixing the kingdom: Political evolution and socio-economic challenges in Bahrain', Occasional Paper No. 3 (Doha: Georgetown University School of Foreign Service in Qatar Center for International and Regional Studies, 2008).

Wolf, Anne, *Political Islam in Tunisia: The History of Ennahda* (Oxford: Oxford University Press, 2017).

World Islamic Front, 'Jihad against Jews and Crusaders', 23 February 1998: https://fas.org/irp/world/para/docs/980223-fatwa.htm

Worth-Dunne, James, *Religious and Political Trends in Modern Egypt* (Washington, DC: The Author's Self, 1950).

Yavuz, Hakan, *Islamic Political Identity in Turkey* (New York: Oxford University Press, 2003).

Yapp, Malcolm, 'The Nineteenth and Twentieth Centuries', in Alvin Cottrell (ed.), *The Persian Gulf States: A General Survey* (Baltimore: Johns Hopkins University Press, 1980).

Young, Crawford, *The African Colonial State in Comparative Perspective* (New Haven: Yale University Press, 1994).

Zahlan, Rosemarie Said, *The Making of the Modern Gulf States* (New York: Routledge, 2016).

Zaman, Muhammad Qasim, *The Ulama in Contemporary Islam: Custodians of Change* (Princeton: Princeton University Press, 2002).

Zollner, Barbara H. E., *The Muslim Brotherhood: Hasan al-Hudaybi and Ideology* (London: Routledge, 2009).

Zubaida, Sami, *Islam, the People and the State: Political Ideas and Movements in the Middle East* (London: I. B. Tauris, 1993).

INDEX

Aba Batain, Abd al-Muhsin, 38
Abd Al-Aziz, Juma Amin, 108
Abd al-Daim, Abdullah, 98–9
Abd al-Khaleq, Ahmad, 182
Abd al-Latif, Es-Seyyid, 38
Abd al-Zahir, Hasan, 99
Abdel Nasser, Gamal, 83, 86–7,
    90–1, 96, 104, 106–8,
    134–5
Abduh, Muhammad, 3, 44, 48, 49,
    50, 51
Abdullah, King of Jordan, 173
Abu al-Izz, Zuhdi, 89
Abu Ghudda, Abd al-Fattah, 106
Abul Futouh, Abdul Moneim, 207
'Adliyya (Justice) Courts (Qatar), 66
Afghani, Jamal al-Din, 3, 42, 44, 50
Ajami, Fuad, 169
Akif, Muhammad Mehdi, 108
Al-Abadi, Abd al-Aziz, 79
Al-Abbad, Abd al-Muhsin bin
    Hamad, 72
Al-Abidin, Muhammad Sourur
    Zein, 110
Al-Adsani, Muhammad, 90
Al-Afifi, Abd al-Razzaq, 76

Al-Ahmadiyyah school (Kuwait),
    50, 51
Al-Ajami, Muhammad al-Dhib, 203
Al-Alim, Mustafa, 106
Al-Alusi, Khair al-Din, 48
Al-Alusi, Mahmoud Shukri, 48, 50, 51
Al-Amin, Sultan, 202
Al-An'am, 9
Al-Anqari, Khalid bin Muhammad, 126
Al-Ansari, Abdullah bin Ibrahim, 33n
Al-Aqil, Abdullah, 97, 108, 109n
Al-Ashmawi, Muhammad, 106
Al-Awdah, Salman, 110, 152, 153,
    154–5, 157–8
    on Arab Spring, 176–81
Al-Azemy, Jaman, 142, 143
Al-Azami, Muhammad Mustafa, 99
Al-Azhar, 36, 40, 52, 76, 81, 105, 106,
    107, 208
Al-Bakir, Muhammad Abd al-Rahman,
    102, 103
Al-Banna, Hasan, 3, 10
    and the Muslim Brotherhood, 43–6
Al-Bassam, Abdullah Abd al-Rahman,
    or *Ulama Najd*, 14, 27, 32, 38
Al Busaidi Family, 22

INDEX 243

Al-Dib, Abd al-Azim, 99
Al-Dirham, Abdullah, 39
Al-Duwaylah, Mubarak Fahad, 139
Al-Faqih, Rashid, 110
Al-Faqih, Saad, 110, 153
Al-Funaisan, Saud, 109
Al-Ghamdi, Said, 109, 151
Al-Ghannushi, Rashid, 152, 169
Al-Ghazali, Zainab, 106
Al-Hajji, Yusuf Jassim, 91, 92, 97, 138
Al-Hajri, Abdullah Rashid, 142, 143
Al-Hammadi, Ali Hussain, 183
Al-Harakan, Muhammad, 71
Al-Harbash, Jaman, 201
Al-Hawali, Safar, 151, 152, 153, 157, 158
Al-Hayat Kalimah (*The Life is Word*), 176, 178, 179
Al-Hidayah school (Bahrain), 48, 50, 92, 93, 94
Al-Hourani, Akram, 49
Al-Hourani, Uthman, 49
Al-Husni, Shahin Abdullah, 183
Al-Irshad magazine, 89
Al-Isal, Ahmad, 99
Al-Islah newsletter/magazine/journal, 91, 94, 103
Al-Jabri, Hasan Munif, 183
Al-Jabri, Hussain Munif, 183
Al-Jazairi, Abd al-Qadir, 48
Al-Jawdar, Abd al-Rahman bin Ali, 50, 93, 94, 96
Al-Jazeera Network, 168, 169, 189, 204, 205
Al-Khaleej newspaper, 104, 105, 147
Al-Khatib, Ahmad, 90
Al-Khatib, Muhib al-Din, 44, 49, 52, 53, 97, 98
Al Khalifa Family, 22, 23, 24, 48, 66
Al Khalifa, Abdullah bin Isa, 93
Al Khalifa, Ahmad Bin Atiyatallah, 164
Al Khalifa, Hamad bin Isa

Al Khalifa, Isa bin Muhammad, 94, 97, 161, 162, 200
Al Khalifa, Isa bin Salman, 159
Al Khalifa, Khalifa bin Salman, 94, 163
Al-Khamis, Hassan Ali, 182
Al-Khawli, Fathi Ahmad, 106
Al-Khuwaitir, Abd al-Aziz, 125
Al-Kuwari, Ali, 203
Al Madhkur Family, 22
Al-Mahmoud, Abdullah bin Zaid, 39, 52, 100
Al-Mahmoud, Ali, 52, 53
Al Maktoum Family, 23
Al Maktoum, Rashid bin Said, 101, 103
Al-Mana, Muhammad bin Abd al-Aziz, 39, 40, 97, 99, 100
Al-Manar journal (Egypt), 44, 50
Al-Mansuri, Muhammad, 149, 184, 185
Al-Marzuqi, Ibrahim Hassan, 183
Al-Masari, Abdullah bin Sulaiman, 71
Al-Massari, Muhammad, 153
Al-Mawdudi, Abu'l Ula, 3
Al-Mayarji, Hasan, 98, 99
Al Mualla Family, 23
Al-Mubarak Family, 36
Al-Mubarak, Ahmad bin Abd al-Aziz, 40
Al-Mubarakiyyah school (Kuwait), 50, 51
Al-Mujtama' journal (Kuwait), 91, 138, 139
Al-Mukhtar al-Islami (Egypt), 137
Al-Mutawa, Abd al-Aziz Abd al-Latif, 139
Al-Mutawa, Abd al-Aziz bin Ali, 51, 88, 89, 92
Al-Mutawa, Abd al-Razzaq al-Salih, 90
Al-Mutawa, Abdullah bin Ali, 51, 88, 90, 108
Al-Nafisi, Abdullah, 139, 140
Al-Nafisi, Yusuf, 91
Al Nahyan or Bani Yas Family, 22–3
Al Nahyan, Abdullah bin Zayed, 184

Al Nahyan, Khalifa bin Zayed, 182, 183
Al Nahyan, Muhammad bin Zayed, 149
Al Nahyan, Nahyan bin Mubarak, 147
Al Nahyan, Zayed bin Sultan, 61, 100, 101, 102, 187, 190
Al-Nashi, Badir al-Nashi, 144, 145, 146
Al Nuaimi Family, 23
Al-Qaeda, 144, 155, 156, 157, 158, 159, 162, 216
Al-Qaeda in the Arabian Peninsula, 157, 158
Al-Qaradawi, Yusuf, 99, 101, 102, 103, 160, 166, 168, 169, 177, 179, 189, 194, 202
  on Arab Spring, 204–9
Al-Qarni, Awad, 109, 151, 152, 153
Al Qasimi or Qawasim Family, 22–3
Al-Qasimi, Jamal al-Din, 48
Al Qasimi, Saqr bin Muhammad, 148
Al Qasimi, Sultan bin Kayid, 103
Al Qasimi, Sultan bin Muhammad, 103–4
Al-Qasimi, Sultan, 184
Al-Qatami, Jassim, 90
Al-Qattan, Mana bin Khalil, 105, 108, 109, 154
Al-Qinai, Yusuf bin Isa, 50, 51, 88
Al-Rasheed, Madawi, 34, 156
Al Rashid Family, 24, 25, 34
Al-Rashid, Abd al-Aziz, 50
Al-Rashid, Muhammad, 125
Al-Rifai, Sayyid Yusuf Sayyid Hashim, 91
Al-Rukn, Muhammad, 146, 149, 150, 184, 185
Al-Rumi, Adnan Salim, 15
Al-Rumi, Hamoud, 139
Al Sabah Family, 22, 23, 26, 38, 66, 76
Al Sabah, Nasser Muhammad, 190
Al-Sabbagh, Nizar Ahmad, 108
Al-Sallabi, Ali, 169, 179
Al-Sane, Naser, 145
Al Saud Family, 21–6, 29, 31–2, 34, 70, 77, 79, 151

Al Saud, Abd al-Aziz bin Abd al-Rahman or Ibn Saud, 25–6, 33–4, 53–4, 57
Al Saud, Abd al-Rahman bin Faisal, 24
Al Saud, Fahd bin Abd al-Aziz, 151
Al Saud, Musaid bin Abd al-Rahman, 71
Al Saud, Nayef bin Abd al-Aziz, 157
Al Saud, Al-Waleed bin Talal, 179, 198
Al-Saqr, Abd al-Badi, 52, 98, 101
Al-Sattar, Abd al-Muiz, 99
Al-Sawwaf, Muhammad Mahmud, 106–7, 108
Al-Shafai, Muhammad, 98
Al-Shaibah, Abdullah, 40
Al-Shahin, Isa Majid, 141, 144
Al-Shanqiti, Muhammad bin Ahmad, 40
Al-Shaqqa, Abd al-Halim, 98
Al-Shariah wa'l-Hayat (The Shariah and the Life), 168
Al-Sharif, Kamil, 106, 108
Al Sharqi Family, 23
Al-Shatti, Ismail, 92, 140, 146
Al-Shaye, Muhammad, 143
Al-Sibai, Mustafa, 106
Al-Siddiq, Muhammad bin Abd al-Razzaq, 146, 183, 184, 185
  on Arab Spring, 185–90
Al-Sheikh Family, 32, 38, 77
Al-Sheikh, Abd al-Aziz bin Abdullah, 70, 71
Al-Sheikh, Abd al-Aziz bin Muhammad bin Ibrahim, 72
Al-Sheikh, Abd al-Latif bin Abd al-Rahman
Al-Sheikh, Abd al-Rahman bin Hasan, 70
Al-Sheikh, Abdullah bin Abd al-Latif, 33
Al-Sheikh, Abdullah bin Hasan, 71
Al-Sheikh, Hasan bin Abdullah, 72, 73
Al-Sheikh, Ibrahim bin Abd al-Latif, 79
Al-Sheikh, Ibrahim bin Muhammad, 71
Al-Sheikh, Ishaq bin Abd al-Rahman, 79

Al-Sheikh, Muhammad bin Abd al-Latif, 79
Al-Sheikh, Muhammad bin Ibrahim, 71, 72, 79
Al-Sheikh, Qasim Yusuf, 96
Al-Sheikh, Ibrahim bin Muhammad
Al-Sheikh, Tarfa bint Abdullah, 33
Al-Sheikh, Umar bin Hasan, 70
Al-Shirbasi, Ahmad, 88, 89
Al-Sisi, Abd al-Aziz, 89
Al-Sisi, Abd al-Fattah, 208
Al-Subae, Abdullah bin Turki, 52, 97, 100
Al-Subeih, Adil Khalid, 144
Al-Sulaifih, Hamad, 109
Al-Suwaidan, Tareq, 92
  on Arab Spring, 191–8
Al-Suwaidi, Ahmad Ghaith, 183, 189
Al-Suwaidi, Ahmad Saqr, 185
Al-Tamim, Dahi Khalfan, 184
Al-Tayer, Ahmad Humaid, 147
Al Thani Family, 24–5, 66, 98
Al Thani, Abdullah bin Jassim, 25, 39, 51
Al Thani, Ahmad bin Ali, 101
Al Thani, Ali bin Abdullah, 101
Al Thani, Hamad bin Jassim, 209, 210
Al Thani, Hamad bin Khalifa, 167
Al Thani, Jassim bin Muhammad, 38
Al Thani, Khalifa bin Hamad, 98, 166
Al Thani, Muhammad bin Hamad, 166
Al Thani, Tamim bin Hamad, 210
Al-Turabi, Hasan, 152, 169
Al-Turki, Abdullah, 109, 154–5
Al-Ubeid, Abdullah, 125
Al-Ummah journal (Qatar), 166
Al-Utaybi, Juhayman, 150, 151
Al-Uthaymin, Muhammad, 157
Al-Wahib clan (of Bani Tamim), 29, 30, 32
Al-Wartlani, Fadil, 89
Al-Wasat newspaper (Bahrain), 165
Al-Wuhaibi, Abd al-Samad, 52

Al-Wuhaibi, Abd al-Wahhab, 52
Al-Yasin, Ahmad Baze, 92, 132
Al-Zinjani, Abd al-Majid, 108
Al-Zufeiry, Salih, 189
Albayrak, Sadık, 15
Ali (Pasha), Muhammad, 23
Arab Spring, 1, 15, 17, 156, 170, 216
  and Bahrain, 199
  and geopolitics of the Middle East, 171–4
  and Kuwait, 190–1
  and Qatar, 203–4, 210–11
  and Saudi Arabia, 174–6
  and the UAE, 182–5
Arabian Peninsula
  climate and economic life, 18–20
  political centralisation in, 21–6
  religious scholarship in, 27–41
Aruba Club (Arabism Club), 95
Ashour, Mustafa, 168

Baath Regime or Party, 83, 85, 91, 96, 98, 104, 106, 137
Badi, Muhammed, 202
Bandar report (Bahrain), 163, 164
Bani Khalid, 21, 22, 29, 33
Bani Tamim, 29, 30, 32
Bayt al-Zakat (The Alms House) (Kuwait), 138
Bayt al-Tamwil al-Kuwait (The Kuwait Finance House), 138
Bedouin, 19–20, 21, 34, 70, 92
Belgrave, Charles, 95
Bin Abd al-Wahhab, Muhammad or ibn Abd al-Wahhab, 30–1, 32, 33, 48, 49, 77, 78
Bin Ali, Sulaiman, 30
Bin Ali, Zein al-Abidin, 171, 176, 192, 205
Bin Atwah, Ahmad bin Yahya, 27
Bin Baz, Abd al-Aziz bin Abdullah, 72, 157

Bin Fairuz, Muhammed bin Abd al-Wahhab, 37
Bin Ghaith, Naser, 182
Bin Ghobash, Mubarak, 40
Bin Ghobash, Muhammad bin Said, 52, 53
Bin Hammadah, Abd al-Aziz bin Qasim, 38
Bin Hamdan, Muhammad, 39
Bin Jame, Uthman, 36
Bin Jame, Ahmad bin Uthman, 36
Bin Jame, Muhammad bin Ahmad, 36
Bin Laden, Osama, 155, 158
Bin Mahza, Qasim, 36
Bin Mahza, Abd al-Rahman, 36
Bin Mahza, Ahmad, 36
Bin Muammer, Uthman, 31
Bin Muhammad, Sulaiman, 31
Bin Rajab, Mansur, 164
Bin Salim, Abdullah bin Muhammad, 79
Bin Salim, Muhammad bin Abdullah, 78
Bin Salim, Umar bin Muhammad, 79
Bin Saud, Muhammad, 31
Bin Sulaiman, Abd al-Wahhab, 30
Bin Thani, Muhammad, 39
British, British Empire or Britain, 5, 15, 41, 48, 49, 50, 58, 59, 69, 86, 90, 95, 111
  intervention into and hegemony in the Gulf, 22–6
  Orders in Council, 58
Bouazizi, Muhammad, 171
Bush, George W., 162

Center for Muslim Contribution to the Civilisation (Qatar), 166
Center for Sirah and Sunnah Research (Qatar), 166

Dar al-Khayrat (UAE), 186
Dar al-Tawhid (House of Unitarian Theology) (Saudi Arabia), 56, 62, 76

Dar al-'Ulum (House of the Sciences) College (Egypt), 44, 45, 106
Dalak, Fahad Salim, 182
Darwish, Qasim, 52, 97, 98
Davutoğlu, Ahmet, 172
Day of Rage (Saudi Arabia), 174, 176
Dhofari rebellion, 135
Diwan al-Mazalim or the Board of Grievances (Saudi Arabia), 65, 68, 71, 112, 113, 119, 120
Diyah, 116, 117, 119

Education City (Qatar), 167, 168, 169
Eisenhower Doctrine, 86
Emirates Human Rights Association (UAE), 101
Erbakan, Necmettin, 152
Erdoğan, Recep Tayyip, 172, 173, 210
Exclusive Agreement, 24, 25

Fraker, Ford, 158
Free Officers, 85
Fundamental Provisions of the Kingdom of Hijaz, 57

Gaddafi, Muammar, 171, 193, 205
geopolitics of the Middle East, 85–7, 134–7, 171–4
Gomaa, Ali, 208
Guantanamo, 163
Gül, Abdullah, 172

Hadith or Prophetic Traditions, 11, 30, 43, 44, 63, 77, 123, 133
Halwabi, Kamal, 108
Hanafi School of Jurisprudence, 59, 115
Hanbalism or Hanbali School of Jurisprudence, 38, 56, 76, 115, 116
Harakat al-Dusturiyya al-Islamiyya or Islamic Constitutional Movement (ICM), 141–6
Harakat al-Nahda (Tunisia), 180
Hasanah, Umar Ubaid, 166, 167

Hawwa, Said, 137
Hay'at al-'amr bi'l ma'ruf wa'l nahyi 'an'il munkar (The Committee for the Promotion of Virtue and the Prevention of Vice) or the Religious Police (Saudi Arabia), 35, 57, 70, 71, 128–9
Hay'at al-Khayriyya al-Islamiyya al-'Alamiyya or the International Islamic Charity Organization (Kuwait), 97, 138
Hay'at Kibar al-'Ulama or the Committee of Senior Religious Scholars (Saudi Arabia), 72, 76, 113, 157, 175
Hay'at al-Tamyiz (Board of Review) (Saudi Arabia), 65
Committee for National Unity (Bahrain), 95–6
Hisbah, 70
Hizb al-Hurriyah wa'l-'Adalah (Freedom and Justice Party) (Egypt), 172, 196
Hobbes, Thomas, 9, 212
Hudud, 116, 117, 118, 119
Hussain, Abd al-Ghaffar, 101
Hussein, Saddam, 140, 152, 163

Ibrahim, Izz al-Din, 98–9, 101–3, 166, 169
Ibrahim, Muhammad Khalid, 163
Ikhwan (Brothers) (Saudi Arabia), 34, 70
Ikhwan al-Hijaz, 109
Ikhwan al-Riyadh, 109
Ikhwan al-Zubair, 110
Iranian or 1979 Revolution, 1, 3, 97, 170, 216
  and geopolitics of the Middle East, 135–9, 150, 159
Iraq's invasion of Kuwait, 1, 216
  and the Muslim Brotherhood in Kuwait, 140–3
  and the Sahwa Movement, 152

Islamism/t, 3, 17, 88, 92, 107, 150, 152, 158, 181, 196, 201, 207, 209
  and Hasan al-Banna, 43–46
  and Islamic Law, 10–12
  ideology of, 8–13
  in the Gulf, 47–54, 137–8, 143–4, 159–60, 164–5, 169, 173
  literature on, 3–8
  origin of, 41–3
  pan-, 107
Islamisation, 8, 153
Ismailism, 35
Ittihad al-'Alemi al-'Ulama' al-Muslimin (International Union of Muslim Scholars), 207

Jam'iyyat al-Akhlaq al-Adabiyya (The Society of Literary Virtues) (Egypt), 46
Jam'iyyat al-Asalah al-Islamiyya (The Islamic Authenticity Society) or al-Asalah (Bahrain), 164–5
Jam'iyyat Ihya' al-Turath al-Islami (Islamic Heritage Revival Society) (Kuwait), 138
Jam'iyyat al-Irshad al-Islami (The Islamic Guidance Society) or al-Irshad Society (Kuwait), 51, 88, 90
Jam'iyyat al-Islah or al-Islah Society (Bahrain), 159, 160, 161, 162, 163
  on the Arab Spring, 200–3
Jam'iyyat al-Islah al-Ijtima'i (The Social Reform Society) or al-Islah Society (Kuwait), 91, 92, 138, 141, 142, 144, 145
Jam'iyyat al-Islah wa'l-Tawjih al-Ijtima'i (The Society of Reform and Social Counselling) or al-Islah Society (UAE), 103, 148, 149, 150, 183, 185, 186, 187, 189
Jam'iyyat Makarim al-Akhlaq al-Islamiyya (The Society of the Noble Islamic Virtues) (Egypt), 46

Jamʿiyyat al-Minbar al-Watani al-Islami (The Society of National Islamic Platform) or al-Minbar (Bahrain), 162, 163, 164, 165, 202
Jamʿiyyat al-Wifaq al-Watani al-Islamiyya (The Concord National Islamic Society) or al-Wifaq (Bahrain), 162, 164–5
Jawfayel, Najib, 89
Jizya, 57
Justice and Development Party (Turkey), 173

Khalifa, Muhammad Abd al-Rahman, 152
Khalil, Abd al-Jalil, 165
Khan, Sayyid Ahmad, 48
Khanfar, Wadhah, 169
Khomeini, Ruhullah, 136, 137, 150, 151, 159
Kuttab, 37
Kuwait Fund for Arab Economic Development, 90

Lajnat al-Daʿwah al-Islamiya (The Islamic Call Committee) (Kuwait), 138, 144

Maʿhad al-ʿAli Liʾl Qadaʾ or the Higher Institute for Jurisprudence, 62, 72
Maʿhad al-Islami (The Islamic Institute), 56
Maʿhad al-ʿIlmi or the Religious Scientific Institute, 62, 72
Maʿhad al-Dini or the Religious Institute, 62, 75, 102, 103
Majlis al-Aʿla al-ʿAlami lʾil-Masajid (The World Supreme Council of Mosques), 108
Majlis al-Qadaʾ al-Aʿla (The Supreme Judicial Council) (Saudi Arabia), 65
Makki, Abd al-Latif, 98

Maliki School of Jurisprudence, 76, 115
Mansour, Adli, 210
Mansur, Ahmad, 182
Markaz al-Qaradawi liʾl Wasatiyya al-Islamiyya waʾl-Tajdid (Al-Qaradawi Center for Islamic Moderation and Renewal), 169
Memorandum of Advice (Saudi Arabia), 153
Meshaal, Khaled, 169
Mithat Pasha, 25
modern (sovereign) state, 2, 6
 and islamism, 10–12
 and religion, 8–9, 212–14, 218
modern state building in the Gulf, 13, 16, 17, 170, 214–16
 and religious scholars, 70–6, 78–9
 and the Muslim Brotherhood, 106–7
 early challenges in, 83–7
 in education, 60–4, 120–6
 in legal system, 65–70, 111–20
 pre-oil efforts of, 55–9
 religious services and religious symbolism, 126–33
Mortal God *see* Hobbes, Thomas
Mouline, Nabil, 76
Mubarak, Hosni, 148, 171, 174, 179, 180, 192, 204
Muhalhel, Jassim, 141, 142
Muhammad, Salah Ali, 162, 163
Murad, Abd al-Halim, 201
Mursi, Muhammad, 172, 174
Muslim Brotherhood (al-Ikhwan al-Muslimun), 1, 2, 6–8, 12, 14, 16, 17, 41, 43, 79
 and Hasan al-Banna, 45–6
 and Islamism in the Gulf, 48, 50–4
 Crescent or Rise to Geopolitical Significance, 171–4
 ideology of, 80–3
 in Bahrain, 92–7, 159–65
 in Kuwait, 88–92, 137–46

in Qatar, 97–100, 165–70
in Saudi Arabia, 105–10, 150–9
in the UAE, 100–5, 146–50

Nadi al-Islah or Islah Club (Bahrain), 50, 93, 94, 95, 96, 97, 159
Nadi al-Talabah or the Student Club (Bahrain), 50, 93
Nadwat al-'Alemiyya li'l Shabab al-Islami (The World Assembly of Muslim Youth), 108
Naji, Kamal, 98, 99, 165, 166
Nasserites, 5, 134
National Action Charter (Bahrain), 161, 162
National Union of Kuwaiti Students (Kuwait), 92
Nizamiye Courts, 56
Nursi, Said, 3

Ottoman or Ottoman Empire, 5, 15, 32, 38, 39, 41, 42, 55–7, 59, 65, 68, 69, 75, 114, 214, 215
  Civil Code, or *Majalla*, 59, 69, 114
  intervention into and rule in the Gulf, 22–6

Pan-Arabism/Arab Nationalism/ Socialism, 1, 49, 80, 83, 174, 216
  and geopolitics of the Middle East, 85–7, 107–8, 134–5
  in the Gulf, 90–2, 96–7, 98, 99, 103–4, 147, 169
Popular Front for the Liberation of the Occupied Arabian Gulf (Oman), 85
Presidency of Girls' Education (Saudi Arabia), 126

Qatar Foundation for Education, Science and Community Development (Qatar), 167
Qisas, 116, 117, 119

Qur'an, 9, 11, 43, 44, 45, 63, 64, 70, 75, 92, 116, 117, 122, 123, 133, 138, 151, 159, 160, 162, 166, 188, 196, 212, 213
Qutb, Muhammad, 107, 151, 166
Qutb, Sayyid, 94, 158

Rabitat al-'Alam al-Islami or the Muslim World League, 96, 107, 108, 154, 155, 174
Ramadan, Said, 106, 108
RAND Corporation, 156, 167
religious scholars or Ulama, 2, 14–15, 17, 192, 193, 194, 206
  and the Gulf's exposure to Islamism, 47–8, 51–3
  in Saudi Arabia, 27–36, 68, 76–9, 120, 125–6, 127, 151–4, 156–7, 175–6, 215–16
  in Bahrain, 36, 75
  in Kuwait, 36–8, 75–6, 205
  in Qatar, 38–9, 75, 99
  in the UAE, 40, 75
  see also modern state building in the Gulf, religious scholars
Renan, Ernst, 42
Rida, Rashid, 3, 44, 48, 49, 50, 52

Saad al-Din, Adnan, 101
Sadat, Anwar, 135, 138
Safavid Empire, 21, 22, 35, 201
Sahwa movement (Saudi Arabia), 151–9, 176; *see also* the Muslim Brotherhood in Saudi Arabia
Salafism/Salafis, 44, 53, 81, 100, 138, 143, 159, 162, 164, 197
Salih, Abdullah, 171
Salman, Said Abdullah, 102, 105, 150
Sawt al-Arab, 107
Sawt al-Islam, 107
Schmitt, Carl, 213

September 11th or 9/11 Attacks, 1, 144, 216
   and Saudi Arabia, 155–6
Shafi School of Jurisprudence, 76, 115
Shafik, Ahmad, 196, 207
Shahatah, Ali, 98
Shariah or Islamic Law, 16, 27, 46, 68–9, 111, 114–17, 119, 127, 128, 133, 139, 141–2, 145, 153, 177, 208, 217
   colleges, 56, 61–3, 72–3, 75, 99, 106–7, 109, 120, 124–6, 154, 166
   courts, 40, 56–9, 65–7, 69–70, 72, 75, 100, 112–13, 118–20, 127, 129, 133, 166
   Islamism, 10–12
Sharif of Mecca, 25
Shia/Shiism, 12, 19, 22, 30, 35, 136–7, 206, 214, 216
   in Bahrain, 58, 66, 94–7, 114, 115, 119–20, 127, 161–5, 199
   in Kuwait, 89, 91
   in Saudi Arabia, 175, 180
Soururism, 110
state–religion relations *see* modern (sovereign) state and religion in the Gulf, 2, 14–15, 57, 69, 111, 214–16; *see also* modern state building in the Gulf
state religiosity, 2, 8, 11, 13, 170
   in the Gulf *see* state–religion relations in the Gulf

state secularisation, 2, 6, 17, 55, 69, 170, 213
Sultan, Jassim, 100, 168

Taliban, 162
Tamarod (Rebellion) movement (Egypt), 197
Taryam, Abdullah Umran, 104, 105, 147, 148
Taryam, Taryam Umran, 105, 105, 147
Tolstoy, Leo, 7
Trucial System, 24, 25
Twelver Shiism, 35, 76

United Nations Educational Scientific and Cultural Organization (UNESCO), 16, 130, 131, 132
US Commission on International Religious Freedom, 157

Wahba, Hafiz, 49, 53
Wahhabi or Wahhabism, 7, 38, 53, 99, 100, 151
   and the Saudi state, 31–4
   origin and theology of, 29–30, 77
   religious scholar(s) *see* religious scholars or ulama in Saudi Arabia
Wehrey, Frederic, 162
Wikileaks, 157, 158, 163

Yariba Imamate, 21, 22

Zakat, 57
Zubair, Muhammad Umar, 109

EU representative:
Easy Access System Europe
Mustamäe tee 50, 10621 Tallinn, Estonia
Gpsr.requests@easproject.com